<small>PRAISE FOR</small>
Reading Like a Writer

"A love letter about the pleasures of reading and how much writers can learn from the careful reading of great writers as diverse as Virginia Woolf and Flannery O'Connor."   —*USA Today*

"A jewel of a companion . . . engrossing—both light and erudite, daringly insightful and, in some places, bust-out-laughing funny."
                    —*Los Angeles Times Book Review*

"Even for those without an inclination to put pen to paper . . . this highly intelligent book is a tutorial in how to read closely. . . . Francine Prose leaves the reader a better reader."
                                —*Chicago Tribune*

"Master teacher Francine Prose details the delights of slowly imbibing a book, savoring every word, sentence, and paragraph, tasting morsels of metaphor. Prose's list of 119 'Books to Be Read Immediately'—by Flannery O'Connor, Anton Chekhov, and Alice Munro, among others—is a mouthwatering treat."
                                —*O, The Oprah Magazine*

"If you love books, or want to write them, you need to read this book at least once. Probably twice. Then put it somewhere within reach. You'll want to go back for more."
                            —*Cleveland Plain Dealer*

"Celebrates the pleasures of close reading and explores the power of well-wrought language . . . refreshing."
                                —*Time Out* (New York)

"Prose masterfully meditates on how quality reading informs great writing. . . . Her guide to reading and writing belongs on ever writer's bookshelf alongside E. M. Forster's *Aspects of the Novel*."   —*Publisher's Weekly* (starred review)

"Witty . . . insightful . . . close reading leads Prose back to the place where all desires 'to read like a writer' start: sputtering fandom."
                    —*Washington Post Book World*

"An absolutely necessary addition to the personal library of anyone who is a writer or dreams of writing, but it's also a terrific choice for anyone who loves to read."   —National Public Radio

"An ode to the value of careful reading. . . . Prose focuses on what makes great fiction, mixing personal narrative with plentiful quotations from her favored writers."   —*Library Journal*

READING
Like a
WRITER

READING
Like a
WRITER

A Guide for People Who Love Books and
for Those Who Want to Write Them

FRANCINE PROSE

HARPER PERENNIAL

NEW YORK • LONDON • TORONTO • SYDNEY

HARPER ● PERENNIAL

Grateful acknowledgment is made to the following for permission to reprint from previously published material:
Jane Bowles, *Two Serious Ladies*. Reprinted by permission of Peter Owen Publishers, London; Gustave Flaubert, *A Sentimental Education*. Translated by Robert Baldick. Published by Penguin. Reprinted by permission of David Higham Associates; David Gates, *The Wonders of the Invisible World*, pages 164–165. Copyright © 1999 David Gates. Reprinted by permission of Alfred A. Knopf, a division of Random House, Inc.; Henry Green, *Loving*. Published by Vintage. Reprinted by permission of The Random House Group Ltd.; Zbigniew Herbert, "Five Men" from *Selected Poems of Zbigniew Herbert*. Edited and translated by Czeslaw Milosz and Peter Dale Scott. English translation copyright © 1968 Czeslaw Milosz and Peter Scott. Introduction copyright © A. Alvarez. Reprinted by permission of HarperCollins Publishers; Vladimir Nabokov, *Lectures on Russian Literature*. Copyright © 1981 Estate of Vladmir Nabokov. Reprinted by permission of Harcourt, Inc. All rights reserved; Vladimir Nabokov, *Lolita*. Copyright © 1955 Vladimir Nabokov. Reprinted by permission of the Estate of Vladimir Nabokov. All rights reserved; Flannery O'Connor, *Wise Blood*. Copyright © 1962 Flannery O'Connor. Copyright renewed 1990 by Regina O'Connor. Reprinted by permission of Farrar, Straus and Giroux, LLC; Juan Rulfo, *Pedro Paramo*. Translated by Lysander Kemp, pages 251–254. Published by Grove Press. Reprinted by permission of Grove / Atlantic Inc; Scott Spencer, *A Ship Made of Paper*, pages 273–283 and 264–267. Copyright © 2003 Scott Spencer. Reprinted by permission of HarperCollins Publishers.

A hardcover edition of this book was published in 2006 by HarperCollins Publishers.

P.S.™ is a trademark of HarperCollins Publishers.

READING LIKE A WRITER. Copyright © 2006 by Francine Prose. All rights reserved. Printed in the United States of America. No part of this book may be used or reproduced in any manner whatsoever without written permission except in the case of brief quotations embodied in critical articles and reviews. For information address HarperCollins Publishers, 10 East 53rd Street, New York, NY 10022.

HarperCollins books may be purchased for educational, business, or sales promotional use. For information please write: Special Markets Department, HarperCollins Publishers, 10 East 53rd Street, New York, NY 10022.

FIRST HARPER PERENNIAL EDITION PUBLISHED 2007.

Designed by Sarah Maya Gubkin

The Library of Congress has catalogued the hardcover edition as follows:
Prose, Francine
 Reading like a writer : a guide for people who love books and for those who want to write them / Francine Prose.—1st ed.
    p. cm.
 ISBN: 978-0-06-077704-3
 ISBN-10: 0-06-077704-4
   1. English language—Rhetoric. 2. Creative Writing. 3. Authors—Books and reading. 4. Prose, Francine—Books and reading. I. Title.
 PE1408.P774 2006
 808'. 02—dc22   2005058457

ISBN: 978-0-06-077705-0 (pbk.)
ISBN-10: 0-06-077705-2 (pbk.)

08 09 10 11 ❖/RRD 10 9 8 7

This book is dedicated to my teachers:
Monroe Engel, Alberta Magzanian, and Phil Schwartz.

CONTENTS

READING
Like a
WRITER

ONE

Close Reading

CAN CREATIVE WRITING BE TAUGHT?

It's a reasonable question, but no matter how often I've been asked it, I never know quite what to say. Because if what people mean is: Can the love of language be taught? Can a gift for story-telling be taught? then the answer is no. Which may be why the question is so often asked in a skeptical tone implying that, un-like the multiplication tables or the principles of auto mechanics, creativity can't be transmitted from teacher to student. Imagine Milton enrolling in a graduate program for help with *Paradise Lost*, or Kafka enduring the seminar in which his classmates in-form him that, frankly, they just don't believe the part about the guy waking up one morning to find he's a giant bug.

What confuses me is not the sensibleness of the question but the fact that it's being asked of a writer who has taught writing, on and off, for almost twenty years. What would it say about me, my students, and the hours we'd spent in the classroom if I said that any attempt to teach the writing of fiction was a complete waste of time? Probably, I should just go ahead and admit that I've been committing criminal fraud.

Instead I answer by recalling my own most valuable experience, not as a teacher but as a student in one of the few fiction workshops I took. This was in the 1970s, during my brief career as a graduate student in medieval English literature, when I was allowed the indulgence of taking one fiction class. Its generous teacher showed me, among other things, how to line edit my work. For any writer, the ability to look at a sentence and see what's superfluous, what can be altered, revised, expanded, and, especially, cut, is essential. It's satisfying to see that sentence shrink, snap into place, and ultimately emerge in a more polished form: clear, economical, sharp.

Meanwhile, my classmates were providing me with my first real audience. In that prehistory, before mass photocopying enabled students to distribute manuscripts in advance, we read our work aloud. That year, I was beginning what would become my first novel. And what made an important difference to me was the attention I felt in the room as the others listened. I was encouraged by their eagerness to hear more.

That's the experience I describe, the answer I give to people who ask about teaching creative writing: A workshop can be useful. A good teacher can show you how to edit your work. The right class can form the basis of a community that will help and sustain you.

But that class, as helpful as it was, was not where I learned to write.

LIKE most—maybe all—writers, I learned to write by writing and, by example, by reading books.

Long before the idea of a writer's conference was a glimmer in anyone's eye, writers learned by reading the work of their predecessors. They studied meter with Ovid, plot construction with Homer, comedy with Aristophanes; they honed their prose style by absorbing the lucid sentences of Montaigne and Samuel Johnson. And who could have asked for better teachers: generous, uncritical, blessed with wisdom and genius, as endlessly forgiving as only the dead can be?

Though writers have learned from the masters in a formal, methodical way—Harry Crews has described taking apart a Graham Greene novel to see how many chapters it contained, how much time it covered, how Greene handled pacing, tone, and point of view—the truth is that this sort of education more often involves a kind of osmosis. After I've written an essay in which I've quoted at length from great writers, so that I've had to copy out long passages of their work, I've noticed that my own work becomes, however briefly, just a little more fluent.

In the ongoing process of becoming a writer, I read and re-read the authors I most loved. I read for pleasure, first, but also more analytically, conscious of style, of diction, of how sentences were formed and information was being conveyed, how the writer was structuring a plot, creating characters, employing detail and dialogue. And as I wrote, I discovered that writing, like reading, was done one word at a time, one punctuation mark at a time. It required what a friend calls "putting every word on trial for its life": changing an adjective, cutting a phrase, removing a comma, and putting the comma back in.

I read closely, word by word, sentence by sentence, pondering each deceptively minor decision the writer had made. And though it's impossible to recall every source of inspiration and instruction, I can remember the novels and stories that seemed to me revelations: wells of beauty and pleasure that were also textbooks, private lessons in the art of fiction.

This book is intended partly as a response to that unavoidable question about how writers learn to do something that cannot be taught. What writers know is that, ultimately, we learn to write by practice, hard work, by repeated trial and error, success and failure, and from the books we admire. And so the book that follows represents an effort to recall my own education as a novelist and to help the passionate reader and would-be writer understand how a writer reads.

WHEN I was a high school junior, our English teacher assigned a term paper on the theme of blindness in *Oedipus Rex* and *King Lear*. We were supposed to go through the two tragedies and circle every reference to eyes, light, darkness, and vision, then draw some conclusion on which we would base our final essay.

It all seemed so dull, so mechanical. We felt we were way beyond it. Without this tedious, time-consuming exercise, all of us knew that blindness played a starring role in both dramas.

Still, we liked our English teacher, and wc wanted to please him. And searching for every relevant word turned out to have an enjoyable treasure-hunt aspect, a *Where's Waldo* detective thrill. Once we started looking for eyes, we found them everywhere, glinting at us, winking from every page.

Long before the blinding of Oedipus or Gloucester, the language of vision and its opposite was preparing us, consciously or unconsciously, for those violent mutilations. It asked us to consider what it meant to be clear-sighted or obtuse, shortsighted or prescient, to heed the signs and warnings, to see or deny what was right in front of one's eyes. Teiresias, Oedipus, Goneril, Kent—all of them could be defined by the sincerity or falseness with which they mused or ranted on the subject of literal or metaphorical blindness.

It was fun to trace those patterns and to make those connections. It was like cracking a code that the playwright had embedded in the text, a riddle that existed just for me to decipher. I felt as if I were engaged in some intimate communication with the writer, as if the ghosts of Sophocles and Shakespeare had been waiting patiently all those centuries for a bookish sixteen-year-old to come along and find them.

I believed that I was learning to read in a whole new way. But this was only partly true. Because in fact I was merely relearning to read in an old way that I had learned, but forgotten.

We all begin as close readers. Even before we learn to read, the process of being read aloud to, and of listening, is one in which we are taking in one word after another, one phrase at a time, in which we are paying attention to whatever each word or phrase is transmitting. Word by word is how we learn to hear and then read, which seems only fitting, because it is how the books we are reading were written in the first place.

The more we read, the faster we can perform that magic trick of seeing how the letters have been combined into words that have meaning. The more we read, the more we comprehend, the more likely we are to discover new ways to read, each one tailored to the reason why we are reading a particular book.

At first, the thrill of our own brand-new expertise is all we ask or expect from Dick and Jane. But soon we begin to ask what else those marks on the page can give us. We begin to want information, entertainment, invention, even truth and beauty. We concentrate, we skim, we skip words, put down the book and daydream, start over, and reread. We finish a book and return to it years later to see what we might have missed, or the ways in which time and age have affected our understanding.

As a child, I was drawn to the works of the great escapist children's writers. I liked trading my familiar world for the London of the four children whose nanny parachuted into their lives with her umbrella and who turned the most routine shopping trip into a magical outing. I would gladly have followed the White Rabbit down into the rabbit hole and had tea with the Mad Hatter. I loved novels in which children stepped through portals—a garden door, a wardrobe—into an alternate universe.

Children love the imagination, with its kaleidoscopic possibilities and its protest against the way that children are always being told exactly what's true and what's false, what's real and what's illusion. Perhaps my taste in reading had something to do with the limitations I was discovering, day by day: the brick walls of time and space, science and probability, to say nothing of whatever messages I was picking up from the culture. I liked novels with plucky heroines like Pippi Longstocking, the astringent Jane Eyre, and the daughters in *Little Women,* girls whose resourcefulness and intelligence don't automatically exclude them from the pleasures of male attention.

Each word of these novels was a yellow brick in the road to Oz. There were chapters I read and reread so as to repeat the dependable, out-of-body sensation of being *somewhere else*. I read addictively, constantly. On one family vacation, my father pleaded with me to close my book long enough to look at the Grand Canyon. I borrowed stacks of books from the public library: novels, biographies, history, anything that looked even remotely engaging.

Along with pre-adolescence came a more pressing desire for escape. I read more widely, more indiscriminately, and mostly with an interest in how far a book could take me from my life and how long it could keep me there: *Gone With the Wind,* Pearl Buck, Edna Ferber, fat bestsellers by James Michener, with a dash of history sprinkled in to cool down the steamy love scenes between the Hawaiian girls and the missionaries, the geishas and the GIs. I also appreciated these books for the often misleading nuggets of information they provided about sex in that innocent era, the 1950s. I turned the pages of these page-turners as fast as

I could. Reading was like eating alone, with that same element of bingeing.

I was fortunate to have good teachers, and friends who were also readers. The books I read became more challenging, better written, more substantial: Steinbeck, Camus, Hemingway, Fitzgerald, Twain, Salinger, Anne Frank. My friends and I, little beatniks, were passionate fans of Jack Kerouac, Allen Ginsberg, Lawrence Ferlinghetti. We read Truman Capote, Carson McCullers, and the proto-hippie classics of Herman Hesse, Carlos Castaneda—*Mary Poppins* for people who thought they'd outgrown the flying nanny. I must have been vaguely aware of the power of language, but only dimly, and only as it applied to whatever effect the book was having on me.

ALL of that that changed with every mark I made on the pages of *King Lear* and *Oedipus Rex*. I still have my old copy of Sophocles, heavily underlined, covered with sweet, embarrassing notes-to-self ("irony?" "recognition of fate?") written in my rounded, heartbreakingly neat schoolgirl print. Like seeing a photograph of yourself as a child, encountering handwriting that you know was once yours but that now seems only dimly familiar can inspire a confrontation with the mystery of time.

Focusing on language proved to be a practical skill, useful the way sight-reading with ease can come in handy for a musician. My high school English teacher had only recently graduated from a college where his own English professors taught what was called New Criticism, a school of thought that favored reading what was on the page with only passing reference to the biography of the writer or the period in which the text was written. Luckily for me, that approach to literature was still in fashion when I graduated and went on to college. At my university there was a well-known professor and critic whose belief in close reading trickled down and influenced the entire humanities program. In French class, we spent an hour each Friday afternoon working our way from *The Song of Roland* to Sartre, paragraph by paragraph, focusing on small sections for what was called the *explication de texte*.

Of course, there were many occasions on which I had to skim as rapidly as I could to get through those survey courses that gave us two weeks to finish *Don Quixote*, ten days for *War and Peace*—courses designed to produce college graduates who could say they'd read the classics. By then I knew enough to regret having to read those books that way. And I promised myself that I would revisit them as soon as I could give them the time and attention they deserved.

ONLY once did my passion for reading steer me in the wrong direction, and that was when I let it persuade me to go to graduate school. There, I soon realized that my love for books was unshared by many of my classmates and professors. I found it hard to understand what they *did* love, exactly, and this gave me an anxious shiver that would later seem like a warning about what would happen to the teaching of literature over the decade or so after I dropped out of my Ph.D. program. That was when literary academia split into warring camps of deconstructionists, Marxists, feminists, and so forth, all battling for the right to tell students that they were reading "texts" in which ideas and politics trumped what the writer had actually written.

I left graduate school and became a writer. I wrote my first novel in India, in Bombay, where I read as omnivorously as I had as a child, rereading classics that I borrowed from the old-fashioned, musty, beautiful university library that seemed to have acquired almost nothing written after 1920. Afraid of running out of books, I decided to slow myself down by reading Proust in French.

Reading a masterpiece in a language for which you need a dictionary is in itself a course in reading word by word. And as I puzzled out the gorgeous, labyrinthine sentences, I discovered how reading a book can make you want to write one.

A work of art can start you thinking about some aesthetic or philosophical problem; it can suggest some new method, some fresh approach to fiction. But the relationship between reading and writing is rarely so clear-cut, and in fact my first novel could hardly have been less Proustian.

More often the connection has to do with whatever mysterious promptings make you want to write. It's like watching someone dance and then secretly, in your own room, trying out a few steps. I often think of learning to write by reading as something like the way I first began to read. I had a few picture books I'd memorized and pretended I could read, as a sort of party trick that I did repeatedly for my parents, who were also pretending—in their case, to be amused. I never knew exactly when I crossed the line from pretending to actually being able, but that was how it happened.

Not long ago, a friend told me that her students had complained that reading masterpieces made them feel stupid. But I've always found that the better the book I'm reading, the smarter I feel, or, at least, the more able I am to imagine that I might, someday, *become* smarter. I've also heard fellow writers say that they cannot read while working on a book of their own, for fear that Tolstoy or Shakespeare might influence them. I've always *hoped* they would influence me, and I wonder if I would have taken so happily to being a writer if it had meant that I couldn't read during the years it might take to complete a novel.

To be truthful, some writers stop you dead in your tracks by making you see your own work in the most unflattering light. Each of us will meet a different harbinger of personal failure, some innocent genius chosen by us for reasons having to do with what we see as our own inadequacies. The only remedy to this

I have found is to read a writer whose work is entirely different
from another, though not necessarily more like your own—a
difference that will remind you of how many rooms there are in
the house of art.

AFTER my novels began to be published, I started to teach, taking
a succession of jobs as a visiting writer at a series of colleges and
universities. Usually, I would teach one creative writing workshop
each semester, together with a literature class entitled something
like "The Modern Short Story"—a course designed for under-
graduates who weren't planning to major in literature or go on
to graduate school and so would not be damaged by my inability
to teach literary theory. Alternately, I would conduct a reading
seminar for MFA students who wanted to be writers rather than
scholars, which meant that it was all right for us to fritter away
our time talking about books rather than politics or ideas.

I enjoyed the reading classes, and the opportunity to func-
tion as a sort of cheerleader for literature. I liked my students,
who were often so eager, bright, and enthusiastic that it took me
years to notice how much trouble they had in reading a fairly
simple short story. Almost simultaneously, I was struck by how
little attention they had been taught to pay to the language, to
the actual words and sentences that a writer had used. Instead,
they had been encouraged to form strong, critical, and often
negative opinions of geniuses who had been read with delight
for centuries before they were born. They had been instructed
to prosecute or defend these authors, as if in a court of law, on
charges having to do with the writers' origins, their racial, cul-
tural, and class backgrounds. They had been encouraged to re-
write the classics into the more acceptable forms that the authors
might have discovered had they only shared their young critics'
level of insight, tolerance, and awareness.

No wonder my students found it so stressful to read! And

possibly because of the harsh judgments they felt required to make about fictional characters and their creators, they didn't seem to *like* reading, which also made me worry for them and wonder why they wanted to become writers. I asked myself how they planned to learn to write, since I had always thought that others learned, as I had, from reading.

Responding to what my students seemed to need, I began to change the way I taught. No more general discussions of this character or that plot turn. No more attempts to talk about how it *felt* to read Borges or Poe or to describe the experience of navigating the fantastic fictional worlds they created. It was a pity, because I'd often enjoyed these wide-ranging discussions, during which my students said things I would always remember. I recall one student saying that reading the stories of Bruno Schulz was like being a child again, hiding behind the door, eavesdropping on the adults, understanding a fraction of what they were saying and inventing the rest. But I assumed that I would still hear such things even if I organized classes around the more pedestrian, halting method of beginning at the beginning, lingering over every word, every phrase, every image, considering how it enhanced and contributed to the story as a whole. In this way, the students and I would get through as much of the text as possible—sometimes three or four, sometimes as many as ten, pages—in a two-hour class.

This remains the way I prefer to teach, partly because it's a method from which I benefit nearly as much as my students. And there are many stories that I have taught for years and from which I learn more each time I read them, word by word.

I've always thought that a close-reading course should at least be a companion, if not an alternative, to the writing workshop. Though it also doles out praise, the workshop most often focuses on what a writer has done wrong, what needs to be fixed, cut, or augmented. Whereas reading a masterpiece can inspire us by showing us how a writer does something brilliantly.

Occasionally, while I was teaching a reading course and simultaneously working on a novel, and when I had reached an impasse in my own work, I began to notice that whatever story I taught that week somehow helped me get past the obstacle that had been in my way. Once, for example, I was struggling with a party scene and happened to be teaching James Joyce's "The Dead," which taught me something about how to orchestrate the voices of the party guests into a chorus from which the principal players step forward, in turn, to take their solos.

On another occasion, I was writing a story that I knew was going to end in an eruption of horrific violence, and I was having trouble getting it to sound natural and inevitable rather than forced and melodramatic. Fortunately, I was teaching the stories of Isaac Babel, whose work so often explores the nature, the causes, and the aftermath of violence. What I noticed, close-reading along with my students, was that frequently in Babel's fiction, a moment of violence is directly preceded by a passage of intense lyricism. It's characteristic of Babel to offer the reader a lovely glimpse of the crescent moon just before all hell breaks loose. I tried it—first the poetry, then the horror—and suddenly everything came together, the pacing seemed right, and the incident I had been struggling with appeared, at least to me, to be plausible and convincing.

Close reading helped me figure out, as I hoped it did for my students, a way to approach a difficult aspect of writing, which is nearly always difficult. Readers of this book will notice that there are writers to whom I keep returning: Chekhov, Joyce, Austen, George Eliot, Kafka, Tolstoy, Flannery O'Connor, Katherine Mansfield, Nabokov, Heinrich von Kleist, Raymond Carver, Jane Bowles, James Baldwin, Alice Munro, Mavis Gallant—the list goes on and on. They are the teachers to whom I go, the authorities I consult, the models that still help to inspire me with the energy and courage it takes to sit down at a desk each day and resume the process of learning, anew, to write.

TWO

Words

WHEN I WAS A CHILD, I HAD A PIANO TEACHER WHO
tried to encourage her uninspired students with a system of re-
wards. A memorized Clementini sonatina or a completed theory
workbook earned us a certain number of stars that added up
to the grand prize: a small, unpainted plaster bust of a famous
composer: Bach, Beethoven, Mozart.

The idea, I suppose, was that we were meant to line up the
statues on the piano as sort of an altar to which we would offer
up our finger exercises in the faint hope of winning these dead
men's approval. I was fascinated by their powdered wigs and their
stern—or in the case of Chopin, dreamy—expressions. They
were like chalky, bodiless dolls I couldn't imagine dressing up.

Unfortunately for my piano teacher and me, I didn't much
care about winning the dead composers' good opinions, perhaps
because I already knew that I never would.

I had my own private pantheon made up not of composers
but of writers: P. L. Travers, Astrid Lindgren, E. Nesbit, the idols
of my childhood. Theirs was the approval I longed for, the com-

pany I longed to join as they floated above me, giving me something to think about during those dreary practice sessions. Over the intervening years, the membership of my literary pantheon has changed. But I have never lost the idea of Tolstoy or George Eliot nodding or frowning over my work, turning thumbs up or down.

I have heard other writers talk about the sensation of writing for an audience made up partly of the dead. In her memoir, *Hope Against Hope*, Nadezhda Mandelstam describes how her husband, Osip, and his friend and fellow poet, Anna Akhmatova participated in a sort of otherworldly communion with their predecessors:

> Both M. and Akhmatova had the astonishing ability of somehow bridging time and space when they read the work of dead poets. By its very nature, such reading is usually anachronistic, but with them it meant entering into personal relations with the poet in question: it was a kind of conversation with someone long since departed. From the way in which he greeted his fellow poets of antiquity in the Inferno, M. suspected that Dante also had this ability. In his article, "On the Nature of Words" he mentions Bergson's search for links between things of the same kind that are separated only by time—in the same way, he thought, one can look for friends and allies across the barriers of both time and space. This would probably have been understood by Keats, who wanted to meet all his friends, living and dead, in a tavern.
>
> Ahkmatova, in resurrecting figures from the past, was always interested in the way they lived and their relations with others. I remember how she made Shelley come alive for me—this was, as it were, her first experiment of this kind. Next began her period of communion with Pushkin. With the thoroughness of a detective or a jealous woman, she ferreted

out everything about the people around him, probing their psy-
chological motives and turning every woman he had ever so
much as smiled at inside out like a glove.

So who are the writers with whom we might want to have
this out-of-time communion? The Brontës, Dickens, Turgenev,
Woolf—the list is long enough to support a lifetime of solid read-
ing. You can assume that if a writer's work has survived for cen-
turies, there are reasons why this is so, explanations that have
nothing to do with a conspiracy of academics plotting to resus-
citate a zombie army of dead white males. Of course, there is
the matter of individual taste. Not all great writers may seem
great to us, regardless of how often and how hard we try to see
their virtues. I know, for example, that Trollope is considered to
have been a brilliant novelist, but I've never quite understood
what makes his fans so fervent. Still, our tastes change as we
ourselves change and grow older, and perhaps in a few months
or so Trollope will have become my new favorite writer.

Part of a reader's job is to find out why certain writers en-
dure. This may require some rewiring, unhooking the connection
that makes you think you have to have an *opinion* about the book
and reconnecting that wire to whatever terminal lets you see
reading as something that might move or delight you. You will
do yourself a disservice if you confine your reading to the rising
star whose six-figure, two-book contract might seem to indicate
where your own work should be heading. I'm not saying you
shouldn't read such writers, some of whom are excellent and
deserving of celebrity. I'm only pointing out that they represent
the dot at the end of the long, glorious, complex sentence in
which literature has been written.

With so much reading ahead of you, the temptation might
be to speed up. But in fact it's essential to slow down and read
every word. Because one important thing that can be learned

by reading slowly is the seemingly obvious but oddly underappreciated fact that language is the medium we use in much the same way a composer uses notes, the way a painter uses paint. I realize it may seem obvious, but it's surprising how easily we lose sight of the fact that words are the raw material out of which literature is crafted.

Every page was once a blank page, just as every word that appears on it now was not always there, but instead reflects the final result of countless large and small deliberations. All the elements of good writing depend on the writer's skill in choosing one word instead of another. And what grabs and keeps our interest has everything to do with those choices.

One way to compel yourself to slow down and stop at every word is to ask yourself what sort of information each word—each word choice—is conveying. Reading with that question in mind, let's consider the wealth of information provided by the first paragraph of Flannery O'Connor's "A Good Man Is Hard to Find":

> *The grandmother didn't want to go to Florida. She wanted to visit some of her connections in east Tennessee and she was seizing at every chance to change Bailey's mind. Bailey was the son she lived with, her only boy. He was sitting on the edge of his chair at the table, bent over the orange sports section of the Journal. "Now look here, Bailey," she said, "see here, read this," and she stood with one hand on her thin hip and the other rattling the newspaper at his bald head. "Here this fellow that calls himself The Misfit is aloose from the Federal Pen and headed toward Florida and you read here what it says he did to these people. Just you read it. I wouldn't take my children in any direction with a criminal like that aloose in it. I couldn't answer to my conscience if I did."*

The first simple declarative sentence could hardly be more plain: subject, verb, infinitive, preposition. There is not one adjective or adverb to distract us from the central fact. But how much is contained in these eight little words!

Here, as in the openings of many stories and novels, we are confronted by one important choice that a writer of fiction needs to make: the question of what to call her characters. Joe, Joe Smith, Mr. Smith? Not, in this case, Grandma or Grandma Smith (no one in this story has a last name) or, let's say, Ethel or Ethel Smith or Mrs. Smith, or any of the myriad terms of address that might have established different degrees of psychic distance and sympathy between the reader and the old woman.

Calling her "the grandmother" at once reduces her to her role in the family, as does the fact that her daughter-in-law is never called anything but "the children's mother." At the same time, the title gives her (like The Misfit) an archetypal, mythic role that elevates her and keeps us from getting too chummy with this woman whose name we never learn, even as the writer is preparing our hearts to break at the critical moment to which the grandmother's whole life and the events of the story have led her.

The grandmother didn't want to go to Florida. The first sentence is a refusal, which, in its very simplicity, emphasizes the force with which the old woman is digging in her heels. It's a concentrated act of negative will, which we will come to understand in all its tragic folly—that is, the foolishness of attempting to exert one's will when fate or destiny (or as O'Connor would argue, God) has other plans for us. And finally, the no-nonsense austerity of the sentence's construction gives it a kind of authority that—like *Moby Dick*'s first sentence, "Call me Ishmael"—makes us feel that the author is in control, an authority that draws us farther into the story.

The first part of the second sentence—"She wanted to visit some of her connections in east Tennessee"—locates us in geography, that is, in the South. And that one word, *connections* (as opposed to *relatives* or *family* or *people*), reveals the grandmother's sense of her own faded gentility, of having come down in the world, a semi-deluded self-image that, like the illusions of many other O'Connor characters, will contribute to the character's downfall.

The sentence's second half—"she was seizing at every chance to change Bailey's mind"—seizes our own attention more strongly than it would have had O'Connor written, say, "*taking* every chance." The verb quietly but succinctly telegraphs both the grandmother's fierceness and the passivity of Bailey, "the son she lived with, her only boy," two phrases that convey their domestic situation as well as the infantilizing dominance and the simultaneous tenderness that the grandmother feels toward her son. That word *boy* will take on tragic resonance later. "Bailey Boy!" the old woman will cry after her son is killed by The Misfit, who is already about to make his appearance in the newspaper that the grandmother is "rattling" at her boy's bald head. Meanwhile, the paradox of a bald, presumably middle-aged boy leads us to make certain accurate conclusions about the family constellation.

The Misfit is "aloose"—here we find one of those words by which O'Connor conveys the rhythm and flavor of a local dialect without subjecting us to the annoying apostrophes, dropped *g*'s, the shootin' and talkin' and cussin,' and the bad grammar with which other authors attempt to transcribe regional speech. The final sentences of the paragraph—"I wouldn't take my children in any direction with a criminal like that aloose in it. I couldn't answer to my conscience if I did"—encapsulate the hilarious and maddening quality of the grandmother's manipulativeness. She'll use *anything*, even an imagined encounter with an escaped criminal, to divert the family vacation from Florida to east

Tennessee. And her apparently unlikely fantasy of encountering The Misfit may cause us to reflect on the peculiar egocentrism and narcissism of those people who are constantly convinced that, however minuscule the odds, the stray bullet will somehow find *them*. Meanwhile, again because of word choice, the final sentence is already alluding to those questions of conscience, morality, the spirit and soul that will reveal themselves as being at the heart of O'Connor's story.

Given the size of the country, we think, they can't *possibly* run into the criminal about whom the grandmother has warned them. And yet we may recall Chekhov's remark that the gun we see onstage in an early scene should probably go off by the play's end. So what *is* going to happen? This short passage has already ushered us into a world that is realistic but at the same time beyond the reach of ordinary logic, and into a narrative that we will follow from this introduction as inexorably as the grandmother is destined to meet a fate that (we *do* suspect) will involve The Misfit. Pared and edited down, highly concentrated, a model of compression from which it would be hard to excise one word, this single passage achieves all this, or more, since there will be additional subtleties and complexities obvious only to each individual reader.

Skimming just won't suffice if we hope to extract one fraction, such as the fraction above, of what a writer's words can teach us about how to use the language. And reading quickly— for plot, for ideas, even for the psychological truths that a story reveals—can be a hindrance when the crucial revelations are in the spaces *between* words, in what has been left out. Such is the case with the opening of Katherine Mansfield's "The Daughters of the Late Colonel":

> *The week after was one of the busiest weeks of their lives.*
> *Even when they went to bed, it was only their bodies that lay*
> *down and rested; their minds went on, thinking things out,*

> *talking things over, wondering, deciding, trying to remember*
> *where . . .*

Again, the story begins with a simple declarative sentence that establishes a sense of competence and control: a story is about to be told by someone who knows what she's doing. But if you read it quickly, you might skip right past the fact that there is no object for that temporal preposition *after*. The week after . . . what? Our heroines—two sisters, whom we have not yet met, who have not been named for us (Josephine and Constantia) or referred to in any way except as *they*—cannot supply the necessary words, *after their father's funeral*, because they have not yet been able to convince themselves that this momentous and terrifying event has really occurred. They simply cannot get their minds around the fact that their feared, tyrannical father, the late colonel, could be gone and is no longer dictating exactly what they will do and feel and think every moment of every day.

By leaving out the object of *after* in the very first sentence, Katherine Mansfield establishes the rules or the lack of rules that allow the story to adopt a distanced third-person point of view along with a fluidity that lets it penetrate the dusty, peculiar recesses of the two sisters' psyches. The second and final sentence of that paragraph is all participles—thinking, wondering, deciding, trying to remember—that describe thought rather than action, until the sentence exhausts itself and peters out in an ellipsis that prefigures the dead end that the sisters' attempts to think things through will ultimately reach.

These two low-key sentences have already ushered us into the paradoxically rich and claustrophobic realm (both outside and inside the sisters) in which the story occurs. They enable us to see their world from a perspective at once so objective and so closely identified with these child-women that everything about their actions (giggling, squirming in their beds, worrying about the little mouse scurrying about their room) makes us think they *might* be children until, almost five pages into the story, the maid, Kate, comes into the dining room, and—in just two words—the story dazzles us with a flash of harsh sunlight that reveals the age of the "old tabbies":

> *And proud young Kate, the enchanted princess, came in to see what the old tabbies wanted now. She snatched away their plates of mock something or other and slapped down a white, terrified blancmange.*

(Note, too, how ingeniously and economically that "terrified blancmange" reflects the mental state of the "old tabbies" in the trembling of the gelatinous pudding.)

Mansfield is one of those stylists whose work you can open anywhere to discover some inspired word choice. Here, the sisters hear a barrel organ playing outside in the street and for the first time realize that they don't have to pay the organ-grinder to go away so his music won't annoy Father. "A perfect fountain of bubbling notes shook from the barrel-organ, round bright notes, carelessly scattered." And how precise and inventive are the words in which the women respond to Father's live-in nurse, who has stayed on after his death. Nurse Andrews's table manners alarm and enrage the sisters, who suddenly have no idea how, economically, they are supposed to survive without their father:

> *Nurse Andrews was simply fearful about butter. Really they couldn't help feeling that about butter, at least, she took advantage of their kindness. And she had that maddening habit of asking for just an inch more bread to finish what she had on her plate, and then, at the last mouthful, absent-mindedly—of course it wasn't absent-mindedly—taking an-*

other helping. Josephine got very red when this happened, and
she fastened her small, bead-like eyes on the tablecloth, as if she
saw a minute strange insect creeping through the web of it.

Again, it's a matter of the word by word—this time, of adjectives and adverbs. Though we remain in the third person, the *simply fearful* and *maddening* are the sister's words. We can hardly miss the rage and despair being generated by that "just an inch more bread," that "absent-mindedly—of course it wasn't absent-mindedly." And we can see with absolute clarity the look of horror, concentration, and suppressed disgust on Josephine's face as she "fastens her small bead-like eyes" on the "minute strange insect" she imagines crawling through the web of the tablecloth. Along the way, *web* informs us that the cloth is made of lace.

"The Daughters of the Late Colonel" rewards rereading at different points in our lives. For years, I assumed I understood it. I believed that the sisters' inability to supply an object for that *after*, to comprehend their father's mysterious departure, had to do with their eccentric natures, with their childlike inability (or refusal) to face the complexities of adult life. And then I happened to reread it not long after a death in my own family, and for the first time I understood that the sisters' perplexity is not so unlike the astonishment and bewilderment that all of us (regardless of how "grown-up" or sophisticated we imagine ourselves to be) feel in the face of the shocking finality, the absence, the mystery of death.

THOUGH their subject matter, their characters, and their approaches to fiction could hardly seem more different, both Flannery O'Connor and Katherine Mansfield share a certain pyrotechnical aspect, deploying metaphors, similes, and sharp turns of phrase that are the literary equivalent of a fireworks

READING LIKE A WRITER   23

display. But there are also writers whose vocabulary and whose approach to language is plain, spare, even Spartan.

Alice Munro writes with the simplicity and beauty of a Shaker box. Everything about her style is meant to attract *no* notice, to make you *not* pay attention. But if you read her work closely, every word challenges you to think of a more direct, less fussy or tarted-up way to say what she is saying.

Hers is such a seemingly effortless style that it presents another sort of challenge: the challenge of imagining the drafts and revisions, the calculations required to end up with something so apparently uncalculated. This is not spontaneous, automatic writing but, again, the end product of numerous decisions, of words tried on, tried out, eliminated, replaced with better words—until, as in the opening of "Dulse," we have a compressed, complete, and painfully honest rendering of the complexities of a woman's entire life, her professional and romantic circumstances, her psychological state, as well as the point at which she stands along the continuum from the beginning of life to the end:

> At the end of the summer Lydia took a boat to an island off the southern coast of New Brunswick, where she was going to stay overnight. She had just a few days left until she had to be back in Ontario. She worked as an editor, for a publisher in Toronto. She was also a poet, but she did not refer to that unless it was something people knew already. For the past eighteen months she had been living with a man in Kingston. As far as she could see, that was over.
>
> She had noticed something about herself on this trip to the Maritimes. It was that people were no longer so interested in getting to know her. It wasn't that she had created such a stir before, but something had been there that she could rely on. She was forty-five, and had been divorced for nine years. Her two children had started on their own lives, though there were still

retreats and confusions. She hadn't gotten fatter or thinner, her looks had not deteriorated in any alarming way, but neverthe- less she had stopped being one sort of woman and had become another, and she had noticed it on this trip.

Observe the relative intimacy that results from the writer's choosing to call our heroine by her first name, the rapid deft strokes—in language almost as plain as that of the newspaper— with which the essential questions (who, what, when, where, if not why) are addressed. Lydia has the resources to take a boat somewhere just to stay overnight, but not enough leisure or free- dom to extend her vacation past the few days she has left. We hear not only about her work as an editor but also about her vocation, and the fact that there might be people around her who might know, or not know, that she is also a poet. In one sentence, we are informed about her romantic life and the undramatic res- ignation ("As far as she could see, that was over.") with which our heroine looks back on eighteen months spent living with a lover whom she chooses to think about not by name but only as "a man in Kingston."

We discover her age, her marital status; she has two children. How much verbiage could have been squandered in summariz- ing the periodic "retreats and confusions" that have stalled Lydia's grown children in their progress toward adulthood. And how much less convincing and moving the last part of the passage would be if Munro had chosen to couch her heroine's assess- ment of her mysteriously altered effect on others ("people were no longer interested in getting to know her") in words that were more emotional, more highly charged, more heavily freighted with self-pity, grief, or regret.

Finally, the passage contradicts a form of bad advice often given young writers—namely, that the job of the author is to show, not tell. Needless to say, many great novelists combine "dramatic" showing with long sections of the flat-out authorial narration that is, I guess, what is meant by telling. And the warning against telling leads to a confusion that causes novice writers to think that everything should be acted out—don't tell us a character is happy, show us how she screams "yay" and jumps up and down for joy—when in fact the responsibility of showing should be assumed by the energetic and specific use of language. There are many occasions in literature in which telling is far more effective than showing. A lot of time would have been wasted had Alice Munro believed that she could not begin her story until she had *shown* us Lydia working as an editor, writing poetry, breaking up with her lover, dealing with her children, getting divorced, growing older, and taking all the steps that led up to the moment at which the story rightly begins.

Richard Yates was equally direct, as devastating, and similarly adept at making everything turn and balance on the apt word choice. Here, in the opening paragraph of *Revolutionary Road*, he warns us that the amateur theatrical performance in the novel's first chapter may not be quite the triumph for which the Laurel Players are hoping:

> The final dying sounds of their dress rehearsal left the Laurel Players with nothing to do but stand there, silent and helpless, blinking out over the footlights of an empty auditorium. They hardly dared to breathe as the short, solemn figure of their director emerged from the naked seats to join them on stage, as he pulled a stepladder raspingly from the wings and climbed halfway up its rungs to turn and tell them, with several clearings of his throat, that they were a damned talented group of people and a wonderful group of people to work with.

When we ask ourselves how we know as much as we know—that is, that the performance is likely to be something of an embarrassment—we notice that individual words have given us all the information we need. *The final dying sounds . . . silent and helpless . . . blinking . . . hardly dared to breathe . . . naked seats . . . raspingly.* Even the name of the group—the Laurel Players—seems banal. Is that laurel as in the *tree,* or as in the laurel *wreath* with which the Greeks honored victory, or an unthinking conflation of the two in some arty theatrical terminology? Then come the director's throat clearings and, in indirect dialogue, the equivalent of the group's first bad review. The fake enthusiasm and bravado of that *"damned* talented" (as opposed to merely "talented"), the immediate retreat into the noncommittal "wonderful," and the repetition of "group of people" tells us, sadly, all we need to know about these actors' gifts and the likelihood that their dreams will come true. Meanwhile, we're very aware of what the director's not saying, which is that their performance was brilliant, or even passably good.

Some writers can write both meticulously and carelessly, sometimes on the same page. At lazy moments, F. Scott Fitzgerald could resort to strings of clichés, but in the next paragraph he could give a familiar word the sort of new slant that totally reinvents the language. That reinvention occurs, beginning with his use of the word *deferential,* in the description of the rose-colored grand hotel that opens *Tender Is the Night*:

> *Deferential palms cool its flushed façade, and before it stretches a short dazzling beach. . . . Now, many bungalows cluster near it, but when this story begins only the cupolas of a dozen old villas rotted like water lilies among the massed pines between Gausses Hôtel des Étrangers and Cannes, five miles away.*

Each adjective (*flushed, dazzling*) strikes us as apt. And the simile "rotted like water lilies" will come to seem increasingly applicable to much of what happens in a novel that is partly about the dissolution and decay of romance and beauty.

Students instructed to ransack *The Great Gatsby* for its narrator's unreliability, for a historical portrait of a bygone era, and for a discussion of social class and the power of lost love might miss the word-by-word gorgeousness of the first time Nick Carraway sees Daisy and her friend Jordan. Every word helps to render a particular moment in, or out of, time, and to capture the convergence of beauty, youth, confidence, money, and privilege. Fitzgerald not only describes but makes us experience what it looks and feels like to be *in* a beautiful room by the sea:

> The windows were ajar and gleaming white against the fresh grass outside that seemed to grow a little way into the house. A breeze blew through the room, blew curtains in at one end and out the other like pale flags, twisting them up toward the frosted wedding-cake of the ceiling, and then rippled over the wine-colored rug, making a shadow on it as wind does on the sea.
>
> The only completely stationary object in the room was an enormous couch on which two young women were buoyed up as though upon an anchored balloon. They were both in white, and their dresses were rippling and fluttering as if they had just been blown back after a short flight around the house. I must have stood for a few moments listening to the whip and snap of the curtains and the groan of a picture on the wall. Then there was a boom as Tom Buchanan shut the rear windows and the caught wind died out about the room, and the curtains and the rugs and the two young women ballooned slowly to the floor.

You could almost get a sense of the passage by sorting the words according to what part of speech they represent, the participles and verbs (*gleaming, rippling, ballooned*), the adjectives and adjectival phrases (the white windows and skirts, the fresh grass, the pale flags of the curtains, the frosted wedding cake of a ceiling), the nouns (the *whip* and *snap* of the curtains, the *groan* of the picture, the *caught wind*, the *boom* of the shut window). But you can imagine the same words grouped in far less felicitous combinations. There are at least two places in which words are, as with the deferential palms, used in ways that seem surprising, even incorrect, but absolutely right. It's not exactly a *shadow* that the wind casts over the sea, or the breeze over the rug, but we know what the writer means; there's no better way to describe it. Nor is there a more vivid way to create the image than the seeming improbability of the two women slowly ballooning back to earth without ever having left their couch.

That daring deployment of the incorrect word also occurs in the first sentence of Joyce's "The Dead," in which we are told that Lily, the caretaker's daughter, is literally run off her feet. We know it isn't *literally*. The mistake is one that Lily herself might make, which puts us momentarily in her point of view and prepares us for the ways in which the story will play with viewpoint, with notions of truth and untruth, and with the ways that class background and education affect how we use the language. Such "wrong" words are neither mistakes nor the product of the lazy writer's assumption that one word is as good as another. Nor are they the consequence of a bullying attempt to will the square peg of a wrong word into a round hole of the sentence. Rather, they are the results of conscious, careful deliberations of writers who thought a thousand times before they purposely misused a word, or gave another word a new meaning.

Some writers simply cannot be understood without close reading, not only those like Faulkner, who requires that we parse those wonderfully convoluted sentences, or like Joyce, whom Picasso called "the incomprehensible that everyone can understand," or like Thomas Pynchon, who requires us to put up with long stretches of narrative in which we may have absolutely no idea what is going on, even on the plainest narrative level. I'm talking about more deceptively straightforward stylists who also happen to be masters of subtext, of that place between the lines where so much of the action occurs.

One such writer is Paul Bowles, whose stories you might easily misread if you read them for plot, of which they have plenty, or for psychological truth, which is mostly of the sort that you would rather not think about for too long, if at all. I always feel a little guilty asking students to read Bowles's "A Distant Episode," the literary equivalent of a kick in the head. I justify it to myself by saying that the story is about language as one way to predict when the kick in the head is coming, language as the essence of the self that registers the fact that one's head is getting kicked.

The tale concerns a linguist known only as "the Professor," who travels into the North African desert in search of exotic languages and armed with the arsenal of the timid tourist. The contents of the Professor's "two small overnight bags full of maps, sun lotions, and medicines" provide a tiny mini-course in the importance of close reading. The protagonist's anxiety and cautiousness, his whole psychological makeup, has been communicated in five words ("maps, sun lotions, and medicines") and without the need to use one descriptive adjective or phrase. (He was an anxious man, who worried about getting lost or sunburned or sick, and so forth.) What very different conclusions we might form about a man who carries a bag filled with dice, syringes, and a hand gun.

By the end of the story, the Professor will have been captured and mutilated by the Reguibat, a tribe of bandits who turn him into a mute clown and sell him to a group of men who are, or have some connection with, fundamentalist revolutionaries. A casual perusal of the story suggests that the Professor's misfortune is the accidental result of his being in the wrong place at the wrong time, of having left "civilization." There are some places where you just shouldn't go, or go at your own peril. Bad things happen there: the normal rules no longer apply. But a closer reading reveals that the Professor is not entirely blameless, though the harshness of his punishment hardly fits his crime.

From the start, the Professor is coolly observed making an escalating series of simultaneously innocent and arrogant cultural mistakes. He takes the darker and more dismal of the two rooms he is offered at the hotel because it is a few pennies cheaper, and because he has "gone native" and does not want to be taken for the tourist he is—and possibly cheated. He insults the waiter at a café by suggesting that the man might be willing to do business with the bandits and help the Professor buy some of the camel-udder boxes he knows are sold in the region. And he insists on this even after the waiter has made it very clear that to consort with the outcast tribe would be so far beneath his dignity as to constitute a personal degradation. There is also a moment at which the Professor fails to offer a cigarette to his guide: a serious breach of decorum. The Professor's miscalculations result in, or contribute to, his being delivered directly into the hands of those same outlaws. None (or few) of these serious social mistakes would be apparent unless you stopped at every word and asked yourself what was being communicated, understood, misunderstood, said, and not being said.

Reading this way requires a certain amount of stamina, concentration, and patience. But it also has its great rewards, among them the excitement of approaching, as nearly as you can hope to come, the hand and mind of the artist. It's something like the way you experience a master painting, a Rembrandt or a Velasquez, by viewing it from not only far away but also up close, in order to see the brushstrokes.

I'VE heard the way a writer reads described as "reading carnivorously." What I've always assumed that this means is not, as the expression might seem to imply, reading for what can be ingested, stolen, or borrowed, but rather for what can be admired, absorbed, and learned. It involves reading for sheer pleasure but also with an eye and a memory for which author happens to do which thing particularly well. Let's say you are facing the challenges of populating a room with a large cast of characters all talking at once. Having read the ballroom scene in *Anna Karenina*, or the wild party that winds through so many pages of William Gaddis's *The Recognitions*, you have sources to which you can go not just for inspiration but for technical assistance.

Or let's imagine that you want to write a scene in which someone is telling a lie, and turns out to be an excellent liar, foreseeing his listeners' doubts and covering himself in case anyone might want to challenge his story. The difficulty of getting this sort of moment onto the page might direct you to Tatyana Tolstaya's "Heavenly Flame." The story is set in a summer dacha outside Moscow, in the post-glasnost years. A sculptor named Dmitry Ilich, who has spent two years in a Soviet prison camp, libels a hapless invalid named Korobeinikov, a man whom Dmitry feels he is competing with for the attention and affections of the other guests at the dacha:

> They were in school together, as it happens. In different classes. Korobeinikov, of course, has forgotten Dmitry Ilich—well, it's been forty years now, that's only natural. But Dmitry Ilich hasn't forgotten, no sir, because at one time this Korobeinikov pulled a really dirty trick on him! You see, in his youth Dmitry Ilich used to write poetry, a sin he still commits even now. They were bad poems, he knows that—nothing that would've made a name for him, just little exercises in the fair

*art of letters, you know, for the soul. That's not the point. But,
as it happened, when Dmitry Ilich had his little legal mishap
and went camping for two years, the manuscripts of these im-
mature poems of his ended up in this Korobeinikov's hands.
And the fellow published them under his own name. So, that's
the story. Fate, of course, sorted everything out: Dmitry Ilich
was actually glad that these poems had appeared under some-
one else's name; nowadays he'd be ashamed to show such rub-
bish to a dog; he doesn't need that kind of fame. And it didn't
bring Korobeinikov any happiness: he got neither praise nor
abuse for his reward; nothing came of it. Korobeinikov never
did make it as an artist, either: he changed professions, and
now he does some kind of technical work, it seems. That's the
way the cookie crumbles.*

Until this point in the story, the reader may have been enter-
taining some doubts about the somewhat sketchy sculptor. But
this passage, written in a third-person voice that is actually a sort
of indirect dialogue, convinces us, just as it is meant to convince
Dmitry's listeners, that he is telling the truth.

The chatty, conversational, deceptively casual colloquialisms
("Well," "you see," "no sir," "that's natural") and the concluding
cliché ("That's the way the cookie crumbles") give Dmitry's lie
a sort of folksy authenticity. A story told this spontaneously and
simply, so apparently straight from the heart, must, we feel, be
authentic. The self-deprecating references to his poems as "rub-
bish" and a "sin," "little exercises in the fair art of letters," suggest
that Dmitry, who has no serious stake in his writing, could not
possibly be harboring a serious grudge against Korobeinikov for
having plagiarized something so unimportant. Indeed, Dmitry is
(as he himself would be the first to tell us) too large, too forgiv-
ing, too generous a soul for any emotion so small as bitterness
or resentment.

Unlike Korobeinikov, he is an artist and thus, he suggests, superior to the putative plagiarist, who does "some kind of technical work"—he is in fact an engineer. But what's most noteworthy about the passage—what indeed is the fulcrum on which the entire story turns—is the (also deceptively) lighthearted and euphemistic reference to the sculptor's "little legal mishap" after which he "went camping for two years," which, of course, is a reference to his term in the Soviet labor camp: a grim reality of their recent history that the pleasure-loving, almost hysterically hedonistic dacha crowd cannot bear to mention more directly. Eventually, when Dmitry's story is revealed to be a lie, the reader is shocked, but in a different way than are the characters, who (again because of their history) are so used to concealment, to being lied to, and to being forced to lie that they treat the incident as yet another joke, though the joke has tragic consequences for poor Korobeinikov.

BEFORE I move on from the subject of words to that of sentences and paragraphs, let me say a few more words about those portrait busts of the musicians that presided over my grade-school piano practice. When I told my husband that I was writing this essay, he informed me that we actually had one of those same little composer statues in our house. It turns out that it had gone underground, survived any number of dislocations and losses, and emerged in an upstairs bedroom, where it remains to this day. It's part of a setup, almost like an altar, in the childhood room of our younger son, who has grown up to be a musician and a composer.

THREE

Sentences

NOT LONG AGO, A YOUNG WRITER TOLD ME A STORY ABOUT being taken to dinner by his successful, high-powered agent. The agent asked him what he wanted to write about, what subjects engaged his interest. To which the young writer replied that, to tell the truth, subject matter wasn't all that important to him. What he really cared about, what he wanted most of all was to write . . . really great sentences.

The agent sighed. His eyelids fluttered. After a moment he said, "Promise me that you will never, *ever* in your life say that to an American publisher."

Part of what makes the story so funny and so poignant, aside from the gratuitous swipe at American publishers, at least a few of whom must still care about great sentences, is that many writers might well say the same thing. They too might say that they care about writing great sentences more than they care about other, more obvious aspects of their work—for example, plot. But what prevents them from saying so is probably not the fear of ruining their careers (without a sensible agent to advise them, most writers might not even realize how self-sabotaging such an admission might be) but rather the fact that to talk about sentences is to have a conversation about something far more meaningful and personal to most authors than the questions they're more often asked, such as: Do you have a work schedule? Do you use a computer? Where do you get your ideas?

To talk to another writer about sentences feels like forging a connection based on the most intimate and arcane sort of shoptalk, much the way mathematicians might bond on the basis of a shared admiration for some obscure, elegant theorem. Every so often I'll hear writers say that there are other writers they would read if for no other reason than to marvel at the skill with which they can put together the sort of sentences that move us to read closely, to disassemble and reassemble them, much the way a mechanic might learn about an engine by taking it apart.

The well-made sentence transcends time and genre. A beautiful sentence is a beautiful sentence, regardless of when it was written, or whether it appears in a play or a magazine article. Which is just one of the many reasons why it's pleasurable and useful to read outside of one's own genre. The writer of the lyrical fiction or of the quirkiest, most free-form stream-of-consciousness novel can learn by paying close attention to the sentences of the most logical author of the exactingly reasoned personal essay. Indeed, the brilliant sentences in Rebecca West's journalism and travel writing often outsparkle those with which she composed her novels. This may suggest the possibility that certain writers' sentences improve in proportion to the density and the gravity of the information they have to impart.

These characteristically lucid sentences from the opening of West's novel *The Birds Fall Down* introduce two of the novel's main characters, sketch in the outlines of their social, psychological, and domestic situation, and end with a flourish guaranteed to persuade the reader to turn the page:

One afternoon, in the early summer of this century, when Laura Rowan was just eighteen, she sat, embroidering a handkerchief, on the steps leading down from the terrace of her father's house to the gardens communally owned by the residents in Radnage Square. She liked embroidery. It was a solitary pastime and nobody bothered to interfere with it. The terrace had been empty till ten minutes before, when her father had come out of the house. She had known without looking up that it was he. He had shifted a chair quite a distance to a new position and as he settled in it had grumbled at its failure to comply with his high standards of comfort; and as he had thereafter kept up a derisive mutter she assumed he was reading a book. He could not see her. She was sitting on the bottom step, and she was content that it should be so, as otherwise he would have told her either to sit up straight or not so straight. His criticism was not so urgent as other people's was apt to be, but it was continuous. Presently she heard the click of the french window which opened on the terrace, and she set down her embroidery and prepared to eavesdrop. For the last year or so everybody in the house had been eavesdropping whenever they had a chance.

Yet even this shimmering passage seems to pale slightly in comparison to this section from West's masterpiece, *Black Lamb and Grey Falcon*, in which she describes the moments leading up to the assassination of Grand Duke Franz Ferdinand at Sarajevo:

Princip heard the noise of Chabrinovitch's bomb and thought the work was done, so stood still. When the car went by and he saw that the royal party was still alive, he was dazed with astonishment and walked away to a cafe, where he sat down and had a cup of coffee and pulled himself together. Granezh was also deceived by the explosion and let his oppor-

tunity go by. Franz Ferdinand would have gone from Sarajevo untouched had it not been for the actions of his staff, who by blunder after blunder contrived that his car should be slowed down and that he should be presented as a stationary target in front of Princip, the one conspirator of real and mature deliberation, who had finished his cup of coffee and was walking back through the streets, aghast at the failure of himself and his friends, which would expose the country to terrible punishment without having inflicted any loss on authority. At last the bullets had been coaxed out of the reluctant revolver to the bodies of the eager victims.

By now you may be asking: what *is* a beautiful sentence? The answer is that beauty, in a sentence, is ultimately as difficult to quantify or describe as beauty in a painting or a human face. Perhaps a more accurate explanation might be something like Emily Dickinson's well-known definition of poetry: "If I feel physically as if the top of my head were taken off, I know this is poetry." I realize that this is not as precise a definition as the would-be beautiful-sentence-writer might wish. But perhaps it will offer some comfort if I say that if you are even thinking in these terms—that is, if you are even considering what might constitute strong, vigorous, energetic, and clear sentences—you are already far in advance of wherever you were before you were conscious of the sentence as something deserving our deep respect and enraptured attention.

Among the many authors whose names crop up in this context are—to choose three who are widely separated not only by the centuries by also by genre, gender, background, and temperament—Samuel Johnson, Virginia Woolf, and Philip Roth. Here is the sentence that begins Samuel Johnson's brief biography *The Life of Savage.*

> *It has been observed in all ages that the advantages of na-*
> *ture or of fortune have contributed very little to the promotion*
> *of happiness; and that those whom the splendour of their rank,*
> *or the extent of their capacity, have placed upon the summits*
> *of human life, have not often given any just occasion to envy*
> *in those who look up to them from a lower station; whether it*
> *be that apparent superiority incites great designs, and great*
> *designs are naturally liable to fatal miscarriages; or that the*
> *general lot of mankind is misery, and the misfortunes of those*
> *whose eminence drew upon them an universal attention, have*
> *been more carefully recorded, because they were more generally*
> *observed, and have in reality only been more conspicuous than*
> *others, not more frequent, or more severe.*

The quality that this sentence shares in common with all good sentences is first and most obviously clarity. Between its initial capital letter and its final period are 134 words, ten commas, and three semicolons, and yet the average reader, or at least the reader who has the patience to read and consider every word, will have no trouble understanding what Doctor Johnson is saying.

Despite its length, the sentence is economical. To remove even one word would make it less lucid and less complete, as Johnson takes an observation so common as to have become a cliché (money and fame don't by themselves make us happy) and turns it, then turns it again, considering the possible explanations, the reasons why this perception may be true or merely *appear* to be true. The sentence combines a sort of magisterial authority with an almost offhand wit, in part because of the casual ease with which it tosses off sweeping philosophical generalizations ("great designs are naturally liable to fatal miscarriages," "the general lot of mankind is misery") compressed into subordinate clauses, as if the truth of these statements is so obvious to both the writer and the reader that there is no need to pause over these pronouncements, let alone give them sentences of their own.

Possibly the principal reason why the sentence so delights us is that to read it is to take part in the process—the successive qualifications and considerations—of thought itself, of a lively mind at work, or in any case a mind as lively as Doctor Johnson's. Finally—and there is no way to convey this unless you read the sentence aloud or at least, as your first grade teacher cautioned you not to do, say it silently, word by word, in your mind—the cadence and rhythm of the sentence (a subject to which I'll return later) are as measured and pleasing as those of poetry or music.

It's necessary to quote a longer passage from Philip Roth, since part of what is so extraordinary about his sentences is how energetic and varied they are, how they differ in length, in tone, in pitch, how rapidly and seamlessly they shift from the explanatory to the incantatory, from the inquisitive to the rhetorical to the reportorial. This paragraph from *American Pastoral* encapsulates the meditation that lies at the center of the book. It's the question of how a man like Seymour "Swede" Levov could do everything in his power to ensure that the American dream, the "longed-for American pastoral," would become a reality for himself and his family—and find himself in a hellish "counterpastoral . . . the indigenous American berserk":

> *The old intergenerational give-and-take of the country-that-used-to-be, when everyone knew his role and took the rules dead seriously, the acculturating back-and-forth that all of us here grew up with, the ritual postimmigrant struggle for success turning pathological in, of all places, the gentleman farmer's castle of our superordinary Swede. A guy stacked like a deck of cards for things to unfold entirely differently. In no way prepared for what is going to hit him. How could he, with all his carefully calibrated goodness, have known that*

the stakes of living obediently were so high? Obedience is em-
braced to lower the stakes. A beautiful wife. A beautiful house.
Runs his business like a charm. . . . This is how successful
people live. They're good citizens. They feel lucky. They feel
grateful. God is smiling down on them. There are problems,
they adjust. And then everything changes and it becomes im-
possible. Nothing is smiling down on anybody. And who can
adjust then? Here is someone not set up for life's working out
poorly, let alone for the impossible. But who is set up for the im-
possible that is going to happen? Who is set up for tragedy and
the incomprehensibility of suffering? Nobody. The tragedy of
the man not set up for tragedy—that is every man's tragedy.

Strictly speaking, these are not all complete sentences.
Sentence fragments are scattered in among the full sentences.
The first long fragment has everything but a verb—the one ele-
ment that, as we learned in school, is, along with the subject,
the most basic necessity for a sentence. But why would it *need* a
verb when it has, packed into fifty-two words and six clauses, a
lament for an old order, for a lost security and predictability, and
a hint that this order will fail "our superordinary Swede." Then
comes the start of the brief, percussive declarative sentences and
fragments. "A guy stacked like a deck of cards . . . In no way
prepared . . ." Immediately the passage swings into a kind of call
and response, an argument with itself, a series of questions and
answers, or, more accurately, answers that acknowledge the fact
that there *are* no answers for the questions being asked. The chain
of three-word sentences: "They're good citizens. They feel lucky.
They feel grateful." Then the parallel sentences: "God is smiling
down on them . . . Nothing is smiling down on anybody."
The questions grow larger, more demanding and despair-
ing, closer to the questions Job asked God. Who is set up for
tragedy and the incomprehensibility of suffering? The question

is answered: nobody. And at last we get the beautiful and unimpeachably wise final sentence: "The tragedy of the man not set up for tragedy—that is every man's tragedy." It's helpful to read the section aloud in order to get the effect of the impassioned debate that Roth has constructed, word by word, sentence by sentence.

Finally, let's look at one of the most complex and virtuosic sentences in all of literature, which appears at the opening of Virginia Woolf's essay "On Being Ill":

> *Considering how common illness is, how tremendous the spiritual change that it brings, how astonishing, when the lights of health go down, the undiscovered countries that are then disclosed, what wastes and deserts of the soul a slight attack of influenza brings to view, what precipices and lawns sprinkled with bright flowers a little rise of temperature reveals, what ancient and obdurate oaks are uprooted in us by the act of sickness, how we go down into the pit of death and feel the waters of annihilation close above our heads and wake thinking to find ourselves in the presence of the angels and the harpers when we have a tooth out and come to the surface in the dentist's arm-chair and confuse his "Rinse the mouth—rinse the mouth" with the greeting of the Deity stooping from the floor of Heaven to welcome us—when we think of this, as we are so frequently forced to think of it, it becomes strange indeed that illness has not taken its place with love and battle and jealousy among the prime themes of literature.*

The marvel, of course, is not how long the sentence is—181 words!—but how perfectly comprehensible, graceful, witty, intelligent, and pleasurable we find it to read. It's not the sentence's gigantism but rather its lucidity that makes it so worth studying and breaking down into its component parts. It makes us wish that students were still taught to diagram sentences, to map them into instantly visible, comprehensible charts that make it not only easy but necessary to account for each word and to keep track of which phrase is modifying which noun, which clause follows which antecedent. As Gertrude Stein wrote, "I really do not know that anything has ever been more exciting than diagramming sentences. I like the feeling the everlasting feeling of sentences as they diagram themselves."

Among the questions that writers need to ask themselves in the process of revision—Is this the best word I can find? Is my meaning clear? Can a word or phrase be cut from this without sacrificing anything essential?—perhaps the most important question is: Is this grammatical? What's strange is how many beginning writers seem to think that grammar is irrelevant, or that they are somehow above or beyond this subject more fit for a schoolchild than the future author of great literature. Or possibly they worry that they will be distracted from their focus on art if they permit themselves to be sidetracked by the dull requirements of English usage. But the truth is that grammar is always interesting, always useful. Mastering the logic of grammar contributes, in a mysterious way that again evokes some process of osmosis, to the logic of thought.

A novelist friend compares the rules of grammar, punctuation, and usage to a sort of old-fashioned etiquette. He says that writing is a bit like inviting someone to your house. The writer is the host, the reader the guest, and you, the writer, follow the etiquette because you want your readers to be more comfortable, especially if you're planning to serve them something they might not be expecting.

For help with this specialized etiquette, I'd recommend a grammar manual such as Strunk and White's *The Elements of Style*. It's a book to which I return from time to time, the way I periodically reread Shakespeare. I always discover something new, settle a question that has been puzzling me, or learn a principle of usage that I have been pretending to know, a pretense that has resulted in inconsistency and in the sort of errors from which I can only pray some saintly copy editor will save me. Only recently, breezing through *The Elements of Style*, I finally nailed down the proper way to form the possessive of a word like Keats. (It's Keats's, but there are exceptions worth looking into.)

The crucial thing, in seeking out a congenial grammar book, is to find one whose authors have an ear for the way language evolves and changes, and show good judgment about the point at which we might want to adopt or surrender to neologisms and new usages. It's also essential to find a manual with a loose interpretation of the whole concept of style, lest you be advised against ever writing the sort of sentence fragment that animates the Philip Roth passage. Which is why, I believe, it's necessary to hold the concept of clarity as an even higher ideal than grammatical correctness, and why it's essential to read great sentences—that is, the sentences of great sentence-writers—along with your style book.

One essential and telling difference between learning from a style manual and learning from literature is that any how-to book will, almost by definition, tell you *how not to* write. In that way, manuals of style are a little like writing workshops, and have the same disadvantage—a pedagogy that involves warnings about what might be broken and directions on how to fix it—as opposed to learning from literature, which teaches by positive model.

We can thank our lucky stars that no one told Virginia Woolf that a sentence as long as the one with which she begins "On Being Ill" might turn out to be hopelessly clumsy or unclear. Because as her sentence winds on, everything proceeds in an orderly progression from that participle "considering" and that introduction of "illness" as the noun that can subsequently be summoned up by the pronoun "it." Pausing to breathe at each

READING LIKE A WRITER   45

comma, we find ourselves amid a series of dependent clauses that break over us like waves, clauses that increase in length, complexity, and intensity as the aspects of illness that we are invited to consider grow more elaborate and imaginative, whisking us from undiscovered countries to deserts to flowered lawns and down into the abyss from which we are lifted by the voice of the dentist whom we mistake for God welcoming us into heaven. Until at last it all comes together in a single word, *this*: "when we think of this." Followed by a sly suggestion that we ourselves might often think of the ease with which the dentist can be mistaken for a heavenly messenger—as in fact we don't often, or at least *I* don't. And only then does this glorious sentence arrive at its apparent point: the oddness of the fact that illness is not more commonly treated in literature.

Once again it's worth mentioning that the composition of a sentence such as this one—or any sentence, really—is the end result of many minute decisions, and that a different sort of writer might have decided to make the same point in a dozen or so words that could have gotten the idea across as understandably but not nearly so enchantingly, nor so intelligently. Nor would such a sentence have been nearly so much fun to read. Another author could have said, simply: Considering how frequently people get sick, it's strange that writers don't write about illness more often.

But that sentence would be a far less revealing and reliable introduction to the essay. Because it's not just the content—the meaning—of the sentence that prepares us for what is to come. What's in store for us is not a straightforward examination, a glorified statistical analysis of the inexplicable infrequency of illness as a literary subject, but rather an opportunity to watch Woolf's mind skipping from subject to subject in a simultaneously imaginative and logical way, crossing gossamer bridges that never seem like non sequiturs but rather like stepping stones from one clear stream of thought to another, from one engaging observation to the next.

By the end of the twenty-five-page essay, at which point Woolf will have gotten to her *real* subject, which is the bravery that it requires to continue living in the presence and the face of loss and death, she will have touched on several dozen topics that include reading, language, faith, solitude, science, Shakespeare, the animal kingdom, insanity, suicide, and a brief biography of the third Marchioness of Waterford. In just a few words, the essay skips from a discussion about how hard it is for us to envision heaven to a very different kind of difficulty, reading *The Decline and Fall of the Roman Empire* when we are feeling less than up to par. And so by the time you have come to the end of the essay, you will have realized that a sentence that may have seemed to involve a sort of showing-off was rather an admirably accurate promise about, or introduction to, the sparkling wit and the deep seriousness of everything that has followed.

Just to demonstrate that this sort of sentence—the complex, introductory sentence that not only establishes the tone but also encapsulates something essential about the remainder of the work—can exist in fiction as well as in the speculative essay, let's look at the opening of Heinrich von Kleist's story "The Earthquake in Chile":

> *In Santiago, the capital of the kingdom of Chile, at the very moment of the great earthquake of 1647 in which many thousands of lives were lost, a young Spaniard by the name of Jéronimo Rugera, who had been locked up on a criminal charge, was standing against a prison pillar, about to hang himself.*

It's a sentence so full of bravado and playful assurance that it's the literary equivalent of a poker player opening with a gigantic bet. How can we not stay in to find out what he's holding in his hand? What will happen during the earthquake, which, we already know, involved a catastrophic loss of life? What "criminal charge" has caused the young Spaniard to be locked up? And why is he about to hang himself? Meanwhile, we can't help noting, along the way, how odd it is: the idea of a suicide happening at the "very moment" of disaster and mass death.

Throughout Kleist's work, there are sentences, particularly first sentences, that startle us with how much sheer storytelling they pack into a few brief phrases. Kafka, himself a master of opening lines ("Someone must have betrayed Joseph K., for one fine morning, he was arrested without having done anything wrong" or, "During these last decades the interest in professional fasting has markedly diminished") is said to have learned to write first sentences by reading those of Kleist.

It's a good idea to have a designated section of your bookshelf (perhaps the one nearest your desk) for books by writers who have obviously worked on their sentences, revising and polishing them into gems that continue to dazzle us. These are works you can turn to whenever you feel that your own style is getting a little slack or lazy or vague. You can open such books anywhere and read a sentence that will move you to labor longer, try harder, to return to that trouble spot and rework that imprecise or awkward sentence until it is something to be proud of instead of something you hope that the reader won't notice.

On that part of my bookshelf—the library of inspirational sentences—there are, among others, the books of Stanley Elkin. To prove my point, I opened *Searches and Seizures* at random and discovered this passage in "The Making of Ashenden," a short novel about a rich man's besotted and highly inappropriate love affair with a bear:

All my adult life I have been a guest in other people's houses, following the sun and seasons like a migratory bird, an instinct in me, the rich man's cunning feel for ripeness, some oyster-in-an-r-month notion working there which knows without reference to anything outside itself when to pack the tennis racket, when to bring along the German field glasses to look at a friend's birds, the telescope to stare at his stars, the wet suit to swim in beneath his waters when the exotic fish are running. It's not in the Times *when the black dinner jacket comes off and the white one goes on; it's something surer, subtler the delicate guidance system of the privileged, my playboy astronomy.*

Compressed into a single sentence is an entire way of life, a stratum of our class and caste system, a key to the narrator's character, a window on his existence, along with all manner of little throwaway extras tossed in, for instance the satisfaction of figuring out the meaning of an "oyster-in-an-r-month notion" or "my playboy astronomy." The sentence gives us a fairly accurate sense of the narrator's confidence, his boastfulness, his sense of entitlement—aspects of his character that will be humbled by his unexpected and overpowering sexual attraction to the bear. Once again, it's useful to imagine the boring summary phrases with which a less skillful author might have conveyed the same information.

I suspect that many Raymond Chandler fans are more attracted to his sentences, those wonders of snappy, outrageously excessive tough-guy prose, than they are to his detective plots, which can be a little hard to follow, and more rapidly slip our minds than the lines for which we remember Philip Marlowe. The fondness we feel for Chandler's detective has more to do with how he uses the language than how he solves a murder or shoots a gun. It's nearly impossible to resist the appeal of lines such as these, from *The Big Sleep*:

> *There was no fear in the scream. It had a sound of half-pleasurable shock, an accent of drunkenness, an overtone of pure idiocy. It was a nasty sound. It made me think of men in white and barred windows and hard narrow cots with leather wrist and ankle straps fastened to them. The Geiger hideaway was perfectly silent again when I hit the gap in the hedge and dodged around the angle that masked the front door. There was an iron ring in a lion's mouth for a knocker. I reached for it, I had hold of it. At that exact instant, as if somebody had been waiting for the cue, three shots boomed in the house. There was a sound that might have been a long harsh sigh. Then a soft messy thump. And then rapid footsteps in the house—going away."*

Perhaps I have been leaning toward sentences, like Woolf's or Kleist's, like butterflies gliding from flower to flower, or those quick uppercuts like Chandler's, sentences like a poke in the ribs, or the rapid-fire sentences of Stanley Elkin or Philip Roth. But there are also wonderful sentences that take the quickest, simplest, clearest route from point A to point B.

It's all but impossible to talk about literary plain speech and the simple (or the unadorned compound) sentence without mentioning Hemingway. Along with Twain, Hemingway can take partial credit for demonstrating that a vast ocean separated the voice of the nineteenth-century European novel from the voice of the average American on the street.

Reading Hemingway, you soon discover that his sentences are neither simple nor mannered in that almost self-parodic, easily satirized way you may remember. His writing is far more varied than those passages constructed from phrases that echo and repeat, joined by conjunctions into a sing-song rhythm halfway between baby talk and the King James Bible. *The Sun Also Rises* contains the following long sentence about a bullfight, just the sort of physical, violent event that another writer might have rendered in shorter, punchier prose. I suppose these cadences more accurately capture the ceremonial aspects of the blood sport, the sweep of the cape, and so forth. It's also a description of a bullfighter whose career is on its way down, a situation partly conveyed through the sentence's vaguely lugubrious tone:

> *Sometimes he turned to smile that toothed, long-jawed, lipless smile when he was called something particularly insulting, and always the pain that any movement produced grew stronger and stronger, until finally his yellow face was parchment color, and after his second bull was dead and the throwing of bread and cushions was over, after he had saluted the President with the same wolf-jawed smile and contemptuous eyes, and handed his sword over the barrera to be wiped, and put back in its case, he passed through into the callejon and leaned on the barrera below us, his head on his arms, not seeing, not hearing anything, only going through his pain.*

Again, we can easily follow the sentence despite its length, though it might have been no less rhythmic and a little more transparent if the phrase "when he was called something particularly insulting" had been put up front after "sometimes," where it properly belongs.

In the very next paragraph are passages of more familiar, more "Hemingwayesque" prose:

> *Belmonte was no longer well enough. He no longer had his greatest moments in the bull-ring. He was not sure that there were any great moments. Things were not the same and now life only came only in flashes.*

Soon after, in the same scene, but now with a different fighter—this one on his way up—we find the sort of sentences for which Hemingway is rightly admired, sentences that know how to get out of their own way and communicate a feeling or a mood or an action with only minimal distraction and maximum verisimilitude. Note how he at once sticks to the facts and at the same time—through word choice, rhythm, and syntax—captures the balletic sexuality of the deadly pas de deux between the matador and the bull:

> The bull's tail went up and he charged, and Romero moved his arms ahead of the bull, wheeling, his feet firmed. The dampened, mud-weighted cape swung open and full as a sail fills, and Romero pivoted with it just ahead of the bull. At the end of the pass they were facing each other again. Romero smiled. The bull wanted it again, and Romero's cape filled again, this time on the other side. Each time he let the bull pass so close that the man and the bull and the cape that filled and pivoted ahead of the bull were all one sharply etched mass. It was all so slow and so controlled. It was as though he were rocking the bull to sleep. He made four veronicas like that, and finished with a half-veronica that turned his back on the bull and came away toward the applause, his hand on his hip, his cape on his arm, and the bull watching his back go away.

In search of both the roots and the end-stage form of the conjunction-heavy, sing-songy Hemingway sentence to which I refer earlier, we need to go back to Gertrude Stein. "Sentences not only words but always sentences have been Gertrude Stein's lifelong passion," she wrote about herself in *The Autobiography of Alice B. Toklas*. From Stein, Hemingway learned much beside what he credits her for in his Paris memoir, *A Moveable Feast*: that is, the advice not to write anything dirty or what she called *inaccrochable*, the idea that male homosexuality is disgusting, and the general principle that one should buy paintings instead of clothes. His debts to her are expressed not only in the content but in the form of the sentence in which Hemingway says, "She had also discovered the truths about rhythms and the use of words in repetition that were valid and valuable and she talked well about them."

In this characteristic passage from *The Autobiography of Alice B. Toklas*—a passage, in fact, about Hemingway, and about sentences—we can see the origins of what Hemingway assimilated and adapted for his own use. We recognize the familiar "rhythms and the use of words in repetition," the conversationality, and the language that forges an amalgam of poetry, plain speech, and eccentric personality:

> *In those early days Hemingway liked all his contemporaries except Cummings. He accused Cummings of having copied everything, not from anybody but from somebody. Gertrude Stein who had been much impressed by* The Enormous Room *said that Cummings did not copy, he was the natural heir of the New England tradition with its aridity and its sterility, but also with its individuality. They disagreed about this. They also disagreed about Sherwood Anderson. Gertrude Stein contended that Sherwood Anderson had a genius for using a sentence to convey a direct emotion, this was in the great American tradition, and that really except Sherwood there was no one in America who could write a clear and passionate sentence. Hemingway did not believe this, he did not like Sherwood's taste. Taste has nothing to do with sentences, contended Gertrude Stein. She also added that Fitzgerald was the only one of the younger writers who wrote naturally in sentences.*

Like her predecessors Sterne and Twain and her contemporaries, Joyce and Woolf, Stein wished, at least in *The Autobiography of Alice B. Toklas*, to construct sentences and use language in a way that reproduced, on the page, the operation of consciousness, the chatter of the inner voice that propels us through the day, the voice in which we understand and explain our own lives to ourselves. More recently, Raymond Carver explored yet another sort of consciousness—usually male, working class, American, reasonably observant, defensive, self-conscious and self-aware though hardly sophisticated—and in the process documented a very different sort of inner life from that of, say, Virginia Woolf's Clarissa Dalloway.

Carver's story "Feathers" concerns an evening that the narrator and his wife, Fran, spend at the home of his co-worker, Bud, his wife, Olla, their baby, and a pet peacock. The beautiful Fran and our narrator are happily in love, contentedly childless, wanting nothing in particular except to be together.

The evening, which Fran approaches with considerable reluctance, turns out to be full of surprises, among them the spectacular ugliness of Bud and Olla's baby, and the couple's odd ideas on the use of family memorabilia as interior-decorating accents. On top of Bud and Olla's TV is a plaster cast of the malformed teeth that Olla was born with and that Bud arranged for her to have fixed. But the biggest surprise of all is the vision of domestic bliss that the visitors are shown, the picture of a household suffused by a love that doesn't require physical beauty or money, a home in which the atmosphere of tenderness, kindness, and care is so palpable and so rich that even the peacock, a notoriously ill-tempered bird, has a frolicsome and sweetly custodial relationship with Bud and Olla's baby.

Here's how Carver describes the effect of that visit in a passage so direct and straight from the narrator's heart that we can tell, simply from the tone and the composition of the sentences, how deeply our normally guarded protagonist has been moved:

*That evening at Bud and Olla's was special. I knew it was
special. That evening I felt good about almost everything in my
life. I couldn't wait to be alone with Fran to talk to her about
what I was feeling. I made a wish that evening. Sitting there
at the table, I closed my eyes for a minute and thought hard.
What I wished for was that I'd never forget or otherwise let go
of that evening. That's one wish of mine that came true. And
it was bad luck for me that it did. But, of course, I couldn't
know that then.*

By repeating that *special* twice, Carver manages to breathe
new freshness and vigor into a word that has, by now, been
blunted out of meaning. The evening is so important that the
word *evening* is repeated three times in the paragraph, though
the evening's pleasures are already offset by the slight ominous-
ness of the "*almost* everything in my life," as well as the complex
emotions—self-pity, resignation, bitterness—contained in that
"*one* wish of mine that came true" (as opposed to, say, "And that
wish came true"). The last three sentences of the paragraph carry
us into the future, or, actually, the present moment in which the
story is being told; by then, the necessity of being careful about
what you wish for will have long become apparent. Finally, the
narrative skips back again into the past, to that evening charac-
terized by so much sheer goodwill that our narrator could never
have imagined how much his life was about to change, and not
for the better.

What follows is a page or so that contains a rapid summary
of those changes. That same night, Bud and Olla's example in-
spire the narrator and his wife to start a family of their own, with
considerably less happy results, a situation that is summed up in
the story's final paragraph, which begins with the narrator oc-
casionally having lunch with Bud at the plant where they work:

Once in a blue moon, he asks about my family. When he
does, I tell him everybody's fine. . . . The truth is, my kid has
a conniving streak in him. But I don't talk about it. Not even
with his mother. Especially her. She and I talk less and less as
it is. Mostly it's just the TV. But I remember that night. I recall
the way the peacock picked up its gray feet and inched around
the table. And then my friend and his wife saying good night
to us on the porch. Olla giving Fran some peacock feathers to
take home. I remember all of us shaking hands, hugging each
other, saying things. In the car, Fran sat close to me as we drove
away. She kept her hand on my leg. We drove home like that
from my friend's house.

The sentences could hardly be more plain. There are hardly
any adjectives except for the gray of the peacock's feet. And there
is that chilling phrase, "conniving streak," which is all the narra-
tor chooses to tell us about his kid. The lovely Fran has become
"his mother," "Her." "Especially her"—two words that convey a
universe of resentment and estrangement. The sentences break
down into sentence fragments, just as they would in speech—in
this guy's speech—punctuating the long bass notes of the sen-
tences that begin: "I remember . . . I recall . . . I remember . . ."
(I've always heard that it's bad luck to have peacock feathers in
the house, and I've always wondered if Carver had this in mind
when he made Olla, unaware of the superstition and with all the
best intentions, give some to Fran.) And finally there are three
short sentences in which the narrator recalls the lost happiness
of that night, a state of blessedness and bliss so hard for him to
recall at this distance that he convinces himself and us with a trio
of statements barely long enough to contain the small, intimate
gesture they describe.

So it's not only the long Latinate sentence that rewards study
and close reading. The brief sentence can be just as effective,

since what matters is not complexity or decoration but rather intelligibility, grace, and the fact that the sentence should strike us as the perfect vehicle for expressing what it aims to express; the sentence should seem ideally suited to whatever story or novel or essay it happens to appear in.

Before we leave the subject of sentences, we should say something more about the subject of rhythm. Rhythm is nearly as important in prose as it is in poetry. I have heard a number of writers say that they would rather choose the slightly wrong word that made their sentence more musical than the precisely right one that made it more awkward and clunky.

Read your work aloud, if you can, if you aren't too embarrassed by the sound of your own voice ringing out when you are alone in a room. Chances are that the sentence you can hardly pronounce without stumbling is a sentence that needs to be reworked to make it smoother and more fluent. A poet once told me that he was reading a draft of a new poem aloud to himself when a thief broke into his Manhattan loft. Instantly surmising that he had entered the dwelling of a madman, the thief turned and ran without taking anything, and without harming the poet. So it may be that reading your work aloud will not only improve its quality but save your life in the process.

Some of the most celebrated passages in literature are those whose cadences move us in ways that reinforce and finally transcend their content. The sentences affect us much as music does, in ways that cannot be explained. Rhythm gives words a power that cannot be reduced to, or described by, mere words.

The haunting, dirgelike force of Tim O'Brien's *The Things They Carried* is created by the repetition of the words *necessity*, *carried*, and *each man*, and by the rhythm established by the obsessive listing, first of objects, then of proper names, then of a quality of each man, followed by more objects, and by the succession of phrases beginning with *because*. Notice how many characters are created in a relatively brief space by the exact and telling choice of what each soldier carried; observe the way that equipment functions as a sort of mini-biography, and the way that, by the end of the passage, *necessity* and *carried* will have taken on a newer, darker meaning. And note how each character is introduced, fleshed out, and humanized by the objects to which he is attached, regardless of how cumbersome they are to carry: canned peaches in heavy syrup, hotel-sized bars of soap. With this recitation of paraphernalia and detritus, O'Brien manages to encapsulate the experience of an army and of a particular war, of a mined and booby-trapped landscape, of cold nights and hot days, of soaking monsoons and rice paddies, and of the possibility of being shot, like Ted Lavender, suddenly and out of nowhere: not only in the middle of a sentence but in the midst of a subordinate clause.

> *The things they carried were largely determined by necessity. Among the necessities or near-necessities were P-38 can openers, pocket knives, heat tabs, wristwatches, dog tags, mosquito repellent, chewing gum, candy, cigarettes, salt tabs. . . . Henry Dobbins, who was a big man, carried extra rations; he was especially fond of canned peaches in heavy syrup over pound cake. Dave Jensen, who practiced field hygiene, carried a toothbrush, dental floss, and several hotel-sized bars of soap he'd stolen on R&R in Sydney, Australia. Ted Lavender, who was scared, carried tranquilizers until he was shot in the head outside the village of Than Ke in mid-April. By necessity, and because it was SOP, they all carried steel helmets that weighed 5 pounds including the lining and camouflage cover. . . . Necessity dictated. Because the land was mined and booby-trapped, it was SOP for each man to carry a steel-centered, nylon-covered flak jacket, which weighed 6.7 pounds, but which on hot days seemed much heavier. Because you could die so quickly,*

each man carried at least one large compress bandage, usually in the helmet band for easy access. Because the nights were cold, and because the monsoons were wet, each carried a green plastic poncho that could be used as a raincoat or groundsheet or makeshift tent. With its quilted liner, the poncho weighed almost two pounds, but it was worth every ounce. In April, for instance, when Ted Lavender was shot, they used his poncho to wrap him up, then to carry him across the paddy, then to lift him into the chopper that took him away.

Among the most well known cadenced sentences are those that end James Joyce's "The Dead." Read them aloud, and there's little that I need to add to what you yourself will discover from the experience of saying them, and hearing them, one word after another:

> *The time had come for him to set out on his journey westward. Yes, the newspapers were right: snow was general all over Ireland. It was falling on every part of the dark central plain, on the treeless hills, falling softly upon the Bog of Allen and, farther westward, softly falling into the dark mutinous Shannon waves. It was falling, too, upon every part of the lonely churchyard on the hill where Michael Furey lay buried. It lay thickly drifted on the crooked crosses and headstones, on the spears of the little gate, on the barren thorns. His soul swooned slowly as he heard the snow falling faintly through the universe and faintly falling, like the descent of their last end, upon all the living and the dead.*

Many of the devices of poetry: meter, alliteration, assonance— swooned slowly, faintly falling—are employed here, as well as the repetitions of the words *falling, falling faintly*, and *faintly falling*, in a series of sentences that at once tie together the themes of the story and lift the narrative to a higher level.

A similarly powerful use of rhythm, in this case to achieve an effect that's a cross between an incantation, a lamentation, and the sort of sermon that might have been delivered by the narrator's Puritan ancestors appears at the end of John Cheever's "Goodbye, My Brother." The family tensions that have simmered throughout this story about a terrible family reunion have, by now, boiled over and more or less evaporated. The unpleasant, difficult brother who functions as the scapegoat for the family's private grievances, and who permits all the buried truths and unspoken dissatisfactions to remain deflected and repressed, has left home yet again. And the narrator, by no means an entirely attractive character himself, rises above that cramped and untrustworthy self to deliver these final lines:

> Oh, what can you do with a man like that? What can you do? How can you dissuade his eye in a crowd from seeking out the cheek with acne, the infirm hand: how can you teach him to respond to the inestimable greatness of the race, the harsh surface beauty of life; how can you put his finger for him on the obdurate truths before which fear and horror are powerless? The sea that morning was iridescent and dark. My wife and my sister were swimming—Diana and Helen—and I saw their uncovered heads, black and gold in the dark water. I saw them come out and I saw that they were naked, unshy, beautiful, and full of grace, and I watched the naked women walk out of the sea.

We're struck by the energy, the grace, and the variety of the sentences, to say nothing of the high oratorical mode in which the passage begins, with the series of questions asking (Who? The reader? The deity?) what is to be done with "a man like that." They are, of course, rhetorical questions. Nothing can be done, and the queries are a literary form of throwing up one's hands. The questions vary in length. The shortest, a mere four words, repeats and emphasizes the first. The longest requires fifty-eight words, and a cascading succession of dependent clauses. This final question begins with what the sinner does wrong—seeking out the pimples, the lameness, the flaws in nature and human nature—before moving on to what he does not do right: that is, celebrating the harsh surface beauty of life, acknowledging the obdurate (note even how the vocabulary and diction has changed, soaring up from the more plainspoken body of the story) truths.

And as we switch from the lengthy and interrogatory to the brief and declarative, the passage shifts from the Puritan to the pagan, or at least the Homeric, from the sermon to the celebration of the women whose names have been borrowed from the beauties of Greek mythology. And still the rhythms faintly echo those of the bible, specifically the early verses of Genesis, in that repetition of "I saw . . . I saw . . . I saw . . . "

All of which contributes not only to the beauty of the ending but also to its strangeness and its mystery, as we leave the story wondering how—how much and for how long—the experience that it describes has transformed the narrator from a not particularly compassionate or self-aware high school teacher into a metaphysician and a poet. The stylistic changes make us even more acutely aware of the alteration that has come over Cheever's protagonist, and we remember the relief we ourselves may have felt after the difficult social occasion, after the troublesome guest has gone home, and the horizon looks briefly unclouded. What makes the passage even more provocative is the fact that it is directly preceded by a horrific act of violence perpetrated by the same narrator who then rises to such heights of poetic diction.

It's also worth noting how both passages from the Joyce and Cheever stories employ rhythm and cadence to signal to the reader that the story is ending. Again, it's helpful to consider the parallels to music, the way that, at the end of a symphony, the tempo slows down and the chords become more sustained or dramatic, with overtones that reverberate and echo after the musicians have stopped playing. Try opening your favorite books and reading the endings aloud. Chances are you'll find yourself reading more slowly, and perhaps more softly, as the sentences themselves telegraph the arrival of a grand or muted finale.

Finally, before we leave the subject of sentences, let's return once more to Hemingway, and to the passage from his memoir of his youth in Paris, *A Moveable Feast*, in which he describes his working method and which subsequent generations of writers have taken as a form of implicit literary advice:

> *Sometimes when I was starting a new story and I could not get it going . . . I would stand and look out over the roofs of Paris and think, "Do not worry. You have always written before and you will write now. All you have to do is write one true sentence. Write the truest sentence that you know." So finally I would write one true sentence, and then go on from there. It was easy then because there was always one true sentence that I knew or had seen or had heard someone say. If I started to write elaborately, or like someone introducing or presenting something, I found that I could cut that scrollwork or ornament out and throw it away and start with the first true simple declarative sentence I had written.*

For years, I've heard this passage about the one true sentence cited as a sort of credo. And I've nodded my head, not wanting to admit that I honestly had no idea what in the world Hemingway was talking about. What is a "true" sentence in this context—that is, the context of fiction? What makes Hemingway's advice so hard to follow is that he never quite explains what "true" means.

Perhaps it's wisest to assume that Hemingway, like countless others, was simply confusing truth with beauty. Possibly what he really meant was a beautiful sentence—a concept that, as we have seen, is almost as hard to define as the one true sentence.

In any case, it should encourage us. Hemingway was not only thinking about the good and beautiful and true sentence, but also using it as sustenance—as a goal to focus on, as a way to keep himself going. And though it's obvious that times have changed, that what was true in Hemingway's era may no longer be true today, the fact remains that Hemingway not only cared about sentences, not only told his publishers that they mattered to him, but told his readers, and told the world.

The young would-be writer of great sentences can perhaps take comfort in the fact that Hemingway's interest in the sentence did not appear to have hurt his career.

FOUR

Paragraphs

IN HIS MEMOIR *Years of Hope* KONSTANTIN PAUSTOVSKY describes a visit to the study of Isaac Babel, an occasion during which the memoirist glimpsed a tall stack of manuscript pages on Babel's desk. Could it be that the celebrated master of the short story was finally writing a novel? No, replied Babel, the mass of paper merely represented the twenty-two most recent drafts of his new story. His friend's surprise inspired Babel to deliver a lengthy disquisition on writing in general and revision in particular.

During his mini-lecture, Babel addressed the subject of the paragraph: "The breaking up into paragraphs and the punctuation have to be done properly but only for the effect on the reader. A set of dead rules is no good. A new paragraph is a wonderful thing. It lets you quietly change the rhythm, and it can be like a flash of lightning that shows the same landscape from a different aspect."

We understand intuitively what Babel means about rhythmic changes and flashes of lightning. But he's not giving us much practical help with the more quotidian problems of how to shape a paragraph or where to end one and begin another. Though once again, as with sentences, merely *thinking* about "the paragraph" puts us ahead of the game, just as being conscious of the sentence as an entity worthy of our attention represents a major step in the right direction.

I asked a friend, a poet who also writes essays and memoirs, if he had any thoughts about the paragraph. He said he thought of the paragraph as a form, like a poetic form, perhaps a bit like a stanza. Then he added something that I myself have noticed. He said that when he was writing an essay, there came a point at which he knew what his first few paragraphs would be. That was the point at which the essay organized itself in his mind and fell, as if with a series of clicks, more or less into place.

But how, precisely, can we tell when these clicks are supposed to occur? Once again, it seems easier to learn by example than by abstraction, by reading Babel's fiction to see how his ideas about electrical storms and rhythm operate in practice.

Let's consider the opening paragraphs of two of his most famous stories, together with the beginning of the paragraphs that follow, and focus on the careful reasoning or the unconscious impulse that might inspire a writer to call up that flash of lightning.

Before I go further, it's necessary to say something about translation. When we read a work in translation, we are, and must remain, aware that certain essential choices—about tone and diction, and among variant synonyms—have been made by the translator, rather than the writer. In that case we can only hope that the translator has decided wisely, and has tried, insofar as possible, somehow to channel what the writer would have wished. Babel in English is, needless to say, different from Babel in Russian. So when I quote Babel in the Walter Morrison translation, I am quoting something that is not entirely Babel but rather the product of a sort of collaboration between Morrison and Babel. Obviously, I would prefer to have read the stories in the original. But Morrison's was the first translation I read, and it is still what comes to mind when I think of the work of Isaac Babel, just as I have come to think of Kleist in the Martin Greenberg translation and Chekhov as rendered by Constance Garnett in a style about which others often complain, but which I have always found to be perfectly adequate.

This, then, is the opening passage of the Babel-Morrison "Crossing into Poland."

> *The Commander of the VI Division reported: Novograd-Volynsk was taken at dawn today. The Staff had left Krapivno, and our baggage train was spread out in a noisy rearguard over the highroad from Brest to Warsaw built by Nicholas I upon the bones of peasants.*
>
> *Fields flowered around us, crimson with poppies; a noon-tide breeze played in the yellowing rye; on the horizon virginal buckwheat rose like the wall of a distant monastery. . . . The orange sun rolled down the sky like a lopped-off head, and mild light glowed from the cloud gorges. The standards of the sunset flew above our heads. Into the cool of evening dripped the smell of yesterday's blood, of slaughtered horses.*

And here is the beginning of "My First Goose":

> *Savitsky, Commander of the VI Division, rose when he saw me, and I wondered at the beauty of his giant's body. He rose, the purple of his riding breeches and the crimson of his little tilted cap and the decorations stuck on his chest cleaving the hut as a standard cleaves the sky. A smell of scent and the sickly sweet freshness of soap emanated from him. His long legs*

were like girls sheathed to the neck in shining riding boots.

He smiled at me, struck his riding whip on the table, and drew toward him an order that the Chief of Staff had just finished dictating.

What may impress us most strongly about both of these first paragraphs is not how they begin but rather how they end—with little climaxes of disquiet toward which they seem to be leading. In general, I would suggest, the paragraph could be understood as a sort of literary respiration, with each paragraph as an extended—in some cases, very extended—breath. Inhale at the beginning of the paragraph, exhale at the end. Inhale again at the start of the next. But by introducing some element of unease, Babel's paragraphs make us catch our breath in the final sentence, so that we are still a little breathless in the midst of that rhythmic change, that shift of perspective.

"Crossing into Poland" begins with straightforward, unadorned narration, a reportorial (Babel worked for many years as a journalist) reference to a victory. There are no adjectives in the sentence, and only one, *noisy,* appears in the paragraph. We might almost be reading a memo, a military briefing, until we get to that last phrase, "upon the bones of peasants," which, in just a few words, lifts us from the realm of the newspaper report, in which no such phrase is likely to appear, into that of fiction. It's worth noting how differently that paragraph would read if its final sentence ended as it does in the more recent Peter Constantine translation, "The staff is now withdrawing from Krapivno, and our cavalry transport stretches along the high road that goes from Brest to Warsaw, a high road built on the bones of muzhiks by Czar Nicholas I."

In any case, those bones continue to rattle through the subsequent paragraph, in which the alternation between a lush, lyrical description of nature and glancing references to such nasty things as horse blood and lopped-off heads evokes the horrors of a military campaign, of traveling through an ordinary or even gorgeous landscape in which something terrible may at any moment happen—as it does by the end of the story.

Something similar occurs in the opening of "My First Goose," though here the faint notes of discord and unease begin from the very first sentence, with the narrator's response to Division Commander Savitsky. His initial impulse is to admire the beauty of the man's giant's body. The entire paragraph represents a transfixed instant during which our protagonist—who, we will soon learn, is a law graduate of St. Petersburg University, an intellectual, an idealistic follower of Lenin, a writer with a trunkful of manuscripts—loses his awareness of everything but what the commander is wearing and the smell of his perfume. The perverse polymorphic eroticism of that moment, which will resonate throughout a story that is partly about the interconnection of military comradery, sex, and violence, builds toward the perception of the commander's long legs "like girls sheathed to the neck in shining riding boots."

This disturbing image will resurface in the story's last sentences, when the bespectacled narrator has, by committing a violent act, gained the acceptance of the brutal Cossacks with whom he is riding. Finally, the men fall asleep in a hayloft:

> We slept, all six of us, beneath a wooden roof that let in the stars, warming one another, our legs intermingled. I dreamed: and in my dreams saw women. But my heart, stained with bloodshed, grated and brimmed over.

What the break at the end of the story's first paragraph does is startle us, along with the narrator, out of our reverie. The commander's smile, the snap of his whip against his table, and the movement he makes in reaching for the newly dictated report combine to break the dreamy spell that has given the paragraph its aspect of frozen bewitchment. The flash of lightning, the rhythm change set the story in motion. The smile, the whip, the military report signal that it's time to get down to business, which, we learn in just a few words, is the business of killing. The second paragraph ends with the orders that the report contains, which are expressed in what we imagine to be the language of the military directive: "to make contact with the enemy and destroy the same."

At this point we might want to return to the quote from *Years of Hope*, in which Babel begins his discussion of the paragraph by warning against a set of dead rules, because the temptation here might be to suppose that the opening paragraphs from his own two stories suggest a rule of sorts—namely, that the paragraph should build toward some kind of climax, toward that little intake of breath that carries you over into the next paragraph. But the advantage of reading widely, as opposed to trying to formulate a series of general rules, is that we learn there *are* no general rules, only individual examples to help point you in a direction in which you might want to go.

In one of Rex Stout's mysteries, *Plot It Yourself*, Nero Wolfe is called upon to determine if three manuscripts that figure in a case involving accusations of plagiarism could have been written by the same person. His conclusion—that they are indeed by the same author—is based on the telltale repetition of characteristic words (*aver*) and phrases such as "not for nothing." There are also similarities in punctuation; the writer shows a preference for semicolons instead of commas or dashes. But the most telling feature, the great detective claims, are the paragraphs:

> *A clever man might successfully disguise every element of his style but one—the paragraphing. Diction and syntax may be determined and controlled by rational processes in*

full consciousness, but paragraphing—the decision whether to take short hops or long ones, and whether to hop in the middle of a thought or action or finish it first—that comes from instinct, from the depths of personality. I will concede the possibility that the verbal similarities, and even the punctuation, could be coincidence, though it is highly improbable; but not the paragraphing. These three stories were paragraphed by the same person.

Soon afterward, Archie Goodwin, Wolfe's loyal sidekick, returns to his desk, which is covered with paperwork that needs to be attended to. He spends a half hour or so studying the paragraphing of the three manuscripts in question. He concludes that Wolfe is right about their having been written by the same person. Archie tells us so in the second sentence of a very long paragraph, then goes on to say, "I put the stories in the safe and then considered the problem of the table-load of paper." Still within the same paragraph, he lists the various members of Nero Wolfe's household, and what their functions are. The paragraph ends with a succession of sentences that succinctly capture the whole dilemma of where to put the paragraph break, and how not only the emphasis but the implied meaning of a sentence can differ, depending on whether it appears at the end of a paragraph, or the start of a new one:

> *... My status and function are whatever a given situation calls for, and the question of who decides what it calls for is what occasionally creates an atmosphere in which Wolfe and I are not speaking. The next sentence is to be, "But the table-load of paper, being in the office, was clearly up to me," and I have to decide whether to put it here or start a new paragraph with it. You see how subtle it is. Paragraph it yourself.*
>
> *I stood surveying the stacks of paper ...*

It is, as Archie says, subtle. If the sentence about the paper-work being up to him goes at the end of the preceding paragraph, it seems to be a sort of addenda to that paragraph's consideration of professional responsibility, and of who exactly decides what a situation requires. At the start of the next paragraph, it sounds more as if Archie has taken a deep breath and finally turned his attention to the stack of paper that he will now begin to work on.

Presumably, Nero Wolfe would have been able to identify Paula Fox as the writer of the paragraph below, which appears in her novel *Desperate Characters*. The justly celebrated passage, which is near the novel's beginning and from which the rest of its plot will follow, describes its heroine feeding a stray cat:

> *The cat had begun to clean its whiskers. Sophie caressed its back again, drawing her fingers along until they met the sharp furry crook where the tail turned up. The cat's back rose convulsively to press against her hand. She smiled, wondering how often, if ever before, the cat had felt a friendly human touch, and she was still smiling as the cat reared up on its hind legs, even as it struck her with extended claws, smiling right up to that second when it sank its teeth into the back of her left hand and hung from her flesh so that she nearly fell forward, stunned and horrified, yet conscious enough of Otto's presence to smother the cry that arose in her throat as she jerked her hand back from that circle of barbed wire. She pushed out with her other hand, and as the sweat broke out on her forehead, as her flesh crawled and tightened, she said, "No, no, stop that!" to the cat, as if it had done nothing more than beg for food, and in the midst of her pain and dismay she was astonished to hear how cool her voice was. Then, all at once, the claws released her and flew back as though to deliver another blow, but then the cat turned—it seemed in mid-air—and sprang from the porch, disappearing into the shadowed yard below.*

The drama peaks in the center of the paragraph, while what comes before and after is devoted to the thoughts and the actions that led up to Sophie's injury, and the shifts of consciousness and the resultant shock with which she responds to it. Along the way, the descriptiveness of that "sharp furry crook" does make you think that someone who had never petted a cat could never have written anything quite so evocative. The sentences in the passage are, as Jonathan Franzen notes in his introduction to the reissue of the novel, "small miracles of compression and specificity, tiny novels in themselves. . . . By imagining a dramatic moment as a series of physical gestures—by paying close attention—Fox makes room here for each aspect of Sophie's complexity: her liberality, her self-delusion, her vulnerability, and, above all, her married person's consciousness."

The beauties of the paragraph are probably obvious, but it's worth pausing to examine the sentence in which the bite occurs. Sophie's shock and humiliation are intensified by the fact that what begins the sentence and continues throughout is the smile that lingers on her face—described in a series of parallel temporal clauses beginning with *as*, *even as*, and *when*. The smile nearly turns to a cry, which is aborted when Sophie, even in the midst of this horrific event, remembers her husband's presence and controls herself so as not to alarm him. Or perhaps her self-control owes as much to her reluctance to betray her own weakness, foolishness, culpability, and disobedience. After all, Otto has warned her not to feed the cat.

Her strenuous effort of will takes her through the next paragraphs, in which Otto asks her what's happened, and she answers, "Nothing," a reflexive denial that, like the bite itself, will inform the remainder of the book. What makes the passage so remarkable is how it strikes the perfect balance between action—we always know exactly what the cat is doing, and what Sophie is doing in response—and consciousness, the minute shifts in her awareness and the interior voice that arises from her self-monitoring, her knowledge not only of her own pain but also of her surroundings and of the circumstances that have led up to her misfortune.

The fact that Fox's paragraph is constructed so differently from Babel's might inspire us to question our notion of what a paragraph is, and to consult the manuals of style for help on where to take that breath that the paragraph break encourages. I remember learning in school that each paragraph should begin with a topical sentence, but the truth is that I was never precisely sure what a topical sentence was. And now that I have read so much more, I'm even less certain. Strunk and White are, as usual, helpful in presenting the essential situation and in giving us ways to think about the nuts and bolts of writing:

> *As a rule, begin each paragraph either with a sentence that suggests the topic or with a sentence that helps the transition. . . . In narration and description, the paragraph sometimes begins with a concise, comprehensive statement serving to hold together the details that follow. . . . But when this device, or any device, is too often used, it becomes a mannerism. . . . In animated narrative, the paragraphs are likely to be short and without any semblance of a topic sentence, the writer rushing headlong, event following event in rapid succession. The break between such paragraphs merely serves the purpose of a rhetorical pause, throwing into prominence some detail of the action.*

Strunk and White conclude their meditation on the paragraph with a paragraph of their own that hearkens back to Babel's warning against a set of dead rules, and to his advice that everything should be done with an eye to its effect on the reader:

In general, remember that paragraphing calls for a good eye as well as a logical mind. Enormous blocks of print look formidable to readers, who are often reluctant to tackle them. Therefore, breaking long paragraphs in two, even if it is not necessary to do so for sense, meaning, or logical development, is often a visual help. But remember, too, that firing off many short paragraphs in quick succession can be distracting. . . . Moderation and a sense of order should be the main consideration in paragraphing.

Once again, it's advice to take seriously while at the same time being grateful for those writers who felt compelled to break the rules or who, for whatever reason, failed to take such sensible counsel to heart. Samuel Beckett and José Saramago are just two of the many writers given to constructing extremely long paragraphs.

The first paragraph of Gabriel García Márquez's *One Hundred Years of Solitude* goes on for a page and a half and contains perhaps a dozen places that might, in the work of another writer, seem like natural paragraph breaks. In fact, the entire novel is composed of extremely long paragraphs divided—reluctantly, it would seem—when a passage of dialogue requires a break in the narration. Reading García Márquez, you can almost feel him struggling against the desire to construct the endless paragraph, an urge to which he succumbed in *The Autumn of the Patriarch,* an entire novel in which there are no paragraph breaks at all. Reading it, you feel that García Márquez can do anything he wants, that you would never dare to suggest more conventional paragraphing. Even so, the lack of breaks makes for a somewhat tough read. A neighbor once told me he had trouble with García Márquez's novel because he likes to drink while he reads, and *The Autumn of the Patriarch* gave him no space in which to take a sip of his beer.

Most style books will also caution you against using one-sentence paragraphs, and in general they are right, especially when the sentence in question is only a few words long. A friend says a one-sentence paragraph feels like a punch, and no one wants to get punched. Overused, it can be an annoying tic, a lazy writer's attempt to compel us to pay attention or to inject energy and life into a narrative, of falsely inflating the importance of sentences that our eye might skip over entirely if they were placed, more quietly and modestly, inside a longer paragraph.

A cheesier writer than Rex Stout might have suggested, or employed, a third possibility for Archie's sentence: "But the table-load of papers, being in the office, was clearly up to me." He might have given it its own paragraph, to jack things up, to keep the narrative rolling. Except that the narrative *is* rolling along quite well without such unnecessary assistance.

The one-sentence paragraph should be used sparingly, if at all. But it does have its uses. If a writer is going to draw attention to the stand-alone sentence, the sentence had better be worth it. That is, the sentence should have enough content—enough resonance—to justify this slightly unusual, attention-grabbing device.

Again, it's worth paging through literature for the instances, however few and far between, in which single sentences actually *do* seem to merit paragraphs of their own. The beginning of *Pride and Prejudice*—"It is a truth universally acknowledged, that a single man in possession of a good fortune, must be in want of a wife"—occupies an entire paragraph, as does the following sentence: "However little known the feelings or views of such a man may be on his first entering a neighbourhood, this truth is so well fixed in the minds of the surrounding families, that he is considered as the rightful property of some one or other of their daughters." Clearly, these are not the truncated, abrupt, one-two-punch one-sentence paragraphs that we might sensibly be warned against.

In Melville's "Bartleby the Scrivener," nearly all of Bartleby's demurrals and refusals are given separate paragraphs. His dialogue and his silence, together with the narrator's prompts, are like a call and response in a piece of music, or like an operatic duet. The power and the rhythm of the passage that follows would be markedly decreased if Bartleby's replies and silences were run in with the paragraphs that immediately precede and follow them:

> I buttoned up my coat, balanced myself; advanced slowly towards him, touched his shoulder, and said, "The time has come; you must quit this place; I am sorry for you; here is money; but you must go."
>
> "I would prefer not," he replied, with his back still towards me.
>
> "You must."
>
> He remained silent.
>
> Now I had an unbounded confidence in this man's common honesty. He had frequently restored to me sixpences and shillings carelessly dropped upon the floor, for I am apt to be very reckless in such shirt-button affairs. The proceeding, then, which followed will not be deemed extraordinary.
>
> "Bartleby," said I, "I owe you twelve dollars on account; here are thirty-two; the odd twenty are yours.—Will you take it?" and I handed the bills towards him.
>
> But he made no motion.

In the hands of a master, even the shortest paragraphs can be enormously powerful, as are the last two paragraphs of Raymond Carver's story "Fat":

> It is August.
> My life is going to change. I feel it.

Consider how much less successful this passage would be if all three sentences appeared in the same paragraph. As is, the section seems nearly perfect, because every decision about paragraphing contributes to the strength of the story's ending.

The first sentence-paragraph is a fact. It is August. The reader can't argue with that. And so the following paragraph aims to be another equally straightforward declaration, two sentences that—in a way that we can no more "explain" than we can summarize the "point" of poetry or analyze how it operates on us—manage to combine statement and qualification, certainty and doubt, without ever acknowledging that what is being said is anything but the expression of a truth as simple and inarguable as the information about what month it is. Except that we doubt that the narrator's life *is* going to change. As, in fact, does the narrator. And finally, we're left asking: What else could possibly be added to this section that would not blunt or diminish the force of the three brief sentences that amply fill two paragraphs and resonate beyond them?

Paragraphs are a form of emphasis. What appears at the start and end of the paragraph has (again, if we except passages such as the one from *Desperate Characters*) greater weight than what appears in the middle.

This paragraph from Jonathan Franzen's *The Corrections* begins in what appears to be an omniscient third person, then, at the end, abruptly veers off in a direction that makes us realize that we have been watching the scene through the eyes of a character who is (to say the least) closely involved in what he is observing, and whose view of it alters, or in any case complicates, what we have been seeing. Simultaneously, the last line transforms a simple description of an elderly and rather fragile couple arriving at an airport into a freighted capsule summary of a family relationship. Finally, the paragraph's startling conclusion—in its honesty, its unexpectedness, and above all, in its compression—is itself a lure that pulls us into the narrative:

Down the long concourse they came unsteadily, Enid fa-
voring her damaged hip, Alfred paddling at the air with loose-
hinged hands and slapping the airport carpeting with poorly
controlled feet, both of them carrying Nordic Pleasurelines
shoulder bags and concentrating on the floor in front of them,
measuring out the hazardous distance three paces at a time.
To anyone who saw them averting their eyes from the dark-
haired New Yorkers careering past them, to anyone who caught
a glimpse of Alfred's straw fedora looming at the height of Iowa
corn on Labor Day, or the yellow wool of the slacks stretching over
Enid's outslung hip, it was obvious that they were midwestern
and intimidated. But to Chip Lambert, who was waiting for
them just beyond the security checkpoint, they were killers.

Frequently, each paragraph shift represents a slight change in
point of view—Babel's flash of lightning—or a shift in perspective
that we can conceptualize, cinematically, as a change in camera
angles. In the passage from *The Great Gatsby* that describes the
two beautiful young women seated on the couch, quoted in the
earlier chapter on sentences, the paragraph break occurs at
the moment the eye of the narrator switches focus, from the
room in general to the sofa in particular. It's often easiest to ob-
serve this in the opening pages of a book, as—jumping from
paragraph to paragraph, from page to page—the lens of the nar-
rative zeroes in on its subject. The first paragraphs of Balzac's
Cousin Bette function, to extend the cinematic metaphor, as a suc-
cession of tracking shots, in which we watch one of the novel's
villains, Monsieur Crevel, approach his destination. Meanwhile,
we are receiving a series of cues about what we are meant to
think of this man, as well as the physical location and the social
milieu in which the book's highly unpleasant opening scene is
about to take place. And the novel's principal themes—money,
especially new money, status, class mobility, betrayal, dishonesty,

age, appearance—are all sounded, like phrases of music that will combine to form the concert of the novel.

Like many of Balzac's provincial novels, Stendhal's *The Red and the Black* begins by introducing the reader to the topography of the town before narrowing in on one of its inhabitants. Below are the first lines of the book's first six paragraphs, which occupy the first two pages or so of the narrative. I've also included the entire fifth paragraph, because it is such an elegant example of its form, one of those single paragraphs in which a writer tells us nearly all we need to know about a character:

1. *"The little town of Verrières may be one of the prettiest in all the Franche-Comté . . .*

2. *"To the north, Verrières is sheltered by a great mountain, part of the Jura range . . .*

3. *"Entering town one is deafened by the roar of a noisy, frightening machine . . .*

4. *"If the traveler spends even a few moments on Verrières's main street, which ascends along the banks of the Doub to the top of the hill, the odds are a hundred to one he'll see a tall man with a businesslike and important air . . .*

5. *"When he appears, every hat is raised. His hair is grizzled, he's dressed in gray. He wears the medals of several knightly orders; his forehead is high, his nose aquiline, and all in all there's an orderliness about him. At first sight, one feels that the dignity of his mayoral status is in harmony with the sort to be found in a man of forty-eight or fifty. But soon a Parisian traveler will be shocked by signs of self-satisfaction and smugness, mixed with something limited and unoriginal. Finally, one feels that his talents are confined to making sure he is paid exactly what he is owed, while paying what he himself owes only at the last possible moment.*

6. *"This is the mayor of Verrières, Mayor de Rênal. . . ."*

You can watch something similar happen—the camera eye of the narrative moving in for a close-up—in the opening of Gary Shteyngart's novel *The Russian Debutante's Handbook*. The initial three paragraphs introduce us to the novel's energy and hilarity, to its unlikely hero, and finally to its themes—among them, the absurdities of the immigrant experience, the parallel follies of American and Eastern European society in the 1990s, and the difficulties of cultural assimilation and reconciliation. These cross-cultural exchanges transpire by the "demilitarized water fountain" and, more enjoyably, in our hero's breakfast sandwich:

> The story of Vladimir Girshkin—part P. T. Barnum, part V. I. Lenin, the man who would conquer half of Europe (albeit the wrong half)—begins the way so many other things begin. On a Monday morning. In an office. With the first cup of instant coffee gurgling to life in the common lounge.
>
> His story begins in New York, on the corner of Broadway and Battery Place, the most disheveled, godforsaken, not-for-profit corner of New York's financial district. On the tenth floor, the Emma Lazarus Immigrant Absorption Society greeted its clients with the familiar yellow water–stained walls and dying hydrangeas of a sad Third World government office. In the reception room, under the gentle but insistent prodding of trained Assimilation Facilitators, Turks and Kurds called a truce, Tutsis queued patiently behind Hutus, Serbs chatted up Croats by the demilitarized water fountain.
>
> Meanwhile, in the cluttered back office, junior clerk Vladimir Girshkin—the immigrant's immigrant, the expatriate's expatriate, enduring victim of every practical joke the late twentieth century had to offer and an unlikely hero for our times—was going at it with the morning's first double-cured-spicy-sopressata-and-avocado-sandwich. How Vladimir loved the unforgiving hardness of the sopressata and the fatty under-

tow of the tender avocado! The proliferation of this kind of Janus-faced sandwich, as far as he was concerned, was the best thing about Manhattan in the summer of 1993.

The initial paragraphs of another first novel, Denis Johnson's *Angels*, also convey a series of subtle shifts—first in perspective, then in time. Again, you have the sense that these sentences could not have been paragraphed in any other way, that the breaks are as essential and organic to the narrative as each of the word choices that suffuse it with an almost hallucinatory paranoia that is, at the same time, solidly grounded in exterior reality. The first paragraph surveys the landscape, such as it is, as our heroine looks out the window of a Greyhound bus. The second focuses on the young woman herself, while we continue to see the world around her from her point of view. And the third takes us across a skip in time, and deeper into an almost visionary state induced by exhaustion and anxiety. The paragraphing enhances both the clarity and the disorientation of the opening that captures, with chilling precision, the psychology of a young mother who is in deep trouble, and who is hanging on to exactly as much awareness and stability as is necessary for her to survive and to care for two young daughters:

In the Oakland Greyhound all the people were dwarfs, and they pushed and shoved to get on the bus, even cutting in ahead of the two nuns, who were there first. The two nuns smiled sweetly at Miranda and Baby Ellen and played I-see-you behind their fingers when they'd taken their seats. But Jamie could sense that they found her make-up too thick, her pants too tight. They knew she was leaving her husband, and figured she'd turn for a living to whoring. She wanted to tell them what, was what, but you can't talk to a Catholic. The shorter nun carried a bright cut rose wrapped in her two hands.

Jamie sat by the window looking out and smoking a Kool. People still crowded at the bus's door, people she hoped never to meet—struggling with mutilated luggage and paper sacks that might have contained, the way they handled them, the reasons for their every regretted act and the justifications for their wounds. A black man in a tweed suit and a straw hat held up a sign for his departing relatives: "THE SUN SHALL BE TURNED INTO DARKNESS AND THE MOON INTO BLOOD." (JOEL 2:31). Under the circumstances, Jamie felt close to this stranger.

Around three in the morning Jamie's eyes came open. Headlights on an entrance ramp cut across their flight and swept through the bus, and momentarily in her exhaustion she thought it was the flaming head of a man whipping like a comet through the sleeping darkness of these travellers, hers alone to witness. Suddenly Miranda was awake, jabbering in her ear, excited to be up past bedtime.

Once more, it's writing you want to read word by word, pausing to note how much information is conveyed through ingenious indirection. Though first you might have to recover from the outrageousness of that first statement about the dwarf population of the bus station, a shock mediated, but only slightly, when we realize that these "dwarfs" may just be normal people, viewed from the bus window—that is, from above.

Two words, "Oakland Greyhound," are enough to give us our bearings, both geographically and socioeconomically; we're a long way from the yacht basin at Boca Raton. Baby Ellen's name, and the fact that the nuns are playing I-see-you with the kids, spares the writer from having to tell us that they *are* kids, and when Jamie projects her doubts and fears about her self-presentation (pants, makeup) and her situation (she's left her husband and may have few employment options aside from prostitution) onto the nuns, regarding and judging herself from their viewpoint, Johnson performs the difficult feat of enabling us to see his heroine simultaneously from the inside and the outside.

Every detail—the mentholated cigarette, the casual prejudice against Catholics—grounds the character so firmly in a recognizable reality, however peculiar and altered, that by the second paragraph we're willing to accept the loopy poetry of a consciousness that registers the "mutilated" luggage and expands to embrace the idea that a paper sack could contain a lifetime of regrets, justifications, and wounds. From here on it's straight down toward the apocalypse into which the book will descend, which is already being prepared for us with the, again, credible and frightening quotation from the Bible, a vision of a heavenly messenger leavened by the humor of Jamie's sympathetic identification with the stranger "under the circumstances."

And now, just in case the landscape isn't dark enough already, the third paragraph whisks us into the middle of the night and offers us a vision of the flaming head whipping like a comet, a surreal and lyrical image at once transfiguring and isolating, and one that ends by reassuring us about our character's sanity. Her daughter is jabbering in her ear. Her daughter has a bedtime.

Let's look at one final paragraph, before we leave the subject, in part because it has some qualities (public transportation, flashing lights in the darkness) in common with the passage from *Angels*, but mostly because the two opening paragraphs of James Baldwin's "Sonny's Blues" are such marvelous examples of the paragraph form:

> *I read about it in the paper, in the subway, on my way to work. I read it, and I couldn't believe it, and I read it again. Then perhaps I just stared at it, at the newsprint spelling out his name, spelling out the story. I stared at it in the swinging*

lights of the subway car, and in the faces and bodies of the people, and in my own face, trapped in the darkness which roared outside.

It was not to be believed and I kept telling myself that, as I walked from the subway station to the high school. And at the same time I couldn't doubt it. I was scared, scared for Sonny. He became real to me again. A great block of ice got settled in my belly and kept melting there slowly all day long, while I taught my classes algebra. It was a special kind of ice. It kept melting, sending trickles of ice water all up and down my veins, but it never got less. Sometimes it hardened and seemed to expand until I felt my guts were going to come spilling out or that I was going to choke or scream. This would always be at a moment when I was remembering some specific thing Sonny had once said or done.

As in the passages from Cheever and Joyce, the rhythm of the sentences and the paragraph establish the importance, the high seriousness, the poetry, and (as in the end of "Goodbye, My Brother") the sermon-like quality of the prose. But though the rhythms are no less ecclesiastical, it's a different type of sermon. It's pure gospel music, all of it turning around that *it* in the opening phrase, that thing that, like the father's death in Mansfield's "The Daughters of the Late Colonel," is too momentous, too shocking, too personal to be named.

This mythical and ultimately transcendent story begins in the subway, the underworld, where the narrator has a vision of the faces and bodies of his fellow passengers and finally of his own face, trapped in the darkness. What's impressive is how much Baldwin is doing at once: immersing us in a narrative, starting up the musical rhythms that are at once the story's method and its subject, introducing us to the narrator, and establishing a series of contrasting images—dark and light, inside and outside, imprisonment and freedom, inclusion and exclusion—that will reappear from the story's beginning until the end.

The paragraph shift is, like the rest, masterful. For that *it* is suddenly illuminated by the lightning flash that occurs in the change to the passive voice; the diction becomes more formal, as if the narrative is seeking some higher authority and confirmation. *It was not to be believed*, we read, and so the story swings into that duet of the physical and the cerebral, the rational and the emotional, the logical and the intuitive that it is about to play out. Until (in almost no time at all) we are delivered to the place where we will find out about Sonny, the as-yet-unidentified character (but for his name) for whom the narrator is scared, and who is connected with that *it*.

It's reminiscent of Babel. A similar flash of lightning, a similar rhythm change and shift in perspective, but now all of it has migrated from a Russian village to a New York subway. It's similar, but not the same, because as Nero Wolfe told us, paragraphing is as particular, as individual to each writer, as the fingerprint at the crime scene, as that telltale trace of DNA.

FIVE

Narration

THE ONLY WAY I WAS ABLE TO TRICK MYSELF INTO WRITING a first novel, as well as the first short story I published that I liked (as opposed to the first story I published) was to write both the novel and the story as stories within stories, narratives told by one character to another. Eavesdropped upon by the reader, the storytellers and their audiences appeared at the beginning and end of the works, and occasionally throughout, to interrupt and comment upon the action.

The reason I say "tricked myself" was that this device enabled me to overcome one of the obstacles confronting the novice writer. This hurdle disguises itself as the question of voice and of who is telling the story (should the narrator be first or third person, close or omniscient?) when in fact the truly problematic question is: Who is listening? On what occasion is the story being told, and why? Is the protagonist projecting this heartfelt confession out into the ozone, and, if so, what is the proper tone to assume when the ozone is one's audience?

I had always assumed that I was alone in having discerned that the identity of the listener was a more vexing problem than the voice of the storyteller until I heard a writer say that what enabled him to write a novel from the point of view of a rather complicated middle-aged woman was by pretending that she was telling her story to a close male friend, and that he, the writer, was that friend. What had made the whole thing possible, he added, was that he was fortunate enough to have had several wives, a few daughters, and a host of female friends, all of whom spoke to him that directly.

For me, writing framed stories not only answered all those troubling questions about the narrator's audience, but also neatly integrated the answers into the narrative itself. I knew not only who was speaking but who was being spoken to, where the speaker and listener were, and when and why the event—that is, the telling of the story—was occurring. This permitted me to skip over slow parts of the plot by having the listener become impatient and hurry the narrator along, while, conversely, an expression of doubt or a request for clarification could slow things down and let me explicate some tricky point of causality. At the same time it forced me to confront the painful question of whether what I was telling was actually a story or merely, say, a rumination. Was it something that one character *would* tell another in the way that people tell stories about their lives? Would anyone imagine that these recounted events would hold another human being's interest, and would the reader believe that anyone, even a fictional character, would stay focused and pay attention all the way through?

It was fortunate that I had lived so much in books, and especially in the books of the past. For one thing, I seemed not to know that no one wrote that way anymore. For another, I was somehow unaware that no one *lived* that way any longer—that is, in circumstances that encouraged and facilitated the telling of long stories.

In an era in which air travelers compare notes on how best to prevent their seatmates from making casual conversation (the eyeshade! the earplugs! the open magazine!) it seems far less likely that one passenger would tell another (as happens in Tolstoy's "The Kreutzer Sonata") a long, tormented account of how sexual jealousy ruined his marriage and his life. Perversely, it's *more* likely that someone might "share" this confession with a national TV audience. Now that anyone who talks for more than a few seconds—that is, anyone who prevents *us* from talking for more than a few seconds—is generally regarded as a bore, what are the chances that a group of gentlemen will gather before a fire to exchange the detailed histories of long-past love affairs, as they do in Chekhov's "On Love"? Or that a similar discussion will move one of its participants to transcribe the long account of a coming-of-age that constitutes Turgenev's "First Love," a novella that takes on an added level of intensity when we realize that the love story is being recalled—in exquisite detail and with profound emotion—decades after it occurred.

But why should I have cared how anyone else was writing, or living, when I had *Wuthering Heights* as a model of how to write and of how people lived?

For every reader who remembers Cathy and Heathcliff scrambling over the moors, many will have forgotten that the novel is constructed like a series of Russian nesting dolls. On the outside we have Mr. Lockwood, who is renting property from Mr. Heathcliff for a temporary stay, and who has exactly as much at stake in his surroundings as is often found among those who rent, instead of owning. After a number of startling incidents involving a plaintive ghost, a diary, and his landlord's alarmingly dysfunctional family, Lockwood persuades Nelly, the housekeeper, to tell him the history of the place and of several generations of the house's inhabitants.

Though she herself has been deeply involved in the events

that have occurred at the estate, Nelly has—except for Lockwood and the nearly subverbal servant Joseph—the lowest emotional stake in the family's tragic history. Thus she is the most credible witness to the happenings that, at moments, are not merely dramatic but positively gothic, with all the sublime and supernatural trappings of the gothic romance. Her voice is one of pure narrative, unintrusive and uninflected, and using her to tell the tale allows Emily Brontë to ground these improbable happenings in everyday reality, or at least the reality that can be found at Wuthering Heights. Nelly's relatively organized habit of mind also helps when it becomes necessary to explain some complex issues of genealogy and inheritance, and to glide across the skips in time that propel the plot forward. Imbedded within Nelly's narrative are yet more layers of story, reports by Heathcliff and others of events that Nelly herself could not have witnessed.

It's hard to imagine a more ornate or artificial structure. So what's surprising is how natural it seems, how quickly our awareness of artifice fades before the urgency of the story being narrated, and how fully the various characters emerge through the eyes and in the voice of a woman who is intuitive, wise, but not, strictly speaking, omniscient. Reading closely, you can see that the diction—the standard English of Brontë's era—and the rhythms vary only slightly when Lockwood, Nelly, and Heathcliff are in charge of the story, even as their very different personalities (Nelly's tender sympathies, Heathcliff's passionate impulsiveness, Lockwood's self-regarding dimness) inform every word they utter.

Something similar occurs in *The Turn of the Screw*, another psychological thriller whose readers need all the help they can get in deciding how to interpret the central narrative and, indeed, how much of it to believe. Like *Wuthering Heights*, Henry James's novella about a governess and the two evil—or are they innocent?—children is narrated from the outside in. It's not really

framed, since the end of the story never returns to the initial set-
ting, but rather is introduced by an account of a highly civilized
gathering attended by a first-person narrator who is soon sup-
planted by another first-person narrator, and who subsequently
disappears from the tale.

At a Christmas Eve party, a group of guests are telling ghost
stories around a fire. One of them mentions the horror of an
apparition appearing to a child, and a man named Douglas asks,
"What do you say to *two* children?" The others are intrigued,
especially when Douglas adds that no one but he has ever heard
the story. "It's quite too horrible." And so the section functions
not only as an introduction to the narrative, but as a sort of blurb,
an elegant come-on that Douglas steadily ramps up, as James
raises the bar for himself (that is, for the story that is to follow)
far higher than most writers would dare:

> "It's beyond everything. Nothing at all that I know
> touches it."
> "For sheer terror," I remember asking.
> He seemed to say it was not so simple as that; to be really at
> a loss how to qualify it. He passed his hand over his eyes, made
> a little wincing grimace. "For dreadful—dreadfulness!"
> "Oh how delicious!" cried one of the women.
> He took no notice of her; he looked at me, but as if, instead
> of me, he saw what he spoke of. "For general uncanny ugliness
> and horror and pain."
> "Well then," I said, "just sit right down and begin."

Well then, indeed. Every word of *The Turn of the Screw* needs
to be read attentively, because to do so is to solve (insofar as any-
thing about this puzzling and upsetting tale can be solved) the
debate that has long raged about whether it is a ghost story or
a tale of psychological aberration, whether the apparitions are

"real" or merely figments of the governess's overheated imagi-
nation. To dissect the governess's language—the way that she
describes and interprets events, draws conclusions, and charts
her own escalating panic and hysteria—is to acknowledge that
the ambiguity is not accidental, that James meant to write a story
that could be read in two entirely different ways, both of them
fully supported by evidence from the text. And it's this mystery
that has made the story so fascinating and seductive, inviting us
to return to it again and again, as if this time we will finally come
up with an ultimately conclusive reading of a work designed to
prevent us from reaching any sort of ultimate conclusion.

Little nuggets of economy and compression, interpolated
stories—anecdotes that one character tells another within the
body of a narrative—change the pace of that narrative and il-
luminate a character who is revealed by the content of the story,
by the manner of its telling, and finally by what the reader con-
cludes about the purpose that the story is intended to serve.

Here is one such story from Richard Price's novel *Freedomland*,
an anecdote that a mother tells a reporter about her daughter,
Brenda, a woman who may or may not be guilty of the death
of her child, whom Brenda claims has been kidnapped by a car-
jacker:

> "When she was little, kindergarten age, her father and
> I one time had a fight. Pete, he used to like his cocktails back
> then, and it was real bad. He was never a mean drunk, never
> raised a hand, but it was hell, and I told him I was taking the
> kids and leaving—I had had it—and, he started crying, telling
> me he'll straighten out. He's crying, I'm crying. We're both in
> the kitchen, and Brenda comes in. She comes in, sees us, and
> gets this stricken look on her face. And we had a radio in there
> back then. And the song that was playing was 'September
> Song,' being sung by, if you can believe it, Jimmy Durante.

*Brenda, she looks at us crying, and I say, 'Sweetie, isn't that
a sad song? Me and daddy are crying because that song is so
beautiful and sad.' So of course she starts crying too, so I go
and I pick her up and it kind of broke my train of thought
there with Pete, so I don't go through with it . . .*

"A few years ago, Pete passed on. Brenda came to the house.
*She takes me into the kitchen, says, 'Mom, I have something
for you,' and she gives me a tape she made. She likes to make
music tapes for people. She gives me a tape, it's Jimmy Durante
singing 'September Song.' I have no idea how she remembered,
or where she found it, or, better yet, how she even knew who
the singer had been. She was five years old. She gives me the
tape, says, 'Mom, if you're ever missing Daddy too much
maybe you could play this for yourself.' See, all those years she
believed me, that we were crying because . . . "*

Everything in the paragraph contributes to the speaker's
credibility, as a fictional character and as an honest human being:
the diction, the rhythms, the slight repetitions for emphasis, the
way that the tenses keep shifting from present to past and back.
The choice of words and phrases ("used to like his cocktails,"
"never raised a hand," "passed on") make us feel that this is how
this woman might really recount an incident from her life. The
language, the story itself, the specificity of the details (Jimmy
Durante singing "September Song") convince us that the woman
is telling the truth. Even more important is the character of the
child who emerges from the story, the girl who will grow up to
become Brenda. She is sympathetic (she cries when she sees her
parents crying), generous (she makes music tapes for people, a
time-consuming and personal gift), open-hearted, thoughtful;
this certainly does not seem to be a person who would cold-
heartedly murder her own son and blame it on a stranger. Finally,
what's so moving is the sense of a mother looking back through

her daughters' entire childhood and adult life to find the perfect anecdote to explain who her daughter is, and to offer conclusive evidence that Brenda could not be a criminal. It is a story intended to make a case for the innocence of her daughter.

There are plenty of interpolated stories in Dostoyevsky, possibly because his characters are so often having drunken or sober fits in which they reveal their entire life histories to casual acquaintances or perfect strangers. In the second chapter of *Crime and Punishment*, Raskolnikov enters the tavern in which he first meets Marmeladov, who begins, "May I venture, honored sir, to engage you in polite conversation?" a question that Raskolnikov will at first have reason to regret, and ultimately to be grateful for. Marmeladov's inebriated, impassioned rant goes on for nearly ten pages and introduces several of the novel's principal characters, most notably, Sonia, Marmeladov's daughter, a prostitute who will ultimately help Raskolnikov discover the path to redemption.

Dostoyevsky was painfully familiar with problems of narration, with challenging and even wrong decisions about how a story is to be told. The notebooks in which he sketched out his ideas for *Crime and Punishment* not only document the many projected plot turns that never appear in the finished book and the early conceptions of characters who have utterly different personalities in the completed novel, but also chart his struggle to find the best way to tell his story. Sections of these early drafts of the novel are written in the first person, as a diary, as confession, as memory, and as a combination of journal and drama. But ultimately he realized that, given the problems caused by the fact that his hero was to be semi-delirious for significant portions of the narrative, he could maintain the same intensity and immediacy, while avoiding the technical limitations of the first person, by sticking to a close third-person narration that, at critical junctures, merges with the consciousness of the protagonist.

Though students of writing are usually instructed—with good reason—that it is necessary to pick a point of view and stick to it, this, like any "rule," can be circumvented by any writer skillful enough to get away with it. *Madame Bovary* begins from the perspective of a classmate of Emma Bovary's future husband, a narrator who is never heard from again. Gertrude Stein's *The Autobiography of Alice B. Toklas* is a first-person narrative disguised as someone else's memoir, while Randall Jarrell's *Pictures from an Institution* is a third-person narrative occasionally interrupted by a character who refers to "my wife and I," but about whom we learn very little.

The opening pages of Flannery O'Connor's *Wise Blood* shift perspective every few sentences: we see the train carriage from Hazel Motes's point of view, then we peer at Hazel through the eyes of the woman sitting in the seat across from him, then we are looking out the window from a viewpoint that seems more detached, even omniscient. Diane Johnson's novel *Persian Nights* slips from the consciousness of one character into that of another, so that a single scene may be observed from several variant perspectives. Harold Brodkey's story "S.L." keeps changing: from the present tense to the past, and from the first-person "I" point of view of a small child to a third-person narrator who refers to the story's tiny hero as "the child" and as "Wiley," the boy's proper name, though it's also clear that this more distanced narrator is the child himself, grown up.

The breathtaking conclusion of Mavis Gallant's "The Ice Wagon Going Down the Street" exchanges the dispassionate (if sly) omniscience with which the story has mostly been narrated and enters the inner life of one of its central characters, Peter Frazier. Together with his wife, Sheilah, Peter has retreated from a pretend-glamorous and actually quite shabby life on the fringes of the postwar European expatriate set. He has surrendered and returned to his native Toronto, where the couple is staying, as if in exile, with his decidedly unglamorous sister, Lucille. The story's final section begins like this:

> *When, on Sunday mornings, Sheilah and Peter talk about those times, they take on the glamour of something still to come. It is then he remembers Agnes Brusen. He never says her name. Sheilah wouldn't remember Agnes. Agnes is the only secret Peter has from his wife, the only puzzle he pieces together without her help.*

As the reader knows by now, Agnes Brusen is a mousy, eccentric Canadian woman with whom Peter briefly shared an office when he had a job doing clerical work in Geneva. One night, the prim, repressed, teetotaling Agnes got drunk at a party, and their hostess asked Peter to take her home. The next day, in the office, they shared a moment of communication so intense that—though, as the story repeatedly tells us, "nothing happened"—the event seemed to Peter as momentous and life-changing as if they had had a serious love affair.

Now, years later, back in Canada, he finds himself thinking of Agnes, then of his father, then of Sheilah, and again of Agnes, wondering where she has gone and recalling a story she told him about her childhood in Saskatchewan, when she would wake up early in the morning to watch the ice wagon going down the street. He imagines Agnes carrying the youngest child in her arms.

Then something extraordinary starts to happen in the narrative. Peter thinks, "The child is Peter." Peter's consciousness begins to swoop around, to move through the universe, to inhabit the child in Agnes's arms. He returns briefly to himself, then again leaves his own mind to imagine the mind of Agnes, who in turn is thinking of him. His thoughts travel back to Sheilah and to their diminished lives in Toronto.

> *He touches Sheilah's hand. The children have their aunt*
> *now, and he and Sheilah have each other. Everything works*
> *out, somehow or other. Let Agnes have the start of the day.*
> *Let Agnes think it was invented for her. Who wants to be alone*
> *in the universe? No, begin at the beginning: Peter lost Agnes.*
> *Agnes says to herself somewhere, Peter is lost.*

This is hardly what one would calling choosing a point of view and sticking to it, which is yet more proof that any set of "rules" offers only the loosest of guidelines. Even so, regardless of how blithely and confidently it breaks the rules and expands the third-person form, the Gallant story is in the "third person." That is, it employs third-person pronouns—*he* did this, *she* said that—rather than the "I" form.

When we talk about point of view, we generally assume that a work is written either in the first or third person, though in the 1980s, perhaps partly thanks to the success of Jay McInerney's novel *Bright Lights, Big City*, there was a brief vogue, which has not entirely disappeared, for writing in the second person.

Like the one sentence paragraph, the "you" form can all too easily come to seem like a distracting tic, especially when the "you" is presumed to be you-the-reader. "What do you mean, *me*?" the reader may sensibly wonder. Like the one-sentence paragraph, the second-person point of view can also make us suspect that style is being used as a substitute for content. Or perhaps it is being employed out of fear that the content is thin or insufficient, which is perhaps why the "you" form so often appears in stories that are actually dating advice, or commiserations on the subject of romance, lightly disguised as fiction.

The truth is that marvelous fiction has been written in the second person, though in these cases, the "you" is less likely to be the reader in general than someone in particular, an individual to whom the story (often metaphorically or imaginatively) is being addressed. In William Trevor's novel *Fools of Fortune*, the two main characters narrate alternate sections as if they were speaking, or writing, to each other. Such works are actually closer to the epistolary form in which a number of the very earliest novels, such as Samuel Richardson's *Pamela*, were written. Occasionally, authors still employ the device of the letter, as Donald Barthelme does in his story "The Sandman," in which a man's note to his girlfriend's psychoanalyst, defending her desire to terminate her analysis and buy a piano instead, expands into a meditation on psychology, character, and love.

One virtuosic story, written in the second person and addressed to a particular individual, is also by Mavis Gallant. It's "Mlle. Dias de Corta," and it begins as follows:

> *You moved into my apartment during the summer of the year before abortion became legal in France; that should fix it in past time for you, dear Mlle. Dias de Corta. You had just arrived in Paris from your native city, which you kept insisting was Marseilles, and were looking for work. You said you had studied television-performance techniques at some provincial school (we had never heard of the school, even though my son had one or two actor friends) and received a diploma with "special mention" for vocal expression. The diploma was not among the things we found in your suitcase, after you disappeared, but my son recalled that you carried it in your handbag, in case you had the good luck to sit next to a casting director on the bus.*

The narrator, an old woman, is addressing a former boarder, an actress with whom she has lost contact for decades but whom she recently happened to see on television, in an oven commercial. As it turns out, the reference to the legalization of abortion is not a casual way of placing their acquaintance in time, but a direct reference to something that occurred and will be recalled in the course of the story. It is, moreover, an early indication of the narrator's mixed feelings toward Mlle. Dias de Corta, whom she simultaneously envied, distrusted, condescended to (thus the mention of the "provincial school"), and viewed as an embodiment of the immigrants polluting the purity of the French population, a prejudice underlying the reference to the "native city which *you kept insisting* was Marseilles." At the same time, the older woman clings to the memory of the boarder who brought, however briefly, a breath of mystery, exoticism, glamor, and romance into her dull, narrowly circumscribed existence. Consequently, the story, which consists mostly of a series of thinly veiled reproaches, ends with a heartfelt invitation: "You need not call to make an appointment. I prefer to live in the expectation of hearing the elevator stop at my floor and then your ring, and of having you tell me you have come home."

Stuart Dybek's "We Didn't" is written in the first-person plural: the "we" of its subject is the narrator and his first true love. Note the way that, in the passage that follows, taken from the story's beginning, the rhythms, the repetition of "we didn't," the language, and the imagery establish a high-poetic lyricism ("the snow where moonlight threw down our shadows") that is periodically undercut by specific, quotidian details, such as the kielbasa, that provide information about the narrator's milieu. The fact that the story takes place in the fifties, a circumstance that strongly affects the characters' behavior, is cleverly established by the invocation of car models and movie stars (the rusted Rambler, the Buick Eight, Doris Day). The fact that it occurs in the narrator's distant past comes through the detail of the "now-defunct" theater, while the religion of the "you" being addressed—faith is also, as it will turn out, significant—is neatly conveyed by the convincing detail of the "beaded, black snake" of the rosary twined around the rearview mirror. Finally, the lush eroticism is leavened

throughout by humor: the idea that the lovers' fumblings are be-
ing monitored by the all-seeing eye of Doris Day.

> *We didn't in the light; we didn't in darkness. We didn't in the*
> *fresh-cut summer grass or in the mounds of autumn leaves or on*
> *the snow where moonlight threw down our shadows. We didn't in*
> *your room in the canopy bed you slept in, the bed you slept in as*
> *a child, or on the backseat of my father's rusted Rambler, which*
> *smelled of the smoked chubs and kielbasa he delivered on week-*
> *ends from my uncle Vincent's meat market. We didn't in your*
> *mother's Buick Eight, where a rosary twined the rearview mir-*
> *ror like a beaded, black snake with silver, cruciform fangs.*
>
> *At the dead end of our lover's lane—a side street of aban-*
> *doned factories—where I perfected the pinch that springs open*
> *a bra; behind the lilac bushes in Marquette Park, where you*
> *first touched me through my jeans and your nipples, swollen*
> *against transparent cotton, seemed the shade of lilacs; in the*
> *balcony of the now defunct Clark Theater, where I wiped pop-*
> *corn salt from my palms and slid them up your thighs and you*
> *whispered, "I feel like Doris Day is watching us," we didn't.*

As you may have guessed by now, the story describes a pas-
sionate romance that includes everything but sexual intercourse.
The event around which the plot turns involves a grisly discovery
that the couple make one night on the beach, just when they are
finally about to make love. The aftermath of this event not only
derails the love affair, but casts a long shadow of longing and loss
that persists into the present moment, in which the narrator is
presumably writing the story that ends:

> *But we didn't, not in the moonlight, or by the phosphores-*
> *cent lanterns of lightning bugs in your back yard, not beneath*
> *the constellations we couldn't see, let alone decipher, or in the*

dark glow that replaced the real darkness of the night, a dark-
ness already stolen from us, not with the skyline rising behind
us while a city gradually decayed, not in the heat of summer
while a Cold War raged, despite the freedom of youth and the
license of first love—because of what, karma, luck, what does
it matter?—we made not doing it a wonder, and yet we didn't,
we didn't, we never did.

As in "Mlle. Dias de Corta," the invocation of a listener seems absolutely necessary to make the reader understand and feel what the writer is attempting to communicate, though the Gallant story so typically evades the reaches of the intellect that it is hard to explain what that meaning or what that feeling is. In both stories, the narrative voice creates an urgency, a desperate attempt to maintain and establish contact with a particular human being. That is very different from the impersonal "you," which is more often a way of inventing a listener—personifying the empty space into which the story is being projected.

All of this should begin to give us an idea of the different options available when a writer is choosing to write a story from a particular point of view, or when, as more often seems to be the case, the story is choosing the point of view from which it wishes to be written. To speak as if there were two major points of view—first and third—is like saying that the only thing we need to know in order to prepare and enjoy a delicious multicourse dinner is that there are five basic food groups.

First-person narratives are as variable as the number of characters who can sustain a narrative in the first person—which is to say, an endless variety. And through the skillful deployment of language, writers can not only establish the personality of that narrator within a few sentences or paragraphs, but, more important, in the case of a novel, persuade us that we want to be in that person's company for several hundred pages.

How could we resist the brilliant, inventive, self-dramatizing, self-mocking, obsessive lunatic genius who emerges from the following paragraphs?

> *Lolita, light of my life, fire of my loins, My sin, my soul. Lo-lee-ta: the tip of the tongue taking a trip of three steps down the palate to tap, at three, on the teeth. Lo. Lee. Ta.*
>
> *She was Lo, plain Lo, in the morning, standing four feet ten in one sock. She was Lola in slacks. She was Dolly at school. She was Dolores on the dotted line. But in my arms she was always Lolita.*
>
> *Did she have a precursor? She did, indeed she did. In point of fact, there might have been no Lolita at all had I not loved, one summer, a certain initial girl-child. In a princedom by the sea. Oh when? About as many years before Lolita was born as my age was that summer. You can always count on a murderer for a fancy prose style.*

In the midst of all that flighty exhibitionism, Nabokov has nonetheless managed to give us some hard information. Already we have learned that the narrator's relationship with Lolita (whose name is, fittingly, the first word of the novel) is sexual ("fire of my loins"), that she was little more than a child (a four-foot-ten-inch schoolgirl), that the narrator is capable of not merely quoting but also playing upon the poetry of Edgar Allan Poe ("in a princedom by the sea") and finally, that he has committed a murder.

Now consider how different the voice of Humbert Humbert is from that of Phillip Carver, the middle-aged hero of Peter Taylor's *A Summons to Memphis*, a man who has fled his proper, oppressive family in the South to live a modest, stunted, and finally no less oppressive literary life in New York City. This is how the novel begins:

The courtship and remarriage of an old widower is always made more difficult when middle-aged children are involved—especially when they are unmarried daughters. This seemed particularly true in the landlocked, backwater city of Memphis some forty-odd years ago. At least it is a certainty that remarriage was more difficult for old widowers in Memphis than it was over in Nashville, say, or in Knoxville—or even in Chattanooga, for that matter. One needs to know those other cities only slightly to be absolutely sure of that. Yet one cannot say with equal certainty just why the difficulty was so peculiar to Memphis, unless it is that Memphis, unlike the other Tennessee cities, remains to this day a "land-oriented" place. Nearly everybody there who is anybody is apt still to own some land. He owns it in Arkansas or in West Tennessee or in the Mississippi Delta. And it may be that whenever or wherever land gets involved, any family matter is bound to become more complex, less reasonable, more desperate.

Much of what we need to know about the narrator is suggested by his compulsion to use the words *always, particularly true, certainly, certainty,* and *absolutely* as often as he does. But even in this single paragraph, deeper aspects of his psychology emerge via the phrases "unmarried children" and "unmarried daughters"—Phillip himself is something of a middle-age child and has two unwed sisters—and by the confidence and the "certainty" of the sociological generalization about how things were, at one time, in Memphis. What he is about to describe is something, he reminds us, that happened to an entire group of people in a particular city. Already, we begin to intuit what lies beneath all this: the insecurity and uncertainty that the need to generalize (and the repeated invocations of certitude) implies. And we are reminded of how, when we ourselves are about to confess something unpleasant or embarrassing, we may find ourselves suggesting that many perfectly respectable people have probably had the same experience.

Even more is conveyed by the description of Memphis (a city that, as we will learn, Phillip's family associates with unhappiness) as a landlocked backwater, by the need to make fine distinctions between its customs and those of other cities in Tennessee, by the mild (but only mild) irony of the phrase "everybody there who is anybody," and by the notion that it is the ownership of land that tips garden-variety familial conflict over into desperation. In Phillip's own family, discord will turn out to have less to do with property and real estate than with resentment, revenge, power, the inability to love, and the impulse to control and destroy one another's lives.

Only in the next paragraph does the impersonal pronoun "one" change to an "I," at which point we realize that this story is indeed being told in the first person, by a narrator who is more comfortable using the impersonal pronoun (into which he rapidly slips back) and who again feels the need to reassure us that his is not the only family to have experienced the polite domestic nastiness about which we will soon be reading:

> At any rate, during the time when I was in my teens and had recently been removed from Nashville to Memphis, one was always hearing of some old widower or other whose watchful, middle-aged children had set out to save him from an ill-considered second marriage.

Phillip Carver, in turn, could hardly sound more unlike Isabel Walker, the plucky, intelligent, simultaneously astute and innocent narrator of Diane Johnson's *Le Divorce*. Again, the writer requires only a short time to establish the character of her heroine, who is capable of making incisive observations about how the contradictions of the Métro and its entrance encapsulate the vagaries of the French character, and about the "slightly toxic chemistry" of Americans abroad. The narrator, we learn within moments, is a film school graduate, given to seeing a scene cinematically and thinking metaphorically. She is sensitive to stereotypes and aware of cultural differences. The wit and liveliness of these perceptions draw us into the novel, and we sit back, anticipating the pleasure of being guided around Paris by this charming former film student:

> I suppose because I went to film school, I think of my story as a sort of film. In a film, this part would be under the credits, opening with an establishing shot from a high angle, perhaps the Eiffel Tower, panning tiny scenes far below of the foreign city, life as watched from the wrong end of a telescope. Closer up, the place is identified by clichés of Frenchness—people carrying long baguettes of bread, old men wearing berets, women walking poodles, buses, flower stalls, those Art Nouveau entrances to the Métro that seem to beckon to a nether region of vice and art but actually lead to an efficient transportation system, this contradiction perhaps a clue to the French themselves.
>
> Then, in a series of close shots, we become aware that some of the people we are seeing are not French, that among all the Gallic bustle are many Americans. Far from their native land, their flavor changes ever so slightly as they absorb the new perfumes, just as the slightly toxic chemistry of Americans abroad erodes, just a little, the new place in which they find themselves.

Both Philip Carver and Isabel Walker seem not merely a century, but light years away from Mark Twain's Huckleberry Finn, yet another sort of first-person narrator. Like Flannery O'Connor, Twain conveys the inflections of regional speech with only occasional minor departures from standard English, regionalisms that make us admire the inspired way that Huck colors and personalizes the language ("dismal regular and decent") rather than making us feel that he is ignorant or inarticulate. Meanwhile, Twain manages to suffuse every phrase with Huck's character, his independence and his love for freedom, his delight in the contradictions of respectability as a prerequisite for being allowed to join a gang of thieves, his sympathy for others ("she never meant no harm by it"), and his humor, manifested here in the extended metaphor of pretending to confuse saying grace with complaining about the food:

> *The Widow Douglas, she took me for her son, and allowed she would sivilize me; but it was rough living in the house all the time, considering how dismal regular and decent the widow was in all her ways; and so when I couldn't stand it no longer, I lit out. I got into my old rags, and my sugar-hogshead again, and was free and satisfied. But Tom Sawyer, he hunted me up and said he was going to start a band of robbers, and I might join if I would go back to the widow and be respectable. So I went back.*
>
> *The widow she cried over me, and called me a poor lost lamb, and she called me a lot of other names, too, but she never meant no harm by it. She put me in them new clothes again, and I couldn't do nothing but sweat and sweat, and feel all cramped up. Well, then, the old thing commenced again. The widow rung a bell for supper, and you had to come to time. When you got to the table, you couldn't go right to eating, but you had to wait for the widow to tuck down her head and grumble a little over the victuals, though there warn't really anything the matter with them. That is, nothing only everything was cooked by itself. In a barrel of odds and ends it is different; things get mixed up, and the juice kinds of swaps around, and the things go better.*

Of course, it's hardly surprising that in a first-person narrative, or even in a close third-person narrative (which is often a first-person voice disguised as that of the third person, and is as close to the consciousness of the narrator as the "I" form and no nearer to omniscience) the tone of the narrative will necessarily reflect the personality of the narrator. But what is less generally recognized is how often the omniscient, or godlike, narrator also has a very particular or even quirky personality, much the way the character of God can change (as it does, for example, from the Old to the New Testaments) depending on the needs and intentions of the deity's followers. *Omniscient* merely means all-knowing, but does not suggest that this all-seeing eye is impartial, objective, or free from prejudices and opinions—which, again, are conveyed through word choice, rhythm, sentence length, diction, and so forth—about whatever that eye is observing.

Deborah Eisenberg's "A Cautionary Tale" opens with a scene in which one character (Patty) is saying goodbye to another (Stuart). In one hilariously long, complex, clear, and wise sentence, the narrator (who not only is *not* Patty, but who knows a good deal more than Patty knows, including some things that Patty is only just learning) reveals its seasoned and, as it were, cautionary views on the subject of friendship. At the same time, much is being revealed about the characters' circumstances (Stuart is moving out of an apartment he has shared with Patty); about their separate natures (consider how much information is conveyed by that "enragingly pathetic"); about the history of Stuart and Patty's friendship; and about the analytic intelligence and complex moral sensibilities of everyone involved:

> "Stop that, Stuart," Patty said as Stuart struggled with the suitcases, which were way too heavy for him, she thought. (Almost everything was way too heavy for Stuart.) "Just put those down. Besides," Patty said, "where will you go? You

don't have anyplace to go." But Stuart took her hand and held it for a moment against his closed eyes, and despite the many occasions when Patty had wanted him to go, and the several occasions when she had tried to make him go, despite the fact that he was at his most enragingly pathetic, for once she could think of nothing, nothing at all that he could be trying to shame her into or shame her out of, and so it occurred to her that this time he really would leave—that he was simply saying goodbye. All along, Patty had been unaware that time is as adhesive as love, and that the more time you spend with someone the greater the likelihood of finding yourself with a permanent sort of thing to deal with that people casually refer to as "friendship," as if that were the end of the matter, when the truth is that even if "your friend" does something annoying, or if you and "your friend" decide that you hate each other, or if "your friend" moves away and you lose each other's address, you still have a friendship, and although it can change shape, look different in different lights, become an embarrassment or an encumbrance or a sorrow, it can't simply cease to have existed, no matter how far into the past it sinks, so attempts to disavow or destroy it will not merely constitute betrayals of friendship but, more practically, are bound to be fruitless, causing damage only to the humans involved rather than to that gummy jungle (friendship) in which those humans have entrapped themselves, so if sometime in the future you're not going to want to have been a particular person's friend, or if you're not going to want to have had the particular friendship you and that person can make with one another, then don't be friends with that person at all, don't talk to that person, don't go anywhere near that person, because as soon as you start to see something from that person's point of view (which, inevitably, will be as soon as you stand next to that person) common ground is sure to slide under your feet.

Yet another stylized and unique third-person voice—a voice that suggests the vocabulary and cadence of a highly educated, slightly batty, and neurotic child—narrates Jane Bowles's *Two Serious Ladies*. Here, that voice is describing the behavior of children, but its tone will not alter much as the novel goes on to describe the tremulous forays into adult life attempted by Christina and her friends. Note how the voice keeps veering back and forth between high diction ("generally of a religious nature") and a kind of childish plain speech (that *very* in "very sunny afternoon"); it's also as if the narrator has not yet learned what an adult (let alone an omniscient one) is supposed to say and not say, for instance the reference to the fatness of little Christina's legs:

> (Christina) was in the habit of going through many mental struggles—generally of a religious nature—and she preferred to be with other people and organize games. These games, as a rule, were very moral, and often involved God. However, no one else enjoyed them and she was obliged to spend a great part of the day alone . . .
>
> One very sunny afternoon Sophie went inside for her piano lesson, and Mary remained seated on the grass. . . . Christina . . . took off her shoes and stockings and remained in a short white underslip. This was not a very pleasant sight to behold, because Christina at this time was very heavy and her legs were quite fat . . .
>
> "Now don't take your eyes off me," she said. "I'm going to do a dance of worship to the sun. Then I'm going to show that I'd rather have God and no sun than the sun and no God. Do you understand?"
>
> "Yes," said Mary. "Are you going to do it now?"
>
> "Yes, I'm going to do it right here." She began the dance abruptly. It was a clumsy dance and her gestures were all undecided. When Sophie came out of the house, Christina was

in the act of running backwards and forwards with her hands
joined in prayer.

Even the magisterial third-person voices of the great
eighteenth- and nineteenth-century novels are, on close exami-
nation, not nearly so impartial as we might remember them. The
famous beginning of *Anna Karenina* tells us that, "Happy families
are all alike, but each unhappy family is unhappy in its own way"
is not expressing a scientific fact, but rather an opinion. The om-
niscient voice in Dickens always sounds far more like the voice
of Dickens than the voice of God, as it does here at the start of
Dombey and Son:

> *Dombey sat in the corner of the darkened room in the*
> *great armchair by the bedside, and Son lay tucked up warm*
> *in a little basket bedstead, carefully disposed on a low settee*
> *immediately in front of the fire and close to it, as if his consti-*
> *tution were analogous to that of a muffin, and it was essential*
> *to toast him brown while he was very new.*

What I hope I've managed to show is how much room there
is, how much variation exists, how many possibilities there are
to consider as we choose how to narrate our stories and novels.
Deciding on the narrator's identity, and personality, is an impor-
tant step. But it is only a step. What really matters is what hap-
pens after that—the language that the writer uses to interest and
engage us in the vision and the version of events that we know
as fiction.

SIX

Character

I REALIZED THAT IT WAS A BIT OF A GAMBLE WHEN, IN THE late 1980s, I assigned my undergraduate class at the University of Utah to read Heinrich von Kleist's novella, *The Marquise of O—*. None of my students was a literature major. Most were Mormons. Few had ever left Utah, and not a single one had ever heard of Heinrich von Kleist.

If they'd known him, he would have scared them silly. They were bright, scrubbed, optimistic American kids, and he was a tormented German hypochondriac, who, when he wasn't writing works of genius, was contemplating suicide and longing only for what he called an abyss deep enough to jump into. Eventually he met a terminally ill woman whom he recognized as a soul mate. Their rapturous connection was forged by the shared dream of double suicide, which they finally committed in 1811, in Berlin, on the shore of Lake Wannsee. The description of their suicide—in joyous, almost rapturous moods, Kleist and Henriette Vogel took their innocent-seeming little picnic basket out to the shores of the lake, from which two shots were later heard—is one of the most haunting events in literary biography. Kleist was thirty-five.

Regardless of Kleist's sad history, I thought my students might like his novella, which isn't all that long, and which has a grabby, switchbacking plot that pulls you in, right away, with its famous first sentence—a sentence that may be even more arresting than the opening of Kleist's *The Earthquake in Chile*, quoted in an earlier chapter:

> *In M—, a large town in northern Italy, the widowed Marquise of O—, a lady of unblemished reputation and the mother of several well-bred children, published the following notice in the newspapers: that, without her knowing how, she was in the family way; that she would like the father of the child she was going to bear to report himself; and that her mind was made up, out of consideration for her people, to marry him.*

This single sentence contains more plot and more sheer narrative than many entire novels. Every word is necessary in establishing the setting of the story and the odd situation of its protagonist. The town and our heroine's name are reduced to initials, just as they might if a thoughtful writer were politely trying to conceal the identity and the residence of a real person. And this clever trick is the first of many that will be used to make the unbelievable seem credible. Because, we're encouraged to think, if this incredible premise *weren't* true, why would the writer be at such pains to protect the privacy of the person to whom the embarrassing event has happened? It's not something one would necessarily bother to do for a character who has just been *made up*.

We are about to be told what the unfortunate event is, in fact within the same sentence. But first we learn enough about the Marquise—that she has a spotless reputation and is already a mother—to dispel whatever doubts we might otherwise have harbored about what we subsequently read: namely, that she is pregnant and has no idea how such a thing might have happened. The spotlessness of her reputation, and the fact that she is presumably familiar with the facts of conception and birth, mean that she is neither too innocent nor too guilty for us to doubt automatically the extraordinary claim she is making.

On the other side of the colon, we have the claim itself, in a form that presumably summarizes, and evokes the journalistic style of the notice she published in the paper. We learn that she is "in a family way" with so little knowledge of how this could have happened that she is, in all innocence, requesting the father of her child not merely to declare himself but to *introduce* himself, that not only does she intend to marry him but her intention comes from consideration for her people. This phrase suggests the themes—family, propriety, the bounds of domestic affection—that will inform the narrative as we work toward the solution of the mystery that this first sentence poses, and the consequences for everyone involved when the mystery is ultimately solved.

If all that weren't enough for one sentence to contain, there are also the religious and biblical echoes that will, throughout the tale, hearken back to the most famous example of a woman who is impregnated in a way that is at least initially baffling to her and to the people around her (obviously, the Virgin Mary). And finally, the sentence prefigures the sudden plot turns and switches that will occur throughout the story as each successive shocking event or revelation affects the characters' passions, hopes and fears, the power balance among them, and the complex loyalties that connect and divide them.

By the end of the first three pages, the action has shot back in time to describe a recent siege, a battle, the burning of the Marquise's castle, gunfire, shooting flames, and general mayhem.

The Marquise is nearly raped by a gang of marauding soldiers, then saved at the last minute by a gallant Russian officer, a certain Count F—. The Marquise faints, and her hero returns to battle, in which he is mortally wounded. In fact, the Marquise learns, he has been killed before she has had a chance to thank him.

What follows is a series of twists and turns that keep reversing each one of our assumptions and expectations. The chaste Marquise turns out to be pregnant, the dead Count F— turns out to be alive, a knight in shining armor turns out to be a rapist, an angel turns out to be a devil who must prove himself an angel again. The ground on which we are standing keeps shifting under our feet, jarring our sense of who the characters are, of what happened, of what *will* happen, and of what we *want* to happen. And we may find that our own familiar and dependable moral framework seems to have weakened and been shaken loose. Because by the end of the novella, the reader who has always thought of herself as being very sure about the fact that rape is a crime may be shocked to find herself wondering why the Marquise is so slow to accept as her husband a man who turns out to have impregnated her while she was unconscious and her castle was being sacked and burned.

If for no other reason than its swashbuckling thriller edge, the story had a better chance of engaging my Utah students than, say, *Ulysses* or *The Making of Americans*. But I knew they rarely read anything written so many years ago (the novella was composed in 1806) or anything with a plot that moved so fast you had to read every word just to keep track of what was happening.

Another problem for my students was that Martin Greenberg's translation had retained the complex winding sentences of Kleist's German, a style that even Thomas Mann called

> *hard as steel yet impetuous, totally matter-of-fact yet contorted, twisted, surcharged with matter; a style full of involu-*

tions, periodic and complex, running to constructions like "in such a manner . . . that," which makes for a syntax that is at once closely reasoned and breathless in its intensity. Kleist succeeds in developing an indirect discourse over twenty-five lines without resorting to a single full stop: in this discourse we find no less than thirteen dependent clauses introduced by that and, at the end, a "briefly, in such a manner that . . ."—which, however, fails to pull the sentence up short, but instead gives rise to yet another that clause!

Despite my worries about how my students might respond, I assigned the story. The assignment was also partly, I admit, the result of a mischievous impulse. It's possible to read the novella as a sly comedy about sex, religion, family, the virgin birth, war and peace, good and evil, angels and devils—and I realized that these were subjects about which my students felt so strongly that they might not get the joke.

Finally, just to make things even trickier, there is, near the end of the story, a scene in which the Marquise and her father have a passionate reconciliation after many dramatic family fights. Sitting in his lap, the Marquise embraces and kisses her overjoyed father while her mother eavesdrops from behind a closed door. Even allowing for the different manners and mores of previous centuries, the powerful hint of incest in the scene is immensely disturbing. At the same time, you sense that Kleist is daring you to think so, half persuading you that, as the Marquise's mother seems to think, there is nothing wrong about what is transpiring between the heroine and her overjoyed father. And so your unease can only be the product of your own corrupt imagination.

Ultimately, Kleist gets you past this, in fact he gets you past quite a lot, including your better judgment about the morals of Count F—. Like any great comedy, the novella taps directly into our almost primal longing to have order restored and harmony established. If you read to the story's conclusion, when everything is sorted out in the most clever and satisfying manner imaginable, your wariness about what you are reading melts away (more or less) and you feel that small explosion of happiness you get at the end of a Shakespeare comedy or a Mozart opera or the scene in which the jousting couple in the 1940s screwball film finally drop their defenses and admit that they have fallen in love.

The class, I knew, could have gone either way. It could have been a great success or a major disaster.

By the time I arrived, on the morning we were scheduled to discuss the novella, my students were already in their seats. As I took off my jacket, trying to be as unobtrusive as possible in order to gauge the mood of the room, I heard them discussing *The Marquise of O—*.

It was as if they knew her, as if her family lived next door and they were surprised or shocked to hear that their neighbors had behaved in a certain way. They asked one another what they thought about the Marquise's actions at a certain point in the plot, a juncture at which someone else might have acted differently. They discussed her parents' response. And that weird scene with her father—what was *that* about? They compared what they expected to happen, and how soon they'd figured out what *had* happened and what was *going* to happen. They debated whether the Marquise was right to give Count F— such a hard time, and whether she should have forgiven him at all, even after she'd had his child.

Until then, they had not been an especially talkative group. Usually, before class, they were silent, with only a few chatting quietly with their friends. But now they had something to talk about: the life and loves of the Marquise of O—.

On that winter morning, with the snow-covered mountains of Utah rising outside the window, my students had participated in what seemed to me a triumphant experiment in how reading can bring us together. Almost two hundred years after Heinrich von Kleist and Henriette Vogel went skipping off to their final picnic and two shots rang out from the Wannsee shore, twenty Utah kids had entered into another world and met the family that Heinrich von Kleist had brought to life with words.

AMONG the unusual things about the way that Kleist creates his characters is that he does so entirely without physical description. There is no information, not a single detail, about the Marquise's appearance. We never hear how a room looks, or what the latest fashion might be, or what people are eating and drinking. We assume that the Marquise is beautiful, perhaps because her presence exerts such an immediate and violent effect on the Russian soldier that he loses all control and turns from an angel into a devil. But we can only surmise that.

Kleist tells you what sort of people his characters are—often impetuous, wrongheaded, overly emotional, but essentially good at heart—and then lets them run around the narrative at the speed of windup toys. He has no time for their motives, nor do they, as they struggle, like the reader, to keep up with the pace at which one surprise follows another.

From the first sentence, we know that unless we are willing to believe that another virgin birth took place in M—, a small town in northern Italy, this story is going to be at least partly about sex. And yet we are constantly being told that the story is about virtue and probity, which in fact it also is. From the language of the opening, you would think that moral beauty was the only sort of beauty that counted. What we are intended to note and admire is not how these people look but rather the decency and good conscience with which everyone in the story is trying to act, and does act—with a few dramatic exceptions.

The first few pages fire off a barrage of adjectives on the

theme of purity and nobility: "a lady of unblemished reputation," "the mother of several well-bred children." There is a reference to the Marquise's bravery in placing the newspaper ad that is likely to subject her to general derision, and to her having been "devoted heart and soul" to her husband, who died three years before, during a business trip to Paris.

We learn that the Marquise has spent her widowhood "in strict seclusion, occupying her time with painting, reading, educating her children, and caring for her parents: until the ___ War suddenly filled the neighborhood with the troops of nearly all the powers, including those of Russia." (Typically, Kleist hardly gives us time to take a breath, there is only that colon separating the Marquise's tranquil existence from the outbreak of war.) There follows a long paragraph of complex, energized, action-packed sentences describing the siege of the castle, the near-assault, and the rescue of the Marquise. In the midst of all this is one short sentence that will become increasingly important as the story continues. Indeed it is essential in order for us to understand the conclusion and again shows how closely we must read Kleist in order not to miss anything.

The sentence, which creates a kind of hush, a moment of stasis in the midst of the raging battle, concerns the Marquise's response to her savior, Count F— . "To the Marquise he seemed a very angel from heaven."

The action instantly picks up again:

> *He smashed the last of the murderous brutes, whose arms were wound about her slender figure, in the face with the hilt of his sword and made him reel back with the blood gushing from his mouth; then, saluting her courteously in French, he offered her his arm and led her, speechless from all she had gone through, to the other wing of the residence, which had not caught fire yet, where she fainted dead away. A little while*

after, when her terrified women appeared, he told them to call
a doctor; promised them, as he put his hat on, that she would
soon recover; and returned to the fray.

Even as we are watching this dramatic scene play out, we are also being given a sense of the Count's character: impulsive and violent on the one hand, courageous and honorable on the other. And our strong first impression of him will turn out to have underestimated the extremes to which his dual nature can take him.

The Marquise's father begs the Count to stay so the family can thank him, but he rides off and is reported killed, shot in battle. And the astonished family hears that his dying words were, "Julietta, with this shot you are avenged!"

In the midst of her own regret over not having sufficiently thanked the Count for having saved her, the Marquise pities the unfortunate woman, with the same name as herself, whom the Count thought about during his final hour. She even attempts to find out where this lady is, so that she can get in touch with her and relay the tragic news. In the case that Kleist is making for the Marquise's innocence, this is still more evidence of her being trusting, naïve, and utterly unaware of any connection between the Count and the pregnancy that we have heard about in the novella's first sentence. She does not suspect that this other Julietta, the object of the Count's last cry, is actually she. Nor can she imagine any reason why she might have inspired such passion.

Meanwhile, attentive readers will notice that this is the first time we hear the Marquise's first name—which is, in fact, the only first name we learn in the novella. By contrast, the Marquise's brother is never referred to as anything but the Forest Warden.

It certainly seems a little strange to *us,* if not to the Marquise, that the Count's last words refer to another woman with the same name as the one he has just rescued and who has already caused him to behave so impetuously. And even on the slim chance that he *is* referring to another woman, what does he mean by crying that the shot that kills him will avenge this *other* Julietta? To say nothing of the fact that for him to call the Marquise (or any other woman) by her first name implies a more intimate connection than whatever (apparently) occurred when he saved her from the brutish soldiers. So it *must* be another Julietta. But still . . . we know that the Marquise is mysteriously pregnant, though, in the flashback that this section represents, she herself has yet to find out. Like the Marquise and her family, we are constantly being challenged to weigh the evidence and consider what is likely, probable, and impossible.

At this point we may find ourselves paging back to see what *did* happen between Julietta and Count F—, who by now does seem like the prime suspect, indeed the only one, in the mystery of the Marquise's embarrassing condition. Everything, we realize, must turn on that moment during the battle just after the Count saves the Marquise. So let's look at it again:

> *He offered her his arm and led her, speechless from all she had gone through, to the other wing of the residence, which had not caught fire yet, where she fainted dead away. A little while after, when her terrified women appeared, he told them to call a doctor; promised them, as he put his hat on, that she would soon recover; and returned to the fray.*

Never has a writer told us so much and so little in that temporal phrase "a little while after." If Kleist is what we would now call a cinematic writer, this may be one of literary history's most masterful fades to black.

In any case, the Marquise is soon distracted from her past troubles when she begins feeling unwell. Her symptoms and sensations remind her of what she felt before the birth of her second child. From here on, her response to the gap between what she suspects and what she knows is handled with so much lightness and charm that, if the emphatic and repeated testimony to her character and virtue hasn't already won us over, we are moved not only to sympathize with her but to hope that we would act half as well in a similar situation. As the Marquise is forced to deal with her own increasing certainty and confusion, she is further confounded by the expertise and the skepticism of the doctor and the midwife, who are called in to diagnose her problem and corroborate her suspicion. If we have doubts about any or all of this, these minor characters are our stand-ins, expressing the sensible reservations that any rational person might have about the mother of two children who doesn't know how she got pregnant.

By now the Count has begun charging in and out of the household, declaring his undying love, asking the Marquise to marry him. And even without his help, the mood at home is becoming more volatile . . .

I've revealed too much of the plot already, but what I am trying to demonstrate is that Kleist tells us just as much as we need to know about his characters, then releases them into a narrative that doesn't stop spinning until the last sentence, which is almost as complex as the first sentence, and which refers back to it. The conclusion hurtles us forward in time. The Marquise and Count F— are happily married, and have been for a while:

> A whole line of young Russians now followed the first; and when the Count once asked his wife, in a happy moment, why on that terrible third of the month, when she seemed ready to accept any villain of a fellow that came along, she had fled from him as if from the Devil, she threw her arms around his neck and said: he wouldn't have looked like a devil

*to her then if he had not seemed like an angel to her at his first
appearance.*

Whatever we may think we know about the best way to create a character, literature shows us that it differs from writer to writer, sometimes from book to book. Even the most seemingly disparate writers turn out to share certain skills in common: for example, the ability to create a minor character with just a few quick strokes.

So, in *Sense and Sensibility*, Jane Austen speedily and almost offhandedly dispatches Mr. and Mrs. John Dashwood, the half brother and sister-in-law who treat his half sisters so uncharitably after he inherits all the family money:

> *He was not an ill-disposed young man, unless to be rather
> cold hearted, and rather selfish, is to be ill-disposed: but he
> was, in general, well respected; for he conducted himself with
> propriety in the discharge of his ordinary duties. Had he mar-
> ried a more amiable woman, he might have been made still
> more respectable than he was: he might even have been made
> amiable himself; for he was very young when he married, and
> very fond of his wife. But Mrs. John Dashwood was a strong
> caricature of himself;—more narrow-minded and selfish.*

Part of what's so delightful about the paragraph is how the narrator seems to be making such an effort to be fair and to present such a balanced view of the John Dashwoods that she begins by denying that he is "ill-disposed" but only "rather selfish and rather cold hearted"—adjectives far more damning than "ill-disposed." How different the section would be if Austen had written, more plainly but less elegantly, that John Dashwood was cold hearted and selfish. Mostly what Mr. Dashwood has to recommend him is his respect for the propriety (as opposed, say, to generosity or largeness of spirit) with which he fulfills his basic obligations. Again, in the apparent interest of fairness, the narrator explains how Mr. Dashwood might have been more amiable "had he married a more amiable woman." And even as we are distracted by considering the truth of the observation about how readily the faults of one spouse can rub off on the other, particularly if they marry when they are young and in love, and how it sometimes happens that one partner can come to seem like a caricature of the other, Austen zeroes in for the kill and effectively finishes off the conniving Mrs. Dashwood. Gone is all pretense of fairness: Mrs. John Dashwood is simply *more* narrow-minded and *more* selfish.

This accurate assessment is almost immediately borne out by the characters' thoughts and actions. In the next paragraph, we find Mr. Dashwood demonstrating the minimal propriety for which he is so well respected, which in this case means not evicting his own stepmother and half sisters and forcing them to live on the street.

> *When he gave his promise to his father, he meditated within himself to increase the fortunes of his sisters by the present of a thousand pounds a-piece. He then really thought himself equal to it. The prospect of four thousand a year, in addition to his present income, besides the remaining half of his own mother's fortune, warmed his heart, and made him feel capable of generosity.—"Yes, he would give them three thousand pounds: it would be liberal and handsome! It would be enough to make them completely easy. Three thousand pounds! he could spare so considerable a sum with little inconvenience."—He thought of it all day long, and for many days successively, and he did not repent.*

In Kleist, as we've seen, characters tend to be defined by their actions. But Austen is more likely to create her men and women by telling us what they *think*, what they have done, and what they plan to do. What matters most is how Mr. Dashwood views his own good deed. In that marvelous barbed sentence in which everything hinges on one word, *then*—"He then really thought himself equal to it"—Austen hints at how long his generosity will last, how long he will continue to rise above himself. Mr. John Dashwood is thrilled by his charity, which, it should be emphasized, is in fact *not* magnanimity but fairness. He meditates on his benevolence with such self-regard and self-congratulation, with such acute awareness of how his actions will seem to others, and with so much unacknowledged regret and obsessiveness that we can easily imagine how strongly his resolve will withstand his wife's suggestion that he may have been a bit hasty. *That* unattractive conversation takes place in a paragraph of indirect discourse that brilliantly portrays the seemingly delicate but actually ham-fisted persuasions of someone manipulating a spouse into doing something that he himself more than half wants to do, even though he knows that it is wrong.

> *Mrs. John Dashwood did not at all approve of what her husband intended to do for his sisters. To take three thousand pounds from the fortune of their dear little boy, would be impoverishing him to the most dreadful degree. She begged him to think again on the subject. How could he answer it to himself to rob his child, and his only child too, of so large a sum? And what possible claim could the Miss Dashwoods, who were related to him only by half blood, which she considered as no relationship at all, have on his generosity to so large an amount? It was very well known, that no affection was ever supposed to exist between the children of any man by different marriages; and why was he to ruin himself, and their poor little Harry, by giving away all his money to his half sisters?*

Mrs. John Dashwood begins by noting that the money in question—the same three thousand pounds that we have already seen her husband decide that he could spare with so "little inconvenience"—is necessary and indispensable for their own family's well-being. Not for the two of *them*, of course, but for their child, his *only* child, whom his foolhardy gesture would "rob" and "impoverish." Then she goes to work on the objects of his charity, first undermining his sense of the bonds connecting him and his sisters. Or, to make a crucial distinction, *half* sisters. Next she appeals to general authority, for "it is very well known" that even if he does feel affection for his sisters, he shouldn't. And now the stakes have escalated to the ruin of himself and "poor little Harry" by giving away "all his money" to women whom he is hardly related to, and isn't supposed to like.

In one sublimely arch and positively murderous sentence, Austen conveys the depth and breadth of Mrs. John Dashwood's family feeling: "Mrs. John Dashwood had never been a favourite with any of her husband's family; but she had had no opportunity, till the present, of shewing them with how little attention to the comfort of other people she could act when occasion required it."

It's in response to this behavior that Mrs. Dashwood senior (that is, Mrs. John Dashwood's mother-in-law) and her three daughters, John's half sisters, are defined for us. Austen describes and distinguishes them in a few brisk paragraphs. The emotional Mrs. Dashwood almost flees from her home, which now belongs to her stepson, but her oldest daughter, Elinor—the creature of sense who prevails over the others' more headlong sensibility—counsels moderation:

Elinor, this eldest daughter, whose advice was so effectual, possessed a strength of understanding, and coolness of judgment, which qualified her, though only nineteen, to be the

*counsellor of her mother, and enabled her frequently to coun-
teract, to the advantage of them all, that eagerness of mind in
Mrs. Dashwood which must generally have led to imprudence.
She had an excellent heart;—her disposition was affectionate,
and her feelings were strong; but she knew how to govern them:
it was a knowledge which her mother had yet to learn, and
which one of her sisters had resolved never to be taught.*

*Marianne's abilities were, in many respects, quite equal to
Elinor's. She was sensible and clever; but eager in everything;
her sorrows, her joys, could have no moderation. She was gener-
ous, amiable, interesting: she was everything but prudent. The
resemblance between her and her mother was strikingly great.*

*Elinor saw, with concern, the excess of her sister's sen-
sibility; but by Mrs. Dashwood it was valued and cherished.
They encouraged each other now in the violence of their af-
fliction. . . .*

*Margaret, the other sister, was a good humoured, well
disposed girl; but as she had already imbibed a good deal of
Marianne's romance, without having much of her sense, she
did not, at thirteen, bid fair to equal her sisters at a more ad-
vanced period of life.*

In *Pride and Prejudice*, Austen proves herself to be a master at
using dialogue to establish character, to delineate the personali-
ties of the speakers, and to acquaint us with the people whom
they are speaking about. Here is the first conversation between
Mr. and Mrs. Bennet.

*"My dear Mr. Bennet," said his lady to him one day, "have
you heard that Netherfield Park is let at last?"*

Mr. Bennet replied that he had not.

*"But it is," returned she; "for Mrs. Long has just been
here, and she told me all about it."*

Mr. Bennet made no answer.

"Do not you want to know who has taken it?" cried his wife impatiently.

"You want to tell me, and I have no objection to hearing it."

This was invitation enough.

"Why, my dear, you must know, Mrs. Long says that Netherfield is taken by a young man of large fortune from the north of England; that he came down on Monday in a chaise and four to see the place, and was so much delighted with it that he agreed with Mr. Morris immediately; that he is to take possession before Michaelmas, and some of his servants are to be in the house by the end of next week."

"What is his name?"

"Bingley."

"Is he married or single?"

"Oh! single, my dear, to be sure! A single man of large fortune; four or five thousand a year. What a fine thing for our girls!"

"How so? How can it affect them?"

"My dear Mr. Bennet," replied his wife, "how can you be so tiresome! You must know that I am thinking of his marrying one of them."

"Is that his design in settling here?"

"Design! nonsense, how can you talk so! But it is very likely that he may fall in love with one of them, and therefore you must visit him as soon as he comes."

"I see no occasion for that. You and the girls may go, or you may send them by themselves, which perhaps will be still better, for as you are as handsome as any of them, Mr. Bingley might like you the best of the party."

"My dear, you flatter me. I certainly have had my share of beauty, but I do not pretend to be anything extraordinary now. When a woman has five grown up daughters, she ought to give over thinking of her own beauty."

"In such cases, a woman has not often much beauty to think of."

"But, my dear, you must indeed go and see Mr. Bingley when he comes into the neighbourhood."

"It is more than I engage for, I assure you."

"But consider your daughters. Only think what an establishment it would be for one of them. Sir William and Lady Lucas are determined to go, merely on that account, for in general you know they visit no newcomers. Indeed you must go, for it will be impossible for us to visit him, if you do not."

"You are overscrupulous, surely. I dare say Mr. Bingley will be very glad to see you; and I will send a few lines by you to assure him of my hearty consent to his marrying which ever he chooses of the girls; though I must throw in a good word for my little Lizzy."

"I desire you will do no such thing. Lizzy is not a bit better than the others; and I am sure she is not half so handsome as Jane, nor half so good humoured as Lydia. But you are always giving her the preference."

"They have none of them much to recommend them," replied he; "they are all silly and ignorant like other girls; but Lizzy has something more of quickness than her sisters."

"Mr. Bennet, how can you abuse your own children in such a way? You take delight in vexing me. You have no compassion on my poor nerves."

"You mistake me, my dear. I have a high respect for your nerves. They are my old friends. I have heard you mention them with consideration these twenty years at least."

"Ah! you do not know what I suffer."

"But I hope you will get over it, and live to see many young men of four thousand a year come into the neighbourhood."

"It will be no use to us, if twenty such should come since you will not visit them."

> *"Depend upon it, my dear, that when there are twenty, I will visit them all."*
>
> *Mr. Bennet was so odd a mixture of quick parts, sarcastic humour, reserve, and caprice, that the experience of three and twenty years had been insufficient to make his wife understand his character. Her mind was less difficult to develop. She was a woman of mean understanding, little information, and uncertain temper. When she was discontented she fancied herself nervous. The business of her life was to get her daughters married; its solace was visiting and news.*

The calm forbearance which Mr. Bennet answers his wife's first question ("he replied that he had not") provides an immediate and reasonably accurate idea of his character. Driven to impatience, she says what he was expecting to hear: namely, that a rich young man has moved into the neighborhood. When Mrs. Bennet crows, "What a fine thing for our girls!" we can assume that Mr. Bennet knows the answer before he asks if their new neighbor is married or single. And he's toying with his wife when he inquires, "How can it affect them?"

Lest we receive a skewed or harsh impression of the Bennets' own marriage, Mr. Bennet compliments his wife by suggesting that she is as handsome as their daughters. In fact, as we are discovering, theirs is a harmonious union, and indeed the whole conversation, with its intimacy, its gentle teasing, and with Mr. Bennet's joking reference to his old friendship with his wife's nerves, is a double portrait of a happy couple. Their exchanges also tell us how many daughters they have, as Mrs. Bennet works toward her real purpose, which is to persuade her husband to call on the newly arrived Mr. Bingley. Now comes the loving but slightly chilling assessment of his "silly and ignorant" daughters, except for Lizzy—Elizabeth—his favorite, the novel's heroine.

The next paragraph establishes Lizzy's role in the family;

she's neither so beautiful as Jane nor so pleasant as Lydia, but she is gifted with an intelligence that endears her to her father. Austen invites us to consider a general truth that we may have observed about what sort of girl becomes her father's favorite in a family of daughters. Elizabeth's intelligence means more to her father than it does to her mother, who is perhaps more attuned to the fact that intelligence may not be a virtue in a young woman whom one hopes to marry off.

As the scene ends, Austen sums up Mr. Bennet, with his odd quirks, and his considerably simpler wife. And we're off to the second chapter, in which Mr. Bennet turns out to have visited Mr. Bingley, but without giving his wife the satisfaction of telling her so.

If Jane Austen's method is to attach to each of her characters the equivalent of a musical theme and then set them dancing minuets to slight variations on those themes, George Eliot begins with crashing overtures that introduce the somewhat larger-than-life personalities who populate her novels:

> *Miss Brooke had that kind of beauty which seems to be thrown into relief by poor dress. Her hand and wrist were so finely formed that she could wear sleeves not less bare of style than those in which the Blessed Virgin appeared to Italian painters; and her profile as well as her stature and bearing seemed to gain the more dignity from her plain garments, which by the side of provincial fashion gave her the impressiveness of a fine quotation from the Bible,—or from one of our elder poets,—in a paragraph of today's newspaper. She was usually spoken of as being remarkably clever, but with the addition that her sister Celia had more common-sense. Nevertheless, Celia wore scarcely more trimmings; and it was only to close observers that her dress differed from her sister's, and had a shade of coquetry in its arrangements; for Miss Brooke's plain dressing was due*

to mixed conditions, in most of which her sister shared. The pride of being ladies had something to do with it: the Brooke connections, though not exactly aristocratic, were unquestionably "good": if you inquired backward for a generation or two, you would not find any yard-measuring or parcel-tying forefathers—anything lower than an admiral or a clergyman; and there was even an ancestor discernible as a Puritan gentleman who served under Cromwell, but afterwards conformed, and managed to come out of all political troubles as the proprietor of a respectable family estate. Young women of such birth, living in a quiet country-house, and attending a village church hardly larger than a parlour, naturally regarded frippery as the ambition of a huckster's daughter. Then there was well-bred economy, which in those days made show in dress the first item to be deducted from, when any margin was required for expenses more distinctive of rank. Such reasons would have been enough to account for plain dress, quite apart from religious feeling; but in Miss Brooke's case, religion alone would have determined it; and Celia mildly acquiesced in all her sister's sentiments, only infusing them with that common-sense which is able to accept momentous doctrines without any eccentric agitation. Dorothea knew many passages of Pascal's Pensées and of Jeremy Taylor by heart; and to her the destinies of mankind, seen by the light of Christianity, made the solicitudes of feminine fashion appear an occupation for Bedlam. She could not reconcile the anxieties of a spiritual life involving eternal consequences, with a keen interest in gump and artificial protrusions of drapery. Her mind was theoretic, and yearned by its nature after some lofty conception of the world which might frankly include the parish of Tipton and her own rule of conduct there; she was enamoured of intensity and greatness, and rash in embracing whatever seemed to her to have those aspects; likely to seek martyrdom, to make retractions,

*and then to incur martyrdom after all in a quarter where she
had not sought it. Certainly such elements in the character of a
marriageable girl tended to interfere with her lot, and hinder it
from being decided according to custom, by good looks, vanity,
and merely canine affection. With all this, she, the elder of the
sisters, was not yet twenty, and they had both been educated,
since they were about twelve years old and had lost their par-
ents, on plans at once narrow and promiscuous, first in an
English family and afterwards in a Swiss family at Lausanne,
their bachelor uncle and guardian trying in this way to remedy
the disadvantages of their orphaned condition.*

One might conclude that, in her approach to creating char-
acter, Eliot is the opposite of Kleist, since the very first thing she
tells you in *Middlemarch* is what her heroine looks like and what
she wears. In fact we're so rapidly whisked past mere appearance
to matters of the spirit that Dorothea's appearance might almost
seem irrelevant, a formal concession to the reality a novelist feels
obliged to create. Meanwhile, these seemingly straightforward
sentences are subtly prefiguring one of the major discoveries that
Dorothea will make later in the book: the fact that human beings
are creatures of the body and the passions as well as of the mind
and the soul.

By the end of this substantial first paragraph, Eliot has cre-
ated a character of great complexity as well as an entire milieu,
"young women of such birth, living in a quiet country-house,
and attending a village church." She has contrasted Dorothea's
nature with that of her sister and provided as much of the history
of both young women as is necessary to bring us to the point at
which the novel begins. After telling us that Dorothea's eligibil-
ity may be hampered by the intensity of her religious preoccu-
pations ("women were expected to have weak opinions"), Eliot
proceeds to relay Dorothea's own ideas on marriage: "The really

delightful marriage must be that where your husband was a sort of father, and could teach you even Hebrew, if you wished it."

And so the novel begins the first and most important of its several parallel explorations of the perils of getting what you want, or in any case what you think you want. By the second chapter, Dorothea will have met a man who promises to be the sort of husband she imagines, the dour Mr. Edward Casaubon, a local clergyman, considerably older than she, who has labored for years over a massive and scholarly work entitled *The Key to All Mythologies*. Invited to dinner at Dorothea's uncle's house, Mr. Casaubon takes no part in the lively chatter, until he offers the following speech, a paragraph of dialogue that solidly establishes his character before the other guests have a chance to weigh in on his virtues and flaws, before Celia has time to tell Dorothea that he is ugly and sallow, and before another family friend and a competitor for Dorothea's affections tells a neighbor that Causabon is "no better than a mummy."

Asked if he has read Southey's *Peninsular War*, Mr. Casaubon replies:

> *"I have little leisure for such literature just now. I have been using up my eyesight on old characters lately; the fact is, I want a reader for my evenings; but I am fastidious in voices, and I cannot endure listening to an imperfect reader. It is a misfortune, in some senses: I feed too much on the inward sources; I live too much with the dead. My mind is something like the ghost of an ancient, wandering about the world and trying mentally to construct it as it used to be, in spite of ruin and confusing changes. But I find it necessary to use the utmost caution about my eyesight."*
>
> *This was the first time that Mr. Casaubon had spoken at any length. He delivered himself with precision, as if he had been called upon to make a public statement; and the balanced*

singsong neatness of his speech, occasionally corresponded to by a movement of his head, was the more conspicuous from its contrast with good Mr. Brooke's scrappy slovenliness. Dorothea said to herself that Mr. Casaubon was the most interesting man she had ever seen, not excepting even Monsieur Liret, the Vaudois clergyman who had given conferences on the history of the Waldenses.

The very first words we hear from Casaubon are enough to make us feel chilled by his pomposity and self-importance, and to be troubled by the very different impression he makes on Dorothea. Nor does the letter in which he proposes to Dorothea much reassure us about his character. What's striking is not only what the letter contains but what it lacks: passion, affection, endearments, the least sign of curiosity or interest in who Dorothea *is*. We can't help but notice how much of it is about *his* life, *his* work, *his* habits: how many of his reasons for proposing marriage have to do entirely with *him*. And we cannot read the letter without doing what we are told that Dorothea cannot do, that is, "to look at it critically as a profession of love."

MY DEAR MISS BROOKE—*I have your guardian's permission to address you on a subject than which I have none more at heart. I am not, I trust, mistaken in the recognition of some deeper correspondence than that of date in the fact that a consciousness of need in my own life had arisen contemporaneously with the possibility of my becoming acquainted with you. For in the first hour of meeting you, I had an impression of your eminent and perhaps exclusive fitness to supply that need (connected, I may say, with such activity of the affections as even the preoccupations of a work too special to be abdicated could not uninterruptedly dissimulate); and each succeeding opportunity for observation has given the impression an added depth by convincing me more emphatically of that fitness which I had preconceived, and thus evoking more decisively those affections to which I have but now referred. Our conversations have, I think, made sufficiently clear to you the tenor of my life and purposes: a tenor unsuited, I am aware, to the commoner order of minds. But I have discerned in you an elevation of thought and a capability of devotedness, which I had hitherto not conceived to be compatible either with the early bloom of youth or with those graces of sex that may be said at once to win and to confer distinction when combined, as they notably are in you, with the mental qualities above indicated. It was, I confess, beyond my hope to meet with this rare combination of elements both solid and attractive, adapted to supply aid in graver labours and to cast a charm over vacant hours; and but for the event of my introduction to you (which, let me again say, I trust not to be superficially coincident with foreshadowing needs, but providentially related thereto as stages towards the completion of a life's plan), I should presumably have gone on to the last without any attempt to lighten my solitariness by a matrimonial union.*

Such, my dear Miss Brooke, is the accurate statement of my feelings; and I rely on your kind indulgence in venturing now to ask you how far your own are of a nature to confirm my happy presentiment. To be accepted by you as your husband and the earthly guardian of your welfare, I should regard as the highest of the providential gifts. In return I can at least offer you an affection hitherto unwasted, and the faithful consecration of a life which, however short in the sequel, has no backward pages whereon, if you choose to turn them, you will find records such as might justly cause you either bitterness or shame. I await the expression of your sentiments with an anxiety which it would be the part of wisdom (were it possible) to divert by a more arduous labour than usual. But in this order of experience I am still young, and in looking forward to an unfavourable possibility I cannot but feel that resignation to solitude will be more difficult after the temporary illumination of hope. In any case, I shall remain, yours with sincere devotion.

EDWARD CASAUBON

The marriage takes place, and next we catch up with Dorothea on her honeymoon in Rome, sobbing bitterly because she has just begun to understand what sort of man she has married: a dried-up depressive with no enthusiasm for the sights of Rome or for the company of his new bride. What's worse is her dawning realization that he has not really *begun* the great book that she married him to help him write. When she makes the mistake of mentioning this, the barely bridled nastiness of her husband's response—with its barbed adjectives (*facile, ignorant, baseless, impatient*), its reference to onlookers and chatterers, and its implication that Dorothea might *be* one of those facile, ignorant, impatient onlookers and chatterers who must be ignored by "scrupulous explorers" such as he—convinces us that we were right to fear for the future of this marriage. The defensiveness and aggression, however "reined in by propriety," of Casaubon's reply is exactly, we feel, how such a man would fight back and lash out when he felt challenged:

> *"My love," he said, with irritation reined in by propriety, "you may rely upon me for knowing the times and the seasons, adapted to the different stages of a work which is not to be measured by the facile conjectures of ignorant onlookers. It had been easy for me to gain a temporary effect by a mirage of*

*baseless opinion; but it is ever the trial of the scrupulous ex-
plorer to be saluted with the impatient scorn of chatterers who
attempt only the smallest achievements, being indeed equipped
for no other. And it were well if all such could be admonished to
discriminate judgments of which the true subject-matter lies
entirely beyond their reach, from those of which the elements
may be compassed by a narrow and superficial survey."*

This scene is closely followed by the entirely different con-
versation that Dorothea has with Casaubon's cousin, the young
artist Will Ladislaw, who carelessly flings around words and
concepts—*feeling, pleasure, enjoyment*—that are simply not in Mr.
Casaubon's vocabulary. And so we begin to intuit our heroine's
dilemma: the necessity of admitting that she has made a mistake
about herself, about the world, and about the man she has mar-
ried, and that she must reassess her youthful notions about the
relative importance and the compatibility of goodness and hap-
piness, of self-indulgence and self-transcendence.

In these scenes, both Austen and Eliot manage to establish
several complex characters at once, partly through narration and
partly through drama and dialogue that allows us to observe the
characters interacting. Something similar happens in the first
chapter of Gustave Flaubert's *Sentimental Education*, which intro-
duces us to the young man and the married couple whose triangu-
lated relationship will form the core of the novel. Appropriately
for a book in which time and history play an important role, we're
told that it's six in the morning on September 15, 1840. A crowded
boat is about to set sail up the Seine from a pier in Paris. Here is
our first sight of the novel's hero, Frédéric Moreau:

*A long-haired man of eighteen, holding a sketchbook
under his arm, stood motionless beside the tiller. He gazed
through the mist at spires and buildings whose names he did*

not know, and took a last look at the Île Saint-Louis, the Cité, and Notre-Dame; and soon, as Paris was lost to view, he heaved a deep sigh.

Monsieur Frédéric Moreau, who had just matriculated, was returning to Nogent-sur-Seine, where he would have to hang about for two months before going to read for the Bar. His mother had sent him to Le Havre, giving him just enough money for the journey, to see an uncle who she hoped would leave his fortune to her son; he had returned to Paris only the previous day, and he was making up for the impossibility of staying in the capital by taking the longest route home.

In the first paragraph, the long hair, the sketchbook, the gaze, the sigh, give us a fairly accurate sense of his romantic character, as does the indolence or self-indulgence that has him filling his vacation time by "hanging about" and by taking the slowest possible boat. The second paragraph sketches in the basics of his educational, professional, economic, and domestic situation. As the riverboat picks up steam, cruising past the landscape, the passengers begin to relax. "Spirits rose. Glasses were brought out and filled."

Now we turn back to Frédéric, once again lost in his self-absorbed dreaminess, tellingly convinced that "the happiness which his nobility of soul deserved was slow in coming" and passing the time by reciting melancholy poems to himself:

Frédéric thought about his room at home, about the plot of a play, about subjects for pictures, about future loves. He considered that the happiness which his nobility of soul deserved was slow in coming. He recited melancholy poems to himself; striding along the deck, he went forward as far as the bell, and there, in a group of passengers and sailors, he noticed a gentleman flirting with a peasant-girl, and toying with the gold cross which she wore on her breast. He was a big fellow of about forty, with crinkly hair. His sturdy figure filled out a black velvet tail-coat, a couple of emeralds glittered in his cambric shirt, and his wide white trousers fell over a pair of strange red boots of Russian leather, which were decorated with a pattern in blue.

Frédéric's presence did not embarrass him. He turned towards him several times, giving him conspiratorial winks; then he offered cigars to all the men around him. But he probably found the company boring, for he moved away. Frédéric followed him.

To begin with, the conversation touched on the different kinds of tobacco, and then turned quite naturally to women. The gentleman in the red boots gave the young man advice, expounded theories, told anecdotes, and quoted himself as an example, reeling all this off in a fatherly tone of voice, with an ingenuous wickedness which was quite amusing.

He was a Republican; he had travelled; he knew the secrets of the theatres, restaurants, and newspapers; and he was acquainted with all the celebrities of the stage, whom he referred to familiarly by their Christian names. Before long Frédéric had confided his plans to him; he took a favourable view of them.

Suddenly he broke off to examine the funnel, and then rapidly muttered a lengthy sum to himself, in order to discover "the force of each piston stroke, at so many a minute." Having found the answer, he expatiated on the beauties of the landscape. He said how happy he was to have escaped from business.

Frédéric felt a certain respect for him, and on a sudden impulse asked his name. The stranger replied all in one breath:

"Jacques Arnoux, proprietor of L'Art Industriel, Boulevard Montmartre."

A servant with gold braid on his cap came up to him and said:

> *"Would Monsieur please go below? Mademoiselle is cry-ing."*
>
> *He disappeared.*
>
> L'Art Industriel *was a hybrid establishment, comprising both an art magazine and a picture shop. Frédéric had seen the title several times in the window of his local bookshop, printed on huge prospectuses which bore the name of Jacques Arnoux in a prominent position.*

So, by the end of this section, we have met another of the novel's principal characters, the art dealer and magazine editor Jacques Arnoux. His outfit—flashy, expensive, a bit Bohemian, complete with emeralds and red leather boots—is almost all we need to know, though we do get a little extra: the information that he is entertaining a group of passengers and sailors by pub-licly flirting with a peasant girl. He's a show-off whose social status allows him to behave like that, just as his privilege permits him to offer cigars to the men. We've met men like this, high rollers, big spenders, simultaneously generous and coarse. And throughout the book we will watch him trying to buy attention, love, and forgiveness.

Of course, he's not embarrassed by Frédéric's presence. They recognize each other. They are both from the same social class; hence, the conspiratorial winks and the fact that they go off together when Arnoux gets bored with his own antics. The moment almost streaks past us, but if it does, we miss seeing Flaubert's notation of how the subtle markers of class govern ev-ery social situation, including the choice of whom one engages in casual conversation on a boat.

The interchange adds another layer to our impression of Frédéric, who is not in the least put off by Arnoux's flashiness, but is, on the contrary (as a young man like Frédéric would be), charmed and flattered when this worldly traveler and well-connected bon vivant consents to talk to him. And when he is moved to confide his own plans, of which Arnoux has a "favourable view," we can practically hear the older man only half paying attention. His mind is too busy tracking the ship's funnel, the mechanics of the engine, the beauty of the landscape, and his own pleasure in the journey. Only now does Frédéric ask who he is, and in one breath the man announces not only his name but his title. He's his own business card. The scene ends abruptly in a way that will be repeated, with variations, later in the book. In the middle-class Arnoux household, the parents are careful to consider what they believe are their children's needs. This contradiction enriches Arnoux's character; the sophisticated man of the world makes a hasty exit because his daughter is crying.

Left alone, Frédéric goes back to observing his fellow passengers, an opportunity for us to register the attention he is paying to how everyone is dressed and for Flaubert to display his particular gift for describing busy crowd scenes. On the way back to his seat in the first-class section, he glimpses a woman whose beauty sends him into a rapture. In this state, he will project all his dreams, feelings, and desires—including his strongest desire, which is to *have* a feeling—onto the woman. The woman is Mme. Arnoux, the wife of the gentleman Frédéric has talked to on deck, the man who personifies everything that Frédéric wants to be, and that no one should want to be. And now his enviable position is solidified in Frédéric's eyes by the fact of the man's having such a magnificent, desirable wife—a woman with whom Frédéric enters into a relationship that will reflect his first response to her on the boat.

> It was like a vision:
> She was sitting in the middle of the bench, all alone; or at least he could not see anybody else in the dazzling light which her eyes cast upon him. Just as he passed her, she raised her

*head; he bowed automatically; and stopping a little way off,
on the same side of the boat, he looked at her.*

    *She was wearing a broad-brimmed straw hat, with pink
ribbons which fluttered behind her in the wind. Her black hair
. . . seemed to caress the oval of her face. Her dress of pale
spotted muslin billowed out in countless folds. She was busy
with a piece of embroidery; and her straight nose, her chin, her
whole figure was silhouetted clearly against the background of
the blue sky.*

    *As she stayed in the same position, he took a few turns to
the right and left, in order to conceal the purpose of his move-
ments; then he stationed himself close to her sunshade, which
was leaning against the bench, and pretended to be watching
a launch on the river.*

    *He had never seen anything to compare with her splendid
dark skin, her ravishing figure, or her delicate, translucent fin-
gers. He looked at her workbasket with eyes full of wonder, as
if it were something out of the ordinary. What was her name,
her home, her life, her past? He longed to know the furniture
in her room, all the dresses she had ever worn, the people she
mixed with; and even the desire for physical possession gave
way to a profounder yearning, a poignant curiosity which
knew no bounds.*

We are only four pages into the novel and already we have a
remarkably full impression of its three central characters, who
will eventually be joined by a large supporting cast. And our sense
of all three of them continues to grow and change with every-
thing we see them say and do, and with everything that happens
to them.

    I realize that I have taken my examples from works of ear-
lier centuries, and that equally useful passages could be gathered
from contemporary fiction in which the characters seem, on the

surface, more like us. In theory, such characters—who wear modern clothes, drive cars like our own, shop in discount stores, and live in our cities and suburbs—would strike us as more familiar, more comprehensible, possibly even more interesting. But I think you would have had a hard time convincing my students of that, in that classroom in Salt Lake City, on that winter morning on which they discussed their new friend, the Marquise of O—.

SEVEN

Dialogue

AMONG THE THINGS I REMEMBER HEARING WHEN I WAS beginning to write was the following rule: you shouldn't, and actually *can't,* make fictional dialogue—conversation on the page—sound like actual speech. The repetitions, meaningless expressions, stammers, and nonsensical monosyllables with which we express hesitation, along with the clichés and banalities that constitute so much of everyday conversation, cannot and should not be used when our characters are talking. Rather, they should speak more fluently than we do, with greater economy and certitude. Unlike us, they should say what they mean, get to the point, avoid circumlocution and digression. The idea, presumably, is that fictional dialogue should be an "improved," cleaned-up, and smoothed-out version of the way people talk. *Better* than "real" dialogue.

Then why is so much written dialogue *less* colorful and interesting than what we can overhear daily in the Internet café, the mall, and on the subway? Many people have a gift for language that flows when they are talking and dries up when they are confronted with the blank page, or when they are trying to make the characters on it speak.

Once I assigned a class to eavesdrop on strangers and transcribe the results. I decided to try it myself, in a university coffee shop. Within moments I overheard a young woman telling her male companion about a dream in which she saw Liza Minnelli arrayed in white robes and a starry crown, dressed as the Queen of Heaven. What made the conversation doubly engaging was that the girl seemed to be romantically attracted to her friend, and was using her story as a means of seduction, unaware that he was, insofar as I could tell, gay. This fact was not unrelated to his lively interest in Liza Minnelli, yet another connection that his companion was preferring not to make.

Like this one, most conversations involve a sort of sophisticated multitasking. When we humans speak, we are not merely communicating information but attempting to make an impression and achieve a goal. And sometimes we are hoping to prevent the listener from noticing what we are *not* saying, which is often not merely distracting but, we fear, as audible as what we *are* saying. As a result, dialogue usually contains as much or even more subtext than it does text. More is going on under the surface than on it. One mark of bad written dialogue is that it is only doing one thing, at most, at once.

A PIECE of *good* advice that beginning writers often receive warns against using dialogue as exposition and inventing those stiff, unlikely, artificial conversations in which facts are being transmitted from one character to another mainly for the benefit of the reader:

> *"Hi, Joe."*
> *"Nice to see you again, Sally."*

"What have you been doing, Joe?"

"Well, Sally, as you know, I'm an insurance investigator. I'm twenty-six years old. I've lived in Philadelphia for twelve years. I'm unmarried and very lonely. I come to this bar twice a week, on average, but so far have failed to meet anyone I particularly like."

And so forth.

In nearly every case, this is a mistake. But there are, as always, exceptions to the rule, instances in which a writer employs dialogue not so much as exposition but as a sort of shorthand that obviates the need for whole paragraphs of exposition.

John Le Carré's *A Perfect Spy* begins:

> *In the small hours of a blustery October morning in a south Devon coastal town that seemed to have been deserted by its inhabitants, Magnus Pym got out of his elderly country taxi-cab and, having paid the driver and waited till he had left, struck out across the church square.*

The paragraph goes on, at length, tracking Magnus Pym, whom we learn, has been en route for sixteen hours and is headed toward one of several "ill-lit Victorian boardinghouses." At last Magnus Pym rings the doorbell, and is greeted by an old woman who says, "Why Mr. Canterbury, it's you."

Thus one line of dialogue informs us that Magnus Pym has been here before and, more important, is traveling under an assumed name.

Even when novice writers avoid the sort of dialogue that is essentially exposition framed by quotation marks, the dialogue they *do* write often serves a single purpose—that is, to advance the plot—rather than the numerous simultaneous aims that it can accomplish. To see how much dialogue *can* achieve, it's instructive to look at the novels of Henry Green, in which many of the important plot developments are conveyed through conversation.

Throughout Green's work, dialogue provides both text and subtext, allowing us to observe the wide range of emotions that his characters feel and display, the ways in which they say and don't say what they mean, attempt to manipulate their spouses, lovers, friends, and children, stake emotional claims, demonstrate sexual interest or unavailability, confess and conceal their hopes and fears. And it all passes by us in such a bright, engaging splash of chatter that only slowly do we realize how widely Green has cast his net, how deeply he has penetrated. Green's work not only demands close reading but also provides a paradise for the close reader who can only marvel at the wealth of information each line of dialogue provides, and the accuracy with which it shows people interacting with one another. No one else so fully inhabits his characters or writes them more from the inside, so that we feel that every line a character speaks expresses, and is fully determined by, the character's circumstances and emotional state.

In this passage from his final novel, *Doting,* nineteen-year-old Annabel Payton has invited Peter Middleton, a student two years younger than herself, to have lunch at an inexpensive Indian restaurant near her office. Annabel has a crush on Peter's father—as the awkward, somewhat thick-headed Peter may or may not be aware—and is attempting to extract information about Peter's parents from her lunch companion. Word by word, the dialogue captures the rhythms of someone trying to discover something without disclosing something else, of an interlocutor who cannot stop pushing until she finds what she is seeking. It's a model of social inquisition carried out by someone who doesn't much care about the person she is interrogating, except that she would like to keep him from forming a low opinion of her and from figuring out what she is doing.

"Did your father happen to mention that he'd taken me out the other afternoon?" she inquired.

"No," the boy said in an uninterested voice. "Should he?"

"We ran across one another in the street. I'm afraid I can't afford anything like the gorgeous meal he provided."

"But curry's my favourite," Peter claimed. "I wish I had it every day. Decent of you to ask me."

"No, because I do truly enjoy seeing you. It takes me out of myself. And you've little idea how few there are I could say that of. Though, d'you know, it could be true about your father. He's so terribly handsome, Peter."

The boy broke into mocking laughter, with his mouth full.

"Look out for the curry," she warned. "You'll blow it all over me and the table."

When he had composed himself he said, "Well I once ate a green fig looked exactly like Dad's face."

After a brief pause to discuss a mutual friend, Annabel persists:

"Are your parents still in love?" she asked.

"My mother and father? God, I suppose so. Are yours?"

"Not a bit. No."

Peter went on eating.

"They don't even share a room."

Annabel describes her parents' endless quarreling and asks Peter if his parents are like that, then goes on:

"How long have they been married?"

"Lord, don't ask me. I wouldn't know."

"All in all, I imagine they were still very much in love,"
she suggested.

"I expect so," he said.

"You won't tell them I mentioned this, will you?"

A few lines later, Annabel asks Peter if he thinks his mother
is beautiful.

"Yes," he said, rather gruff. "As a matter of fact."

"Me too," she echoed, but in a wan little voice. "She has
everything. Hair, teeth, skin, those wide-apart eyes. By any
standard your father's a very lucky man."

"Why?"

"To have such a wife of course. Would you say she liked
me, Peter?"

"Fairly, yes. No reason not to, is there?"

"Oh none," she agreed casually.

It's hard to limit yourself to discussing just one scene from
Green's masterpiece, *Loving*. How can we possibly choose the
passage that best illustrates the subtlety, the depth, the original-
ity and complexity with which Green uses conversation to create
character and to tell the minimally dramatic, low-key story that,
thanks to the dialogue, seems positively riveting? In fact, would-
be dialogue writers might want to close-read this entire novel
about a group of mostly English servants (and in the background,
their employers) on an estate in Ireland during the Second World
War. One reason it's hard to stop quoting this book is that each
scene keeps turning and turning in tiny delightful increments,
and it seems unfair to deprive the reader of the next marvelous
development.

In this touching, sweetly comic, intricately choreographed
moment, the two pretty young housemaids, Edith and Kate,

have gone to the beach with the pantry boy, Albert, who is the assistant to the butler, Raunce. They have taken the three children they have been assigned to watch, one of whom is also named Albert. Raunce's Albert, as he is called, is a melancholy, retiring boy who is unrequitedly in love with Edith, who is in love with Raunce.

In the hierarchy of the estate, a caste system in which gradations of rank and influence are precisely calibrated, Edith enjoys the power (at least, the power to tease) that she has over Albert. But the empathetic, decent Edith has no wish to hurt him. As Edith tells Kate in a later scene, Albert suffers from "calf love," a concept that Kate mocks as something too hoity-toity and time-consuming for the likes of working people like them. Edith explains her kindness as the sympathy one might feel for a mouse that had caught its little leg in a wheel.

At the same time, something extremely complex is being suggested here: namely, the notion that Edith half-welcomes Albert's attention because new love has made her more open to the pleasures and possibilities of the world, including the erotic—a sophisticated observation from life that runs counter to the received notion that the beginning of love always makes one more exclusive, more monogamous, more fixated on the beloved.

Until the following scene on the beach, Albert has hardly said a word about himself, let alone about his background or his personal history. Nor has the book given us much information about the boy, other than that he has yellow hair and often looks ill—though his real malady, we suspect, is an acute case of embarrassment and homesickness rather than any physical ailment.

The quiet interlude on the shore has been immediately preceded by a noisier minor event involving the three children, a "fair-sized" aggressive crab, and a riled-up pet dog named Peter, which Albert has called an ugly bastard and has shrunken from, a bit ignominiously. Now, to protect his brand-new blue serge suit, which (doubtless for Edith's benefit) Albert has inadvisably worn to the beach, the thoughtful Edith invites him to lie beside her on her raincoat. She sits up to watch the children, and Kate snoozes beside them in the sun. It's only a raincoat, so they are very close, though Edith has made it clear that their proximity is for the sake of the suit—which, we feel, is just the sort of thing that Edith would think of, and do.

> He lay down at her side while she sat bolt upright to keep an eye on the children.
>
> "I got a sister over at home," he said low.
>
> "What's that?" she asked careless. "I can't hear you with the sea."
>
> "I got a sister works in an airplane factory," he began. If she heard him she gave no indication. "Madge we call her. They's terrible the hours she puts in."
>
> He lay on his stomach facing inland while Edith watched the ocean.
>
> "I've only her and mum left now," he went on. "Dad, 'e died a month or two afore I came here. He worked in a fruiterer's in Albany Place. It was a cancer took 'im."
>
> When he broke off the heavy Atlantic reverberated in their ears.
>
> "Now Mr Raunce writes to his," he continued, "and can't never get a reply. And there's me writes to mine, every week I do since this terrible bombing started but I don't ever seem to receive no answers though every time 'e comes over I'm afeared mum an' sis must've got theirs. To read the papers you wouldn't think there was anything left of the old town."
>
> "That young Albert," Edith yelled against the sea, "I regret we took him along."

Raunce's Albert looked over his shoulder on the side away from Edith but could not see how his namesake was misbehaving.

"You see with dad gone I feel responsible," he tried again loud. "I know I'm only young but I'm earnin' and there's times I consider I ought to be back to look after them. Not that I don't send the best part of me wages each week. I do that of course."

A silence fell.

"What did you say your sister's name was?" Edith asked.

"Mum had her christened Madge," the lad replied. He tried a glance at Edith but she was not regarding him. "To tell you the truth," he continued, "I did wonder what's the right thing? I thought maybe you could advise me?" He looked at her again. This time she was indeed contemplating him though he could not make out the expression in her enormous eyes behind the black yew branch of windblown hair.

He turned away once more. He spoke in what seemed to be bitterness.

"Of course I'm only young I know," he said.

"Well it's not as if they'd written it for you is it?" she announced, on which he turned over and lay on his side to face her. She was looking out to sea again.

"No but then they're like that. Mum always reckoned she'd rather scrub the house out than take a pen. Madge's the same. It's 'ard to know what's for the best," he ended.

"I should stay put," she said, speaking impartially. "You're learnin' a trade after all. If they should ever come for you into the Army you could be an officer's servant. We're all right here."

"Then you don't reckon there's much in what they say about this invasion? If there's one thing I don't aim at it's being interned by the Jerries."

"Oh that's all a lot of talk in my opinion," she answered. "You don't want to pay attention. Oh me oh my," she said, "but isn't it slow for a picnic. Here," and at this she leant over him, "let's see if we can't set old Kate goin'."

She picked up a stray bit of spent straw which was lying on his other side then lowered all the upper part of her body down onto his, resting her elbow between him and the sleeping girl. Her mouth was open in a soundless laugh so that he could see the wet scarlet roof as she reached over to tickle Kate's sand-coloured eyebrows.

Kate's face twitched. Her arm that was stretched white palm upwards along deep green moss struggled to lift itself as though caught on the surface of a morass. Then still asleep she turned away abrupt till the other cheek showed dented with what she was lain on. She muttered once out loud "Paddy."

At this Edith burst into giggles bringing her hand still with its bit of straw up to her mouth as, eyes welling, she looked direct into Albert's below her. He lay quiet and yellow in a simper. This brought her up sharp.

"Can't you even have a joke?" she asked.

"Well you're a pretty pair no mistake," Kate said and yawned. They found she was sitting to rearrange her tow locks.

"Not so comical as you, you believe me," Edith answered removing herself from off Albert. He turned over onto his stomach again, facing Ireland.

"What have I done now then?" Kate wanted to know. "Can't a girl treat herself a nap?"

"Forget it dear," Edith told her.

"I don't know as I want to forget," Kate replied. "It's not nice finding people makin' fun of you when you're asleep."

"It's only what you brought out love," Edith sweetly said.

"What was that then?"

"You called a name."

"Is that all," Kate announced and blushed, which was unusual with her. "Why from the fuss you two made lain right in each other's arms you'd imagine it might be something serious."

"We wasn't," Albert said sharp, twisting his head towards her. His eyes did not seem to see.

"Oh all right let it pass," Kate replied. Her blush had gone. "But you can take it from me what I witnessed was sufficient to make them precious children look twice if they'd noticed."

"Just let 'im be," Edith said indifferent.

Notice how Albert's confession begins: awkward, mumbled, abrupt, starting with his sister. Perhaps he hopes, though he may not even be conscious of it, that his sister, the family member closest in age to Edith, is the one most likely to pique her interest. Edith doesn't hear him; throughout, the sentimentality on which his story verges is undercut by the gentle comedy of the fact that Edith isn't giving him her complete attention, though she is more or less aware of what he is saying. It's an attitude she assumes partly because she has a job to do, watching the children play at the edge of the sea, partly because she is sparing him the self-consciousness that eye contact and direct interrogation might incur, partly because she is not in the mood to deal with Albert's personal torment, and finally because she has other things on her mind, namely her affair with Raunce and the German bombing of England.

In life, it's rare that we truly are able to listen and find someone who will listen to us. And yet it's unusual to find the more common phenomenon—inattention—appearing on the page. Generally, in fiction, one character speaks, and the other listens, and, having listened and understood, replies. So the fidelity to the way inattention operates in reality is yet another way in which

Henry Green's dialogue may strike us as closer to what we have observed in life than to the dialogue we have read in the work of other writers.

A less assured writer would never allow a character to re-phrase and repeat himself (too lifelike!), but Green has Albert begin again, this time naming his sister, Madge, and informing the industrious Edith about Madge's job at the airplane factory and the long day she works. The word choice is pitch perfect: "They's terrible the hours she puts in." Green's touch never fal-ters as Albert (still without distracting Edith from the ocean and the children) briskly sums up his father's death, without linger-ing over the details, just as, we feel, a boy like Albert would: "It was a cancer took 'im."

Albert steams ahead, or as close as Albert can come to steam-ing, with the mention of Raunce (a name guaranteed to snag Edith's notice) and of Raunce's letters to *his* mother. Albert tells Edith he's worried because his own mother and sister don't an-swer his letters ("I'm afeared mum an' sis must've got theirs"), an anxiety exacerbated by his analysis of what the papers say about the bombing. The reader senses the pressure forcing Albert to blurt this out, and the relief he must be feeling as he finally con-fides in *someone*—someone who seems older, wiser, capable of giving the advice that he is about to solicit, someone whom he not only trusts but whom he is in love with. Moreover, the pas-sage efficiently captures something we recognize from our ex-perience, however different it is from Albert's—namely, the way that love and attraction can inspire us to speak more volubly about ourselves and tell more of the truth than we might have intended.

No sooner has Albert unburdened himself than Edith dem-onstrates that, all this time, she has been focused on her charges, particularly Albert's misbehaving namesake, whose unruliness the older Albert might take as a reflection on himself, thanks to their shared name. Albert soldiers on with the ever so slightly boastful (again, remember that he is speaking to a pretty young woman he wants to impress, to move, and to ask for counsel) reference to himself as a young, wage-earning citizen, unselfishly and responsibly sending most of his weekly salary home. But this too is greeted by silence.

It's this silence that prods Edith into asking his sister's name. It is precisely the sort of response we ourselves have made when we have lost track of the conversation and suddenly realize that we have been asked a question and an answer is required. Now comes the reference to the christening, and the mention of things being done with the proper ceremony. When this too fails to elicit much from Edith, Albert at last asks directly for advice about the right thing to do—that is, if he should leave the estate and return to England to look after his family.

Even reading closely, it's hard to say how exactly Green lets us know (as indeed we do) that this is the sort of situation in which the speaker doesn't really want advice but rather reassurance, that Albert isn't at this point seriously considering leaving the manor house and returning to the city but rather wants the older, attractive female beside him to tell him that inaction wouldn't be wrong, that his staying put won't hurt his mother and sister. Or perhaps what he is seeking, though he really *does* know better, is some indication that Edith would like him to stay.

In any case, the bluntness of his request is enough to make Edith finally turn and look at him with an expression sufficiently blank so that now it is Albert who turns away, saying "in what seemed to be bitterness," that he is only young, he knows. His statement is freighted with meaning and ambiguity. Does he mean that he is too young to do much to help his mother and sister? That his presence will hardly make a difference? That he's too inexperienced to make a decision of this sort? Too young for

Edith to take seriously and to give more than the glancing interest she's shown him? Or merely that he feels foolish for having spoken? If Edith had wanted him to remain, he would have seen that on her face. (Though, later in the novel, when Albert announces his plan to run off and enlist as a gunner, the servants, including Edith, are nearly beside themselves with anxiety.)

Now Albert's tone obliges Edith to reply, though before doing so, she turns away again, speaking toward the ocean. And she gives the sort of advice that we have all offered, at times: help that is not really help, but rather the offer of a way for the person who has asked our help to wriggle off the hook and not have to think about his situation. Not even Albert is going for it. He explains that his family wouldn't, couldn't, write, a fact that reflects back on the supposed premise of the entire conversation: Albert's worry over not having received a letter from relatives who, we now learn, would be unlikely and indeed unable to write back.

Thoughtful Edith doesn't point out the inconsistency, but rather intuits that Albert is looking for some sensible, logical, and definitive response from a slightly older person, preferably a good-looking female. She tells poor Albert what he wants and needs to hear: that there's no need for him to leave, that he's doing the right thing. And she concludes with what he *really* wants to hear, what he has been looking for all along, those four words, that final "We're all right here." And now the real source of Albert's anxiety emerges, the fear of the invasion and of being interned by the Germans, a concern that Edith dismisses as a lot of talk, although this possibility and the uncertainty of the future is a subject that Edith and Kate and the rest of the staff have been fretting over throughout the novel.

Breaking the spell of this moment of relative intimacy, Edith initiates one of those wonderful shifts that propel the scene: "Oh me oh my," she says, "isn't it slow for a picnic?" Albert has just unburdened his heart to her, and Edith is calling it *slow*? Edith isn't cruel or unfeeling, but she's had enough; she wants this unsolicited and troubling confession to be over. And possibly she's even experiencing that fleeting irritation we ourselves may feel when someone shadows our bright day by showing us more loneliness and pain than we want to see. She's ready for Kate to wake up now, to come to her aid, to relieve her of the weight of young Albert's hidden love.

Leaning over to tickle Kate, Edith lies on top of Albert, so close that he can see the "wet scarlet" roof of her mouth when she laughs. As we know by now, the housemaids share a relaxed, polymorphous physicality; they're quite capable of undressing and getting in bed together. Edith's ease with Albert is no more than that. At the same time it's a consequence of, and perhaps also a punishment for, the closeness they've shared. It's also a bit of a sexual taunt, an expression of dominance of a sort, a demonstration of what Edith can do if she wants. The gesture means nothing to her, however much it might signify to the besotted Albert.

Only when Edith looks down at him and sees him "quiet and yellow in a simper" does she realize what she has done, that her action has had an effect on him, that the body underneath hers belongs to a human being. This realization inspires her to ask impatiently, and with as much rancor as she can muster—which is to say, not much—"Can't you even have a joke?" Can't the boy have the pretty young woman he adores lie on top of him without believing or wishing it meant something? Or without becoming aroused, a possibility hinted at by the speed with which, once released, he rolls over onto his stomach?

Kate, it seems, has been dreaming of Paddy, the barely verbal Irish lampman in charge of the flock of peacocks that decorate the estate. This revelation may inspire us to page back through the novel, noting only now the previously unremarked (that is, by us) instances in which Kate solicits Paddy's opinion when the staff is discussing something, or in which she turns out to be familiar with Paddy's daily routine. Kate is cranky at having been awoken, and Edith teases her about her having called out a name, which makes Kate blush and launch a teasing counter-attack, as people do in such situations: "Why from the fuss you two made lain right in each other's arms you'd imagine it might be something serious."

Something *serious*? Kate can't *imagine* how much serious emotional and romantic territory has been covered during her little nap. But now it's Albert who denies it, the boy's pride rising "sharp" to his own defense as he must admit how little the con-versation has meant to Edith, however much it may have meant to him. Again, Green's word choice seems perfect. For, strictly speaking, the denial of Kate's "it might be something serious" should, grammatically, be "it wasn't." But tellingly, Albert sub-stitutes the ungrammatical third-person plural. *We* wasn't. We wasn't *what*? The reader knows, but can't explain. Even to *try* to explain would necessitate repeating every word of the preceding scene in which every word has delivered so much.

Confronted with the fact of her having called out a name, Kate blushes, which embarrasses her even more, and which causes her to want the last word about the fuss Edith and Albert were making in each other's arms, enough to "make the chil-dren look twice." Kate knows exactly how her friend feels about Albert—and Raunce. So it's Albert, the weaker and younger one, whom she is lightly teasing, as Edith knows and communicates in that simultaneously complex, simple, and succinct line "'Just let 'im be,' Edith said indifferent."

As I've mentioned, once you start quoting Henry Green, it's difficult to stop. So, before we leave *Loving*, let's look at one more scene: Raunce's proposal of marriage to Edith, a not entirely un-expected event. The servants' employers have gone to England,

and in their absence, Raunce and Edith have taken to pulling up armchairs in front of the fire in the Red Library. Though neither admits it, they are playing at being the lord and lady of the manor. Throughout the novel, the power of love has gradually been making Raunce a more thoughtful and honorable human being. The Michael whom the couple refer to is the Irish groom and driver; it's also necessary to know that under the cushion of Edith's chair is a sapphire ring that her employer has lost, and that Edith has found, and put there.

Raunce begins by asking Edith if she has ever noticed "that little place this side of the East Gate." And so begins the duet of two people negotiating what is in all likelihood the single most important discussion of their lives so far. Raunce thinks, or hopes, he can predict the outcome of the conversation, but there is always the terrifying prospect that he has been wrong about Edith's feelings, and that the scene will not go as planned. Raunce's leading off with the cottage shows that he has thought long and hard about how to broach the subject of marriage, and has decided to frame the proposal not as the passionate desire of his heart but rather as a practical matter, mostly about housing.

> *"Next time you pass that way you have a look, see."*
>
> *"Why Charley?"*
>
> *"It's empty that's why."*
>
> *"It's empty is it?" She echoed dull but with a sharp glance.*
>
> *"The married butlers used to live there at one time," he explained. Then he lied. "Yesterday mornin'," he went on canny, "Michael stopped me as he came out of the kitchen. You'll never guess what he was onto."*
>
> *"Not something for one of his family again?" she inquired.*
>
> *"That's right," he said. "It was only he's goin' to ask Mrs. T. for it when she gets back, that's all. The roof of their pig sty*

*of a hovel 'as gone an' fallen on 'is blessed sister-in-law's head
and's crushed a finger of one of their kids."*

"The cheek," she exclaimed.

*"A horrid liar the man is," Charley commented. "But it's
not the truth that matters. It's what's believed," he added.*

*"You think she'll credit such a tale?" Edith wanted to
know.*

*"Now love," he began then paused. He was dressed in
black trousers and a stiff shirt with no jacket, the only co-
lour being in his footman's livery waistcoat of pink and white
stripes. He wore no collar on account of his neck. Lying back
he squinted into a blushing rose of that huge turf fire as it
glowed, his bluer eye azure on which was a crescent rose re-
flection. "Love," he went on toneless, "what about you an' me
getting married? There I've said it."*

*"That'll want thinking over Charley," she replied at once.
Her eyes left his face and with what seemed a quadrupling in
depth came following his to rest on those rectangles of warmth
alive like blood. From this peat light her great eyes became
invested with rose incandescence that was soft and soft and
soft.*

*"There's none of this love nonsense," he began again ap-
pearing to strain so as not to look at her. "It's logical dear
that's what. You see I thought to get my old mother over out
of the bombers."*

"And quite right too," she answered prompt.

*"I'm glad you see it my way," he took her up. "Oh honey
you don't know what that means."*

*"I've always said a wife that can't make a home for her
man's mother doesn't merit a place of her own," she an-
nounced gentle.*

*"Then you don't say no?" he asked glancing her way at
last. His white face was shot with green from the lawn.*

"I haven't said yes have I?" she countered and looked straight at him, her heart opening about her lips. Seated as she was back to the light he could see only a blinding space for her head framed in dark hair inhabited by those great eyes on her, fathoms deep.

"No that's right," he murmured obviously lost.

"I'll need to think over it," she gently said. Folding hands she returned her gaze into the peat fire.

"She's a good woman," Raunce began again. "She worked hard to raise us when dad died. There were six in our family. She had a struggle."

Edith sat on quiet.

"Now we're scattered all over," he went on. "There's only my sister Bell with the old lady these days. There's her to consider," he said.

"The one working in the gun factory?" she asked.

"That's right," he replied. Then he waited.

"Well I don't know as she'd need to come to Ireland," Edith said at last. "She's got her job all right? I'd hardly reckon to make the change myself if I was in her position."

"You have it any way you want," Raunce explained. "I thought to just mention her that's all. Mrs Charley Raunce," he announced in educated accents. "There you are eh?" He seemed to be gathering confidence.

She suddenly got up half turned from him.

"I'm not sayin' one way or the other, Charley. Not yet awhile."

"But it's not no for start," he said, also rising.

"No," she replied. She began to blush. Seeing this he grinned with an absurd look of sweet pain. "No," she went on, "I don't say I couldn't." And all at once her mood appeared to change. She whirled about and made a dive at the cushion of the chair she had been using.

By the time Charley Raunce says "empty," Edith guesses what subject he might be broaching, just in case she didn't already know. Hence the dull echo and the sharp glance as Raunce forges ahead with his prepared speech, which involves a lie. At this point Raunce's moral reclamation is only partly complete. In sharp contrast to the way in which she listened to Albert's heartfelt confession—because a good writer understands that characters not only speak differently depending on whom they are speaking to, but also listen differently depending on who is speaking—Edith is hanging onto Raunce's every word, and she guesses correctly when he asks what she supposes Michael was onto. And now, putting words into Michael's mouth that Michael never said, Raunce—for authenticity, to give his lie added credence, and also perhaps out of habit, because the servants often mimic one another—drops his *h*'s and leaves off his *d*'s and gets so caught up in his lie that by the time he's finished the (imaginary) falling roof has crushed a child's finger.

To which Edith replies, hilariously, "The cheek." How dare Michael make a request for better quarters even if the roof fell in on his sister-in-law and his child? Or does she already assume what Charley is about to suggest, that Michael is making the story up. But the facts of the case are beside the point, the point being Edith's expression of sympathy and solidarity with her Charley, as well as the strong possibility that as soon as Charley mentions the empty cottage, she knows where all this is heading.

Charley follows up on his own lie by calling Michael a horrible liar, and then concludes, as well he might under the circumstances, that the truth matters less than what is believed. And Raunce *is* believed, or so Edith is pretending as she asks if he thinks their employer will believe the driver. The problem is that Edith is going further into the details and the probable outcome of Raunce's lie than he might have wished, and in the process pushing him toward what he actually wants to say. He begins, falters, the narrative pulls away to tell us what Raunce is wearing, then he proposes, "toneless," blurting out the proposal and concluding, endearingly, "There, I've said it."

Edith replies, as she feels she must, that she has to think about it, and there follows that lovely passage that ends with the description of her eyes "soft and soft and soft." Her failure to respond more enthusiastically has clearly daunted Charley, who backs off from what might have seemed a declaration of "this love nonsense," which, he hastens to assure her, is not what this conversation is about. Rather, it's a purely practical matter. In fact it's not even *about* Edith. As a good son, he is merely trying to protect his mother. When Edith agrees, Raunce interprets this as her acceptance of his proposal. As in fact it is, but Edith's not ready to make that concession—not quite yet. She prefers to step gradually into it, as it were, by referring to "a wife" and "her man's mother." So Charley is correct in concluding that she hasn't said no, just as Edith is justified in drawing out the moment, which she understands will be among the meaningful moments in her life. Again, it's useful to contrast the expressions playing over Edith's face with the very different and far more opaque looks it assumed when she was on the beach with Albert.

"Obviously lost," Raunce has no idea where to go from here. When Edith repeats that she needs to think, and she gazes into the peat fire so that the thinking process can begin at once, Raunce retreats to a subject that he feels comfortable and secure with, one that makes him feel better—that is, the subject of his mother. He praises his mother's forbearance and the struggles she has endured in raising him after his father's death. It's a bid for sympathy not unlike young Albert's, though Raunce knows better than to utter the equivalent of Albert's "a cancer took 'im."

Then, either very innocently or very craftily, Raunce brings the talk around to his sister Bell, the sister who works in the gun factory and whom Edith knows about. Careful readers may recall the way in which, by contrast, she had to ask Albert to repeat his sister's name, which he'd said only moments before. Her alarm at the prospect that Bell might be invited to join them in the little cottage, and her haste to convince Raunce that, in Bell's position, she would never agree to that sort of dislocation convinces Raunce that Edith has not only accepted his proposal but has reached the point of imagining what her life might be like with two additional members of the Raunce family installed in her new home.

"You have it any way you want," he assures her, then takes the bold step of pronouncing her married name, at which point Edith retreats or feigns retreat again. Just as we, at similarly critical moments, may feel the need to hear the other person say the same thing, reassuringly, over and over, Charley again asks if that means she isn't refusing. And now it's Edith's blush that communicates more than she's willing to say. Because there's nothing more to say. Everything is understood. The reality of the forthcoming event is at last so present in Edith's mind that she allows herself to imagine wearing the found ring, an impossibility while she is still in the employ of its rightful owner. And now, in her excitement, she looks for the ring—and finds it missing, a discovery that will initiate a series of new plot turns.

Reading Green, we're tempted to conclude that he simply had a great ear for the sound and rhythms of speech. But as the critic James Wood points out in an incisive essay on Green's work, Green often minted words that were not in use during the period in which his novels are set (or during any other period) but that nonetheless sound utterly right. So perhaps the correct conclusion is that Green was less attuned to how people *sound* when they speak—the actual words and expressions they employ—than to what they *mean*. This notion of dialogue as a pure expression of character that (like character itself) transcends the specifics of time and place may be partly why the conversations in the works of writers such as Austen and Brontë often sound fresh and astonishingly contemporary, and quite unlike the stiff, mannered, archaic speech we find in bad historical novels and in those medieval fantasies in which young men always seem to be saying things like, "Have I passed the solemn and sacred initiation test, venerable hunt master?"

If we do want to write fiction set in the world in which we live, it's useful to study the works of authors who *do* have an ear for dialogue, for the locutions people use, for the accidental poetry with which humans express and conceal their thoughts and feelings. In the following passage from Bruce Wagner's novel *I'm Losing You*, a young man named Simon, who makes his living removing dead animals from the property of rich Californians, and whose mother, Calliope, is a successful Los Angeles psychiatrist-to-the-stars, encounters his stepfather, Mitch, while rummaging through the contents of Mitch and Calliope's high-end Traulsen refrigerator.

"Does your mother know you're here?"

"That's a negative."

"There's some wonderful cheese in there." Mitch took over the Traulsen, reestablishing supremacy. He grinned, scanning Simon's coveralls. "I hope you're pretty well dusted off." He went to the cabinet and got a plate. "How's business?"

"Things were dead but now they're picking up." Simon heh-heh'ed and gulped a Diet Sprite. "Mom with a patient?"

"You mean client." Mitch smiled correctively at Simple Simon. "Patience is something we lose. We don't lose clients— not hopefully, anyway." Through the window, an Asian girl lingered by a table in front of Mitch's cottage. The stepfather took note, then said, "And yes, she's with a client."

"I probably won't see her then. Need to get home and write."

"I'll tell Calliope you said hello."

"You know, I usually charge sixty-five for that—to say hello," he said, nonsensically. Simon took a parting smear of Brie. "She's getting a real deal. Tell her the Dead Animal Guy stopped by, she hates that. No! Tell her Ace Ventura, Dead Pet Detective, was here."

"I think I'll just say, 'Your son came by to see you.' So long, Simon. And clean up after yourself, okay?"

Every word in this deceptively simple exchange is an artfully choreographed step in an unsavory ballet of territoriality and hostility, of dominance and submission, and again what's *not* being said is as important as what is. Mitch's initial reference to "your mother" (as opposed to "your mom" or "Calliope") is immediately distancing, and the chilliness of "Does your mother know you're here?" could hardly be more palpable. It's easy to understand why Simon answers with facile brittleness (saying "That's a negative" instead of a simpler "No") that falls flat, as does his little joke about business having been dead and his seemingly breezy but actually (under the circumstances) demeaning description of himself as the Dead Animal Guy. His remark about getting sixty-five dollars just for saying hello is embarrassing, even excruciating, given what we imagine Calliope receives for a session with one of *her* clients. Mitch's offer of the "wonderful cheese" is indeed, as the narrative suggests, a declaration of ownership and supremacy, and when Simon says he probably won't see his mother, Mitch fails to suggest that Simon stick around and wait. Finally, a close reading of the exchange in which Mitch condescendingly corrects Simon's use of the word *patient* reveals, rather thrillingly, that Mitch himself is misusing the word *hopefully*. Of course, he means *we hope*. Like Henry Green (the last writer to whom it might seem obvious to compare Bruce Wagner), Wagner captures the way that intention and audience shape everything from word choice to tone, how differently people sound when they are talking to a business contact or a relative, to someone they want to impress or someone they regard with contempt.

The importance that a single word can assume in a fictional conversation propels the following scene from Edward St. Aubyn's novel *Mother's Milk*. On the brink of starting up an adulterous affair, Patrick and his former girlfriend, Laura, find their small children, Robert and Lucy, snuggling in the same bed. As Robert seizes on his father's facile and careless use of the word *subplot*, he not only exposes the romantic situation of the adults but provides the reader with an all-too-recognizable demonstration of the perils of underestimating a child's intelligence, curiosity, instinct, and observational powers:

> "This is the most outrageous subplot," said Patrick. "Still, I don't know why they shouldn't sleep together if they want to."
>
> "What's a subplot?" asked Robert.
>
> "Another part of the main story," said Patrick, "reflecting it in some more or less flagrant way."
>
> "Why are we a subplot?" asked Robert.
>
> "You're not," said Patrick. "You're a plot in your own right."
>
> "We've just got so much to talk about," said Lucy, "we just couldn't wait until tomorrow."
>
> "Is that why you two are still up?" asked Robert. "Because you've got so much to talk about. Is that why you said we were a subplot?"
>
> "Listen, forget I ever said it," said Patrick. "We're all each other's subplots," he added, trying to confuse Robert as much as possible.
>
> "Like the moon going around the Earth," said Robert.

"Exactly. Everyone thinks they're on the Earth, even when they're on somebody else's moon."

"But the Earth goes around the sun," said Robert. "Who's on the sun?"

"The sun is uninhabitable," said Patrick, relieved that they had traveled so far from the original motive of his comment. "Its only plot is to keep us going around and around."

Subtext is everything, or almost everything, in this passage from David Gates's story, "The Wonders of the Invisible World," in which a man meets his much younger, married lover in a bar after she has called to say that she needs to see him about something "kind of important." The current temperature of their affair is taken entirely by gestures: our narrator sets down his clarinet, looks around for a coat rack, and only then reminds himself to kiss Jane, who offers her cheek. She tells him that they have to hurry, that she's lied and told her husband she was going to a movie with a friend. And then she looks down at her glass.

"This has to be quick," she said. "I'm officially at the movies with Mariana."

"All ears," I said.

"It's weird," she said. "I feel like more of a shit lying about that than actually——you know."

"Well, better safe than sorry."

She looked down into her glass and said, "Yeah, right."

"So," I said.

"So," she said. She took a deep breath and let it out. "So yours truly thinks she's pregnant."

"You're shitting me," I said. "What do you mean you think?"

"Well, for one thing I'm like three weeks late. And I'm never late. Plus I've been sick to my stomach the last two

mornings. I went out this afternoon and I bought one of those pregnancy things, you know, at the drugstore. Except I'm too scared to use it."

"Unbelievable," I said.

"Really," she said.

"How could it have happened, though?"

"If I knew that," she said, "it wouldn't have happened. Obviously. I don't know. Some stupid thing, I'm sure."

Billie Holiday was singing "Baby Get Lost."

"Well, look," I said. "Let's not panic. For one thing, you've been under a lot of stress. Which can make people late. Which could also upset your stomach. Anyway, even if anything was wrong, I don't think, as nearly as I can remember, I don't think you'd be feeling sick in the morning this early on, would you?"

She raised her eyes and gave me the look I deserved.

My Jack Daniels arrived.

I looked over at the rows and rows of bottles behind the bar, presumably doubled by a mirror. I looked back at Jane. She was looking down into her glass.

I said, "Whose would it be?"

She shrugged. "Up for grabs," she said.

"Have you told Jonathan?"

She shook her head, still looking down.

"Have you thought what you might do?"

"I'm a married woman," she said. "Married women get pregnant, they have a baby, right?"

"Yes, but when——"

"I mean, that's what you do, right?"

"But isn't this a tad more complicated?" I said.

She shook her head, still staring down. Not no to my question, just no.

"Look," I said. "First thing, you need to go to a doctor.

Forget the kit thing. Until you actually see a doctor and actually find out something concrete, we don't even know what we're talking about."

Now she looked at me. "I know what we're talking about," she said.

Right off, we register the calculation, the discomfort, hesitation, displacement, and the suppressed panic that leads Jane to begin this serious declaration by speaking of herself, with studiedly false casualness, as "yours truly." We understand immediately why she might have chosen the word "thinks"—yours truly *thinks* she might be pregnant—though by the end of the conversation we know that Jane's suspicions have already crystallized into something stronger than a "thought." As happens in life, one speaker may question another's word choice, a particular temptation under the circumstances. *Thinks?* What does she means by *thinks*?

Meanwhile, with every word the narrator speaks, the reader—like Jane, we presume—is aware of what the narrator isn't saying: He's not exactly crowing about the prospect that the baby might be his, in which case he hopes she will leave her husband so they can begin their new life together. Rather more coolly, he asks for symptoms, signs, evidence. He stalls for time. He requests an explanation and offers his own false explanation, finally falling back on the most banal interpretation: "stress."

Tellingly, he describes the possible pregnancy as a potential "something wrong." And with that equally damning "as nearly as I can remember," he consciously or unconsciously reminds Jane that he is speaking from memory and experience, that he already has a child, that he and his former wife have a daughter. And now it's his turn to take refuge in the faux offhand. He avoids the straightforward "Is it mine?" for the jauntier "Whose would it be?"

Well, since they're being so light about this, Jane's "up for grabs" keeps the badminton birdy they're batting around in play.

He asks if she's told her husband, a question that he follows with the careful, measured, anxious delicacy of "Have you thought what you might do?"

Jane's answer makes it clear that whatever she does will involve telling her husband, since, being married, she will need a reason for not having the baby. "Married women get pregnant, they have a baby, right?" By stating her dilemma as if its solution is a foregone conclusion, she's actually underlining how complex and all-but-insoluble her problem is. Suddenly, our hero is all common sense, outlining the steps to be taken so they can be sure of their situation. Once they determine the facts, they will "know what we're talking about." When Jane makes her trenchant response—she knows what they're talking about—we feel, as the narrator must, that we've had our heads spun around, our falseness and shallow self-interest noted and corrected.

Consider how another writer might have written the scene: Hi, I think I'm pregnant. My God. Are you going to get an abortion?

An equivalent amount of meaning is packed into every line of the following two scenes from Scott Spencer's *A Ship Made of Paper*, the work of yet another writer who listens to how people talk and is able to make his characters communicate with all the obviousness and subtlety, all the mixed agendas, the heartfelt feelings and hidden (even from themselves) motives of recognizable human beings.

In the first scene a woman named Kate has arranged a dinner with a country neighbor named Iris Davenport, whose daughter goes to nursery school with Kate's daughter. In the following passage, Kate announces their dinner plans to her boyfriend, Daniel. It's an ordinary moment, though it might be somewhat more ordinary and less freighted if Kate has not begun to suspect—correctly, as it happens—that Daniel has developed a serious crush on Iris, whom he sees when he drives Kate's daughter to preschool. It is, we feel, exactly how two people might sound when one wishes to keep hidden (again, even from himself) the early stirrings of an inconvenient romantic attraction.

"I thought you'd be happy I made these plans," Kate says. "You mention her constantly. I figured it was time we got to know them, another couple, like actual grown-ups."

"I mention her constantly?"

"I don't know, probably not. I'm not trying to give you a hard time. I'm trying to make you happy." With rich, shining brown hair, smooth skin, and the scent of perfume on her, she glides to Daniel's side. She would like to put her arms around him, but it might seem she was forcing the issue.

"You do like them, don't you?" she asks. A surviving bit of her old southern accent stretches the "i" in "like."

"I don't really know him."

"Do you like her?"

"Iris?"

She gives him a look. Of course Iris, who else are they talking about?

"Yes," he says. "Sure. Why not? She's Ruby's best friend's mother. That's got to be worth something. And she's nice. She's funny."

"Tell me something funny she's said. It'll whet my appetite for an evening of unbridled hilarity."

"Okay." He takes a deep breath. "Last spring—"

"Last spring? You have to go that far back in time?"

"Actually, it was the summer. She got a mosquito bite, and I guess she was scratching it and scratching it." His eyes shift away from Kate's; he realizes he is talking himself into a hole. "And she turned the bite into a sore, you know how that happens. And so she took a pen and wrote 'ouch ouch ouch ouch' in a circle all around the bite."

"That's it? She wrote ouch on her arm?"

"You know what, Kate? I think we should call them and say we can't make it."

She wouldn't mind doing just that, but she's already set her course. "Nonsense," she says. She holds her pearls out to him and he comes behind her to fasten them. In her scoop-necked dress, Kate's collarbones look as sturdy as handlebars.

Everything that needs to be clear *is* clear from that first "You mention her constantly." Guilty, surprised, not surprised at all, Daniel repeats the phrase, and—perhaps because hearing him say it is more than either of them is prepared to deal with yet—Kate retreats. Her uncertainty, or perhaps her certainty, breaks the surface again as her southern accent elongates the *i* in that charged word *likes*.

Unwilling to talk about Iris, Daniel redirects the question about "them" to one about "him," Iris's husband. Kate presses on, and, stalling for time, hoping for a moment in which to collect himself, Daniel repeats Iris's name. A look suffices for Kate's reply, and, anxious now, Daniel fires off a series of staccato evasions: She's nice, she's funny, the last of which backfires as he proves unable to report one funny thing Iris has said or done, but in the process reveals that he has been paying rapt attention to every one of her tiny gestures.

By now the mood between them has soured, and the stakes of the evening before them have become risky enough for Daniel to suggest that they cancel. Once more Kate retreats, and the passage ends by shifting from Kate's point of view to Daniel's, to the detached and decidedly unsexy comparison of Kate's collarbones to a sturdy pair of handlebars.

Part of what's so convincing about this scene is that even when the subtext is jealousy and concealment, the tone is one of intimacy. The action takes place in the couple's bedroom. The rhythm of conversation is the easy give-and-take of two people who share a life and know a lot about each other, which may be part of their problem. That alone (as well as much else) differentiates this dialogue from that in the following scene, in which we have moved from the bedroom to the restaurant:

Afterward, the four of them walk to the George Washington Inn, where Iris has made dinner reservations. The Inn is redolent with Colonial history—low, beamed ceilings, wormy old tavern tables, an immense blackened fireplace. A high school girl serves them a basket of rolls, then comes back to fill their water glasses. She pours Hampton's last and accidentally fills it to the very top; in fact, a little of it laps onto the table. "Oops," she says, but Hampton looks away. His jaw is suddenly rigid. Iris touches his knee, pats it, as if to calm him down. With her other hand, she is dabbing the little dime-sized puddle with her napkin.

A moment later, a waiter appears to take their drinks orders. Daniel and Kate are used to this waiter, middle-aged, vain, and formal. Hampton, however, sees the waiter's extreme tact as an extension of the bus-girl's spilling his water, and he orders a vodka martini in a surly voice. "Use Absolut," he says. "I'll know if the bartender uses the house brand."

Iris looks down at her lap; when she raises her gaze again she sees Daniel is looking at her, smiling. It startles her into smiling back. The two of them seem happy to be gazing at each other, and Kate feels like Princess Kitty standing at the edge of the room and noticing the joy that floods their faces when Vronsky's and Anna Karenina's eyes meet. Kate wonders exactly how far along these two really are. Is it too late to stop them?

"So, Hampton," Kate says, "tell me. I hear all about Iris from Daniel, but nothing about you. You're in the city most of the time?"

"I come up here on the weekend," Hampton says. "During the work-week, I stay at the apartment where we used to live before Iris got into Marlowe."

"It's a beautiful apartment," Iris says. She glances at Hampton, who smiles at her.

"So what keeps you down in the city all week?" Kate asks.

"I'm co-managing director of the Atlantic Fund," Hampton says.

"He's an investment banker," Iris says, in the same anxious-to-please tone in which she said their apartment was beautiful. To Kate, Iris sounds like a woman whose husband has complained about how she treats him in public.

"The Atlantic Fund provides capital to African-American business," Hampton says. "It's sometimes difficult for black-owned businesses to get what they need from the white banking structure." He cranes his neck, looks for the waiter. "Just like it's hard to get a white waiter to bring you a drink." He breathes out so hard his cheeks puff for a moment. "I've never come here, and now I know why."

"Have we really been waiting that long?" asks Kate. "It seems like we just sat down." She looks to Daniel for confirmation, but all Daniel can manage is a shrug. He is on a plane and he has just heard something in the pitch of the engine's roar that makes him feel the flight is doomed.

"God, that music was so wonderful," Iris says.

"The first time I heard Handel's Messiah, I was four years old," Hampton says, his eyes on Kate. "My grandmother was in a chorus that performed it for Richard Nixon, at the White House." This comment is in keeping with remarks he's been making since they left the church. Already they'd heard references to his grandfather's Harvard roommate, his great-grandfather's Presbyterian mission in the Congo, his mother's spending five thousand dollars on haute couture in Paris when *she was eleven years old, his aunt Dorothy's short engagement to Colin Powell, the suspicious fire at the Welles vacation compound on Martha's Vineyard. He boasts about his lineage in a way that Kate thinks would simply not be allowed from a white person.*

"Thurgood Marshall was a friend of the family and he was there, too, of course. Unfortunately, he fell asleep after ten minutes. Gramma said they all sang extra loud to cover Justice Marshall's snoring."

Kate wonders if Hampton is trying to put Daniel on alert. He, too, must sense what is happening. She has to admit that she is enjoying this foursome more than she'd dared hope. It captures her imagination in some creepy, achey way, like sucking on a tooth that's just starting to die.

"Is this the same grandmother who played the cello?" *she asks.* Maybe if you thought a little less about your grandmother's pedigree and a little more about your wife, she wouldn't be squirming in her chair and eyeing my boyfriend.

"No, the cellist was Abigail Welles, of Boston, my father's mother. The singing grandma was Lucille Cox, of Atlanta, on my mother's side."

"I have many Coxes in my family," *Kate says.* "On my mother's side, many of them from Georgia, too."

There is a brief silence, and then Kate says what she guesses must be passing through everyone's mind. "Of course, there's a chance that one of my Coxes held one of your Coxes in slavery."

"In that case," *says Daniel, lifting his wine glass,* "dinner's on us."

For the first time that evening, Hampton smiles. Beaming, his face grows younger. His teeth are large, even, and very white, and he casts his eye downward, as if the moment's pleasure makes him shy. Kate can imagine the moment when Iris first saw that smile, how it must have drawn her in and made her want to fathom the secret cave of self that was his smile's source.

"Hampton," Kate says. "That's an interesting name."

"My family's full of Hamptons," he says. "We come from Hampton, Virginia. A few of us attended Hampton University, back when it was Hampton Normal and Agriculture Institute."

"Hampton Hawes," says Daniel.

"What?" says Hampton.

"He's a jazz piano player, West Coast."

"Daniel knows everything about jazz," says Kate. "And blues, and rhythm and blues."

The waitress arrives and presents them with yellowfin tuna, coq au vin, filet mignon, risotto funghi. "Look," says Iris, "everything looks so good!"

"Is that tuna?" Hampton asks, peering at Iris's plate.

Every marriage, Kate thinks, seems to have one person wanting what's on the other's plate.

Iris smiles, but she doesn't look pleased. "Do you want some?"

"Okay, a taste." He watches while she cuts her sesame-encrusted tuna in half and then transports it carefully to his plate, next to his charbroiled slab of steak and French fries and homemade coleslaw. He doesn't offer her so much as a morsel of his food.

"Iris doesn't share my interest in my family traditions," Hampton says, cutting into his steak.

"All I ever said is that sometimes they can be a little limiting," says Iris, trying not to plead, but Kate can tell she would like to. "In America you can make your own history."

"Dream on, my sweet," says Hampton.

"All right, then I will. And in the meantime, can we just relax and enjoy being alive?"

"So you work on Wall Street?" Kate asks.

"Does that surprise you?" asks Hampton. "That I'm an investment banker?"

"Yes" she says, "I thought maybe you were a tap dancer."

Hampton smiles, points his finger at Kate. "That's funny," he says, instead of laughing.

"I wrote a piece last year about the stock exchange," Kate says. "I love all those men crawling over each other and shouting out numbers as if their lives were hanging by a thread. And then the final bell rings and everyone cheers and goes out for drinks. I loved the whole thing, including the bell and the drinks."

"That's not what I do. But I'd like to read your article."

"Oh no, please, no. The only way I can churn that crap out is to tell myself that absolutely no one will ever set eyes on it." She catches the waitress's eye and gestures with a twirl of the finger: more drinks over here. "It's just to pay the bills. And wrap fish."

"Do you mostly write about financial topics?" Hampton asks.

"What I'm supposed to be doing is working on my next novel, but that's been the case for quite a while. So in the meanwhile, editors call me up and I give them whatever they want. It's amazing how easily the stuff comes when you don't really have your heart in it. Right now, I'm doing a piece about the O.J. trial and about this woman artist calling herself Ingrid Newport."

"What kind of artist is she?" Hampton asks.

"She's sewn up her vagina," Kate says. She can practically hear Daniel's heart sinking. He worries about her when she drinks. And then he does something that strikes

her as intolerable. *He actually looks over at Iris and shrugs.*

"They keep on assigning me these sexual mutilation pieces," Kate says. "It's becoming sort of my specialty. My little calling card." *Is this putting Iris in her place? Kate has no idea. Iris may be one of those rare monsters: a person of unshakable sexual confidence.* "I tell them, 'Hey guys, how about a piece about reemergence of the lobotomy as an accepted psychiatric practice,' but, no, they say, 'What we really want is fifteen hundred words on Peter Peterson, that guy in Dover, Delaware, who crucified his own penis.' They all tell me I write so well about gender issues, by which they really mean sex. I guess I should be pleased. No one ever said I did anything well when it came to sex." *Kate laughs.* "But now I'm getting a lot of O.J. assignments, so that's good. Have you all been following the case?"

No one's taking the bait on that one. Getting this crowd to talk about O.J. would be like trying to convince them to take off their clothes right there in the restaurant. Kate feels sour and self-righteous, the way you do when you seem to be the only person willing to face something ugly.

Iris's eyes are locked on her meal. She seems to be hurrying to finish it before Hampton tucks into it again. Kate watches her hands as they delicately maneuver her knife and fork. She finds her cute but hardly irresistible. Lean body, broad shoulders, big behind. Kate feels sorry for black people with freckles, it's like they're getting the worst of both worlds.

"You know what we should have done?" *says Daniel, his voice bright silver.* "Kept the kids together, with just one baby-sitter."

"Wasn't I lucky to have found somebody like Daniel?" *Kate announces.* "When my marriage broke up and I was left with my kid, I thought I'd be alone forever. But Daniel's a better par-*

ent than I am." She waits for Daniel to contradict her, but he doesn't. "Well, maybe not better, *but he is so good to Ruby."*

"She's a great kid," Daniel says softly.

"She is," says Iris.

"And she so loves Nelson," Daniel says. His face colors, and he looks to Kate for relief. "Doesn't she? How many times has she talked about him? Right?"

"Kids can fall in love," Kate says. "In fact, in childhood, we may be at our highest capacity to just go head over heels for another person. I was in love with a little boy when I was five years old. A little black boy with the perfect little black boy name: Leroy. Leroy Sinclair." She signals the waiter for more wine. In for a penny. "His mother cleaned the little medical arts building where my father had his office. He was a real butterball, Leroy. Just as fat as a tick, but with the most charming, lazy smile, a real summer-on-the-Mississippi smile. He wore overalls and high-topped sneakers. His mother had to take him to work and apparently she fed that poor boy sweets all through the day to keep him quiet. I used to go to Daddy's office every Saturday and Mrs. Sinclair——"

"You called her Mrs. Sinclair?" Hampton asks.

"Not at the time. We called her Irma. She weighed two pounds, shoes and all."

"Poor Leroy," says Iris.

"I used to read to Leroy. I was precocious. I'd bring a book every Saturday and read to him while Daddy worked in his office, two hours of paperwork, nine-thirty to eleven-forty-five, every Saturday, to the minute. I used to read Leroy these bedtime books, right there in the middle of the day, sitting on the inside staircase of this little medical arts building out on Calhoun Boulevard. And Leroy had all this candy his mother gave him, stuffed in his pockets, little red-and-white mints, butterscotch sucking candies, all fancy wrapped . . ."

"She probably took them from one of the houses she cleaned during the week," Iris says.

"Yes, I suppose she did. Stolen sweets. What could be better?" She narrows her eyes, lets Iris draw her own damn conclusions. "I read him Goodnight, Moon, and he put his head right in my lap and closed his eyes and I patted and rocked him and he pretended to fall asleep. And when I was finished with whatever I was reading, I kissed the palm of my hand and pressed it against his cheek, over and over, hand to my lips, hand to his cheek. And I remember thinking: I love Leroy. I love Leroy Sinclair. And just saying those words put me into a kind of hypnotic trance."

The high school girl has cleared the plates away. The waiter hovers over to the side, waiting for a break in the conversation.

"And then one day I saw my father talking to Mrs. Sinclair," Kate is saying, "and I knew she would never be allowed to bring Leroy to work with her again. And I was right. The next time I saw him, maybe two years later, he was on his way to his school and I was with a couple of my silly, awful little girlfriends from Beaumont Country Day School, and I called him across the street— Hey, Leroy— and he just looked at me as if I was the most ridiculous thing he had ever seen, and he didn't say a word. But whose fault was it? We were both caught in something so large, and so terrible. His people came over in chains and my people sat on the porch sipping gin. Something that begins that badly can never end well . . ."

Kate looks around the table, smiling.

"How about you, Hampton?" she says. "Did you ever fall in love with someone not of your race?" If he finds this offensive he gives no indication—but Kate quickly looks away from him, throws her slightly bleary gaze first at Iris, and finally at Daniel. "Anyone?"

The reader can easily track the ways and the steady, nerve-jangling pace at which the tension burbles toward the surface. As the unease escalates, what is being left unspoken—issues of race (Iris and her husband Hampton are black, Kate and Daniel white), sex, class, power, territoriality, politics and privilege—add to the mounting pressure that Kate brings to a head with the polite social equivalent of a hand grenade, which here means saying what all of the characters have been thinking, or intuiting. From the very beginning, the tone is set—and the anxiety level ratcheted up—by the waitress's innocent mistake, filling Hampton's glass last and spilling some of the water, a gesture he interprets as something less than innocent.

From here on, everything that happens in the restaurant—for example, how long it takes for the drinks to arrive—will exacerbate the strain as Hampton sees these lapses as racially motivated, a view that we feel is a simultaneously skewed (we've all experienced slow service) and an understandable and accurate reaction to the daily slights involved in being an African-American in white America. Throughout, Hampton works to establish his class position and background, boasting in ways that, as Kate notes, might have seemed less tolerable and certainly less understandable in his white counterpart, while Iris rather meekly and placatingly labors at being "supportive" and winds up sounding like a wife whose husband has complained about how she treats him in public. Throughout, the gestures are precisely observed, and the dialogue zips along from one excruciating topic to another: jazz, sex, genital mutilation, the O.J. Simpson case, and so forth.

This scene illustrates one of the many things that differentiates a passage of this sort from its equivalent in a play. Interspersed with dialogue, narration can provide the benefit of commentary, and the sharply focused lens of point of view. As this painful scene goes on, presumably in the omniscient third person, it's

Kate who is monitoring the action for us, pointing out what we should be watching—for example, that little exchange in which Iris readily forks her husband half of her meal, and he gives back nothing. And it's another example of the wise authorial decision to write a scene from the point of view of a character most likely to notice what's happening, and to mind. As Kate herself remarks, it's reminiscent of the ball scene in *Anna Karenina,* which we see through the eyes of Kitty, who is painfully aware of what is transpiring between Anna and Prince Vronsky.

Before we leave the subject of dialogue, it's worth looking at a few selections that in some ways make no attempt to sound like people "really" sound but rather create exchanges that may establish one aspect of the speakers while at the same time giving their conversation a recognizable resonance that makes it seem less regional and temporal than universal and eternal. A good deal of Joy Williams's fiction features young people who seem absolutely contemporary but whose speech lacks up-to-the-minute cultural references. Instead, every word they say telegraphs a sort of spacey, imaginative alienation that we recognize as the particular province of children and adolescents, anytime, anywhere. Here's the opening dialogue in her story "The Blue Men":

> Bomber Boyd, age thirteen, told his new acquaintances that summer that his father had been executed by the state of Florida for the murder of a sheriff's deputy and his drug-sniffing German shepherd.
>
> "It's a bummer he killed the dog," a girl said.
>
> "Guns, chairs, or lethal injection?" a boy asked.
>
> "Chair," Bomber said. He was sorry he had mentioned the dog in the same breath. The dog had definitely not been necessary.
>
> "Lethal injection is fascist, man; who does lethal injection?" a small, fierce-looking boy said.

"Florida, Florida, Florida," the girl murmured. "We went to Key West once. We did sunset. We did Sloppy's. We bought conch-shell lamps with tiny plastic flamingos and palm trees inside lit up by tiny lights." The girl's hair was cut in a high Mohawk that rose at least half a foot in the air. She was pale, her skin flawless except for one pimple artfully flourishing above her full upper lip.

"Key West isn't Florida," a boy said.

There were six of them standing around, four boys and two girls. Bomber stood there with them, waiting.

From the moment that the girl digests the information that Bomber has supplied and focuses on the death of the dog (as opposed to that of the deputy, or for that matter of Bomber's father) we know, or at least have a strong clue about, what territory we've entered. The boy's cool, clinical inquiry about the method of execution (they are, after all, talking about Bomber's *father*) intensifies our sense of what these kids are like, and the dark humor of the exchange contributes to our sympathy for poor Bomber, who by now is regretting having mentioned the dog. The kids are hardly even paying attention to him; the fierce-looking boy has gone off on a tangent of his own, about the fascist nature of lethal injection. Of course, he's misusing the word *fascist*, but not only do we know what he means, we've heard the word misused just that way, often by kids his age. Meanwhile the girl has entered her own parallel world (are they high?) of a past trip to Florida, a theme that the boy takes up to argue that Key West is hardly typical of the state. All of which leaves Bomber more alone than ever, despite, or perhaps because of, having unwisely volunteered a capsule version of the story of his family tragedy.

The narrative voice of Jane Bowles's work, especially that of *Two Serious Ladies* seems, at moments, to belong to some rather more elegant version of Joy Williams's disconnected children. And when Bowles's characters speak, they tend to orate in language through which we feel the desperation of people with complex, burdensome, intoxicating, and often terrifying inner lives. What we hear in their conversation, along with their frequent inability to escape the prison of self long enough to hold a "normal" conversation, is their fear that they will never succeed in getting through to another living person.

In this scene, Christina Goering, a woman mostly referred to as Miss Goering, goes home with a man named Arnold, whom she has met at a party and who has suggested that since Miss Goering is afraid to go home in the dark, she might wish to spend the night in the spare bedroom in his house. No sooner do they begin to get acquainted than Arnold's father appears, a patriarch straight out of Kafka, an irascible, peremptory, and hugely strange man with nothing but contempt for his son and his son's artist friends. Arnold's father comes into the bedroom, and he and Miss Goering begin their conversation:

> "Well, lady," he said to her, "are you an artist too?"
>
> "No," said Miss Goering. "I wanted to be a religious leader when I was young and now I just reside in my house and try not to be too unhappy. I have a friend living with me, which makes it easier."
>
> "What do you think of my son?" he asked, winking at her.
>
> "I have only just met him," said Miss Goering.
>
> "You'll discover soon enough," said Arnold's father, "that he's a rather inferior person. He has no conception of what it is to fight. I shouldn't think women would like that very much. As a matter of fact, I don't think Arnold has had many women in his life. If you'll forgive me for passing this information on to you, I myself am used to fighting. I've fought my neighbors

*all my life instead of sitting down and having tea with them
like Arnold. And my neighbors have fought me back like tigers
too. Now that's not Arnold's kind of thing. . . . Now, with
Arnold and his friends nothing ever really begins or finishes.
They're like fish in dirty water to me. If life don't please them
one way and nobody likes them one place, then they go some-
place else. They aim to please and be pleased; that's why it's so
easy to come and bop them on the head from behind, because
they've never done any serious hating in their lives."*

"*What a strange doctrine!*" *said Miss Goering.*

Part of the peculiarity comes from the skillful mixing of high
and low diction, the discordant combination of Arnold's father's
plain, almost gangsterish speech ("Well, lady") and grammatical
mistakes and Christina Goering's typically elevated and slightly
archaic word choice, her *reside* instead of *live*. No one seems to
bother much with the ordinary social graces. Arnold's father gets
right to the point, and Miss Goering answers by baldly confess-
ing the truest thing about her life as if she is talking about the
weather. Then we get the wild excesses of Arnold's father's rant,
with its switchbacks of logic, its giddy self-referential obsessive-
ness, the bravado with which it declares the sort of thing that
most people would keep silent—for example, the speculation
about how many women his son has had, and the boast about
his own passion for fighting. Now comes his barbed, hilarious as-
sessment of Arnold and his friends, an analysis that we recognize
even as we resist it, presumably because we may be just the sort
of people Arnold's father is describing. Until everything turns
out to have been leading to his marvelous last sentence.

We have probably never met anyone who sounds like Arnold's
father. And at points we can't help thinking that Arnold's father
and his dialogue are a projection of Miss Goering's anxiety and
discomfort. But Jane Bowles's touch is so sure, her language so

well chosen and controlled, her artifice so dazzling (and so insouciantly ready to acknowledge itself as artificial) that we not only admire but are wholly convinced, or at least beguiled, by a passage of dialogue that we cannot imagine any normal human being speaking.

Nor are we entirely persuaded that, in Nabokov's *Lolita*, Humbert Humbert is transcribing verbatim the speech of Miss Pratt, the headmistress of the school in which Humbert's nymphet true love is enrolled. In her conversations with Humbert, Miss Pratt seizes on every chance to expound upon her freethinking, progressive attitudes about girls, sex, the body, etc., all the time blissfully innocent and ignorant of the true state of the relations between Lolita and her lustful stepfather.

> *We are not so much concerned, Mr. Humbird, with having our students become bookworms or be able to reel off all the capitals of Europe which nobody knows anyway, or learn by heart the dates of forgotten battles. What we are concerned with is adjustment of the child to group life. This is why we stress the four D's: Dramatics, Dance, Debating and Dating. We are confronted by certain facts. Your delightful Dolly will presently enter an age group where dates, dating, date dress, date book, date etiquette, mean as much to her as, say, business, business connections, business success, mean to you, or as much as [smiling] the happiness of my girls means to me. Dorothy Humbird is already involved in a whole system of social life which consists, whether we like it or not, of hot-dog stands, corner drugstores, malts ands cokes, movies, square-dancing, blanket parties on beaches, and even hair-fixing parties! Naturally at Beardsley School we disapprove of some of these activities; and we rechannel others into more constructive directions. But we do try to turn our backs on the fog and squarely face the sunshine. To put it briefly, while adopting*

certain teaching techniques, we are more interested in com-
munication than in composition. That is, with due respect to
Shakespeare and others, we want our girls to communicate
freely with the live world around them rather than plunge into
musty old books. We are still groping perhaps, but we grope
intelligently, like a gynecologist feeling a tumor. We think, Dr.
Humburg, in organismal and organizational terms. We have
done away with the mass of irrelevant topics that have tradi-
tionally been presented to young girls, leaving no place, in for-
mer days, for the knowledges and the skills, and the attitudes
they will need in managing their lives and—as the cynic might
add—the lives of their husbands. Mr. Humberson, let us put
it this way: the position of a star is important, but the most
practical spot for an icebox in the kitchen may be even more
important to the budding housewife. You say all you expect a
child to obtain from school is a sound education. But what do
we mean by education? In the old days it was in the main a ver-
bal phenomenon; I mean, you could have a child learn by heart
a good encyclopedia and he or she would know as much as or
more than a school could offer. Dr. Hummer, do you realize
that for the modern pre-adolescent child, medieval dates are
of less vital value than weekend ones [twinkle]?—to repeat
a pun that I heard the Beardsley college psychoanalyst permit
herself the other day. We live not only in a world of thoughts,
but also in a world of things. Words without experience are
meaningless. What on earth can Dorothy Hummerson care for
Greece and the Orient with their harems and slaves?"

The humor of the passage arises from the ridiculous rhetoric
("in organismal and organizational terms"), the risible psycho-
babble ("we want out girls to *communicate*"), the goofy alliteration
("dates, dating, date dress, date book"), the sheer disgustingness
("we grope intelligently, like a gynecologist feeling a tumor"),

the self-contradictions ("words without experience are meaning-less"), to say nothing of the seemingly endless variations that Miss Pratt works on the theme of Humbert and Lolita's proper names. The passage is mined with little jokes: phrases of meaning-less jargon ("modern pre-adolescent child"), anti-intellectualism (the dismissal of Shakespeare as a bunch of "musty old books"), bad puns (weekend and medieval *dates*), and the kind of sexism (in the name of forthrightness and practicality) that relegates girls to a level at which the most important thing for them to be able to calculate is the position of an icebox.

On the surface, Arnold's father and Miss Pratt could hardly have less in common, but what they share is that neither one is talking so much as ranting. If Scott Spencer's two couples are lobbing tennis balls back and forth, these speakers are hitting them, over and over, against a brick wall.

Ranting is another thing that should be done sparingly in lit-erature, as in life, with an eye to why and how long a reader will stay interested in a character who just keeps on talking. People, we notice, tend to rant when they are in control and don't care much about the approval of the people to whom they're ranting. Perhaps that's why there are several notable literary examples of people ranting to children, most notably, in Harold Brodkey's story "S.L." and Christina Stead's *The Man Who Loved Children*.

In "S.L.," the ranter is the title character, a self-indulgent, decent man who is about to adopt the little orphan to whom he is raving. Reading S.L.'s monologues, we become intensely aware of the way that people often talk to children—as if they aren't sentient, comprehending beings—when in fact children, like the boy in the story, know perfectly well what the adults are saying. Though S.L. wants the child to love and accept him, everything he says increases our sense of the child's isolation, confusion, and desperation. In much the same way, your heart goes out to Christina Stead's Pollit children partly because their parents seem to do nothing *but* rant. Their mother, Henny, tends toward dark fits in which she rambles on about murder and suicide. This is how she talks to her lover, Bert, on the subject of her husband, Sam, and her stepdaughter, Louisa:

> ". . . *the impulse to kill him becomes so strong sometimes, when I think of the way he's stolen my life and trampled all over it and then thinks it's sufficient if he reads a few highbrow books, that I don't know how to get over it. I clench my fists together to keep from rushing at his greasy yellow head, or throwing something into that noisy mouth, forever boasting and screaming. If I could kill him and that child . . . I'd gladly do time for it. But what would the kids do? Go to an asylum? No one would stand it. No one could stand it."*

Sam is apt to rattle on longer and more charmingly, or at least so he imagines, in the monologues that betray high spirits, an essentially good heart, and a chilling, slightly megalomaniacal lack of awareness or interest in whoever happens to be listening. In a typical passage, Sam, who can inflate the most trivial circumstances into a prolonged disquisition, blithers on about the seventh day of the week:

> "*This Sunday-Funday has come a long way . . . It's been coming to us, all day yesterday, all night from the mid-Pacific, from Peking, the Himalayas, from the fishing grounds of the old Leni Lenapes and the deeps of the drowned Susquehanna, over the pond pine ragged in the peat and the lily swamps of Anacostia, by scaffolded marbles and time-bloodied weatherboard, northeast, northwest, Washington Circle, Truxton Circle, Sheridan Circle to Rock Creek and the blunt shoulders of our Georgetown. And what does he find there this morning as every morning, in the midst of the slope, but Tohoga House, the*

little shanty of Gulliver Sam's Lilliputian Pollitry—Gulliver Sam, Mrs. Gulliver Henny, Lugubrious Louisa, whose head is bloody but unbowed, Ernest the calculator, Little-Womey . . . Saul and Sam the boy-twins and Thomas-snowshoe-eye, all suntropes that he come galloping to see."

Later, he rambles on to his daughter, Louisa, again (like Henny) on the topic of murder, and with reckless disregard for the sort of thing that a responsible adult might want to say in front of a child:

"Murder might be beautiful, a self-sacrifice, a sacrifice of someone near and dear, for the good of others—I can conceive of such a thing, Looloo! The extinction of one life, when many are threatened, or when future generations might suffer—wouldn't you, even you, think that a fine thing? Why, we might murder thousands—not indiscriminately as in war now—but picking out the unfit and putting them painlessly into the lethal chamber. This alone would benefit mankind by clearing the way for a eugenic racc."

The Man Who Loved Children is a symphonic novel composed of a series of variations on the dissonance of the Pollit parents' voices. And by the end of the novel, all this casual talk of murder and suicide will have catastrophic repercussions.

Which brings up one final thing that seems important to mention about dialogue on the page. And that is the mysterious way in which it so frequently seems to echo the themes, the tone, and the voice of the work in which it appears. The startling and terrible things that happen in *The Man Who Loved Children* turn out to reflect, and perhaps even to have been generated by, what Sam and Henny say, and by the way they say it.

Dialogue differs from story to story, novel to novel, conversation to conversation. There are as many kinds of dialogue in fiction as the sum total of stories, novels, and characters that exist. And really that shouldn't surprise us. Because what is dialogue, after all, but the speech that could only come from the mouth of one character in all of fiction, and from the mind of one writer?

EIGHT

Details

SOME YEARS AGO I HEARD A TRUE STORY THAT I FOUND disturbing, puzzling, and weirdly cheering, because it is partly about the power of storytelling—and of detail. Perhaps the reason why it continues to intrigue me is that I have never completely understood it.

The story was told to me by a friend whose life in art mostly involved telling versions of his true life story, and who was hired by Esalen, the New Age institute in Big Sur, California, to lead a workshop on the subject of telling true-life stories. The purpose of the workshop was to help the participants (who had been admitted on the basis of letters demonstrating that each of them had a story to tell) find ways to tell their stories better.

On the first day of class, my friend asked for a volunteer, and a woman raised her hand. As soon as she began, my friend remembered her letter. This woman had lost one leg to a bout with childhood cancer, but had gone on to become a world-class downhill skiing champion. Her story was an account of her loss and her triumph, not just over one illness but over several life-threatening diseases that left her not only undefeated but stronger. In fact she made her living as a motivational trainer, revving up burned-out salesmen and sluggish CEOs with a message of encouragement based on her own experience: I did this, so you can do that.

After she'd told her story, my friend asked if she didn't ever want just to go somewhere and scream. The woman said no, she did not. She had no interest in screaming. In fact, it was important to her not to get in touch with her dark side.

In the second class, one of the male students volunteered to begin. This was a former investment broker or former insider trader, someone who had earned millions and then given up his career in high finance to attend spiritual workshops all over California. He waited until the room was silent and then pronounced, in a sort of growl, a graphic term for a sex act that, he said, he liked to do with his wife. As the beginning of a story—or whatever—it cut to the chase, conveying that his story was going to be not only confessional and pornographic but aggressive.

He proceeded to tell an extremely confessional, pornographic, and (my friend said) aggressive story about his sex life with his wife. My friend spared me the details but said that the story was so well told that he couldn't move, he hardly breathed the whole time the guy was talking. When the story finished, the class was dead silent, and, not knowing what else to do, my friend took what he called the "technical route" and told the man that his story had been very well told.

The class went wild. Many of the students were furious, especially the women, several of whom tried to explain why they were so upset, how they'd experienced the story not only as pornography (a subject about which the women in fact had divergent views) but as simple aggression. It says something about manners, about the psychology of taboo, of sex, and of confession that it would have been permissible (in some cases sympathetic) for him to tell a story about tormenting his wife, but outrageous to describe having sex with her in many unlikely settings. Though I suppose you can't blame the students for objecting to paying Esalen tuition to find themselves functioning as unpaid phone-sex workers.

The storyteller had meant to stir up the class and make extra work for the teacher. And now he sat back with his arms crossed: satisfied, delighted.

On the third day of class, the one-legged woman asked if she could tell another story. She said that it was a confession, something she'd never told anyone but her therapist. But the fact was, she'd lied on the first day, about how she'd lost her leg. The truth involved her sister, a deeply wicked person, and her sister's black cat, which—when the narrator was a child—bit her on the leg: a wound she refused to attend to, and which became infected, and festered.

One night at a family dinner—always a tense occasion, because their father was a passionate carnivore and their mother a strict vegetarian—the father began to yell that the dining room stank to high heaven, and that it was the mother's tofu that smelled. Of course it wasn't bean curd, but rather the daughter's leg, which had become gangrenous and had to be amputated.

Many readers may be having doubts about this story, as I did. But my friend assured me: the woman told it with unwavering conviction, and there wasn't one person in the room who didn't believe every word.

Finally, she got to the end of her story. She waited a few beats. Then she smiled and said she was sorry, but she'd invented the story about the cat. For a moment the class was truly shocked. It was, after all, a strange thing to do. But eventually they came around to accept this new plot turn with humor and good grace.

All, that is, except for the man who'd told the pornographic story. He rose to his feet and said they'd been had, tricked, hoodwinked—and frankly he didn't like it. Furthermore, he said that my friend—the workshop leader—was nothing but a bad actor. The guy left the classroom, left Esalen, in fact.

Not since Scheherazade saved her life by telling her spouse the tales from *The Arabian Nights* in enthralling serial installments has there been such conclusive proof of the power of fiction. How oddly brave the woman was to use a story of her disability as a heat-seeking missile, a perfectly aimed weapon of retaliation. The part that I don't claim to understand is how she could have known how well her plan would work, or that it would work at all, or why the pornographic storyteller had heard the cat story as it was meant, as an attack on him.

The reason I've told this story is not to upset the reader with its unsettling aspects, or even to encourage those of us (myself included) who have been laboring away in solitude in our studies and garrets, wondering if our fiction means anything or can *do* anything, if anyone really cares . . . but because of something my friend said. He told me that the whole reason the class believed the woman's story—a gothic tall tale about a gangrenous cat bite—was entirely because of the detail about the father's love for steak and the mother's passion for tofu.

"Trust me on this," my friend said. "God really is in the details."

IF God is in the details, we all must on some deep level believe that the truth is in there, too. Or maybe it *is* that God is truth: Details are what persuade us that someone is telling the truth—a fact that every liar knows instinctively and too well. Bad liars pile on the facts and figures, the corroborating evidence, the improbable digressions ending in blind alleys, while good or (at least better) liars know that it's the single priceless detail that jumps out of the story and tells us to take it easy, we can quit our dreary adult jobs of playing judge and jury and again become as trusting children, hearing the gospel of grown-up knowledge without a single care or doubt.

And what a relief it is when a detail reassures us that a writer is in control and isn't putting us on. Let's say we're a little . . . uncertain about Gregor Samsa waking up from a night of troubling dreams to find himself changed in his bed into a giant beetle. Kafka tells us, "It was no dream," but why should we believe him? The facts of insect anatomy—"He was lying on his hard, as it were armor-plated, back, and when he lifted his head a little he could see his domelike brown belly divided into stiff arched segments. . . . His numerous legs, which were pitifully thin compared to the rest of his bulk, flickered helplessly before his eyes"—are convincing, but still we could be reading the script for a Japanese monster movie or a passage of science fiction by a brilliant but demented beginner. It isn't until Samsa surveys his room, the "regular human bedroom, only rather too small," that we lose our last shred of suspicion that this might be a dream, and know that this can only be the real world of a masterpiece of fiction.

> *Above the table on which a collection of cloth samples was unpacked and spread out—Samsa was a commercial traveler—hung the picture which he had recently cut out of an illustrated magazine and put into a pretty gilt frame. It showed a lady, with a fur cap on and a fur stole, sitting upright and holding out to the spectator a huge fur muff into which the whole of her forearm had vanished!*

This picture is the perfect detail, at once surprising, unexpected, inventive, unpredictable, but entirely plausible, serious but somehow playful, apt—but not in the least heavy-handed or pointedly symbolic. The magazine picture of the lady in furs is exactly what, we imagine, a traveling salesman might choose to brighten up his bachelor's bedroom; sexy, in its way, but not so risqué that it wouldn't be proper for the maid to see when she cleaned. And believing in this picture, we begin to believe in Samsa and in the possibility that he *could* turn into a bug. Also, this detail combines a convincingly nervy mix of irony and plausibility, since the daring sub-detail of the hand disappearing into the fur muff is almost *too* perfect to find in the room of a man who is already having a bit of a problem with anatomical boundaries and species identification.

Great writers painstakingly construct their fictions with small but significant details that, brushstroke by brushstroke, paint the pictures the artists hope to portray, the strange or familiar realities of which they hope to convince us: details of landscape and nature (the facts of marine and whale biology in *Moby Dick*), of weather (the fog in the beginning of Dickens's *Bleak House*), of fashion (the tailors' dummies in Bruno Schulz, the hospital bracelets that the customers of the loser's bar are still wearing in Denis Johnson's *Jesus' Son*), of home decoration (the ancient wedding cake in Miss Havisham's room), of food (the hideous smorgasbord of disgusting candies in *Gravity's Rainbow*), of botany (Colette's mother's sedum plant) of music (the little phrase that haunts Swann in *Swann's Way*), of sports, art, of all the things with which we humans express our complex individuality.

Often, a well-chosen detail can tell us more about a character—his social and economic status, his hopes and dreams, his vision of himself—than a long explanatory passage. In Salinger's *Franny and Zooey*, Bessie Glass's bathrobe not only describes her personality and her entire way of life but also conveys a considerable amount about her family, specifically the cleverness and ironic affection that her children so prize, and with which they discuss and treat their mother, and one another:

She was wearing her usual at-home vesture—what her son Buddy (who was a writer, and consequently, as Kafka, no less, had told us, not a nice man) called her pre-notification-of-death uniform. It consisted mostly of a hoary midnight-blue Japanese kimono. She almost invariably wore it throughout the apartment during the day. With its many occultish-looking folds, it also served as the repository for the paraphernalia of a very heavy cigarette smoker and an amateur handyman: two oversized pockets had been added at the hips, and they usually contained two or three packs of cigarettes, several match folders, a screwdriver, a claw-end hammer, a Boy Scout knife that had once belonged to one of her sons, and an enamel faucet handle or two, plus an assortment of screws, nails, hinges, and ball-bearing casters—all of which tended to make Mrs. Glass clink faintly as she moved around her large apartment. For ten years or more, both of her daughters had often, if impotently, conspired to throw out this veteran kimono. (Her married daughter, Boo Boo, had intimated that it might have to be given a coup de grâce with a blunt instrument before it was laid away in a wastebasket.)

Though I'm usually put off by any use of brand names in fiction (it's a lazy writer's way of "placing" a character, and nothing can date a work more quickly than a reference to a brand of bed linen that no longer exists) it's also true that certain consumer choices can communicate a wealth of information. Anyone who has ever listened to the NPR-syndicated call-in show *Car Talk*, will have noticed how much the Brothers "Click and Clack" can tell about each listener on the basis of what sort of car a caller drives, and the nature of his or her engine-repair or brake-drum problem. Once, I heard a man phone in to ask the brothers' opinion on whether he should buy a red Jeep or a red Miata, a question to which the acutely perceptive reply was "So tell me, when did you get your divorce?"

At the opening of William Trevor's story "Access to the Children," its protagonist, Malcolmson, "a fair, tallish man in a green tweed suit that required pressing," arrives at an apartment house (we sense that it is not his own home) in a ten-year-old Volvo. Who drives a ten-year-old Volvo? Not a terribly rich man, who would have a newer-model car and would be less likely to be wearing a rumpled suit. Nor a very poor one, who might be driving something even older and less glamorous. And the Volvo? It's a family car, implying a very different sort of man from the one who might speed up to the curb in a Lamborghini. Everything we learn about Malcolmson will confirm our first impression. He's a little down on his luck, drinking a bit too much. He's been married (during his Volvo days) but is now divorced, and is going to spend the Sunday on which he has visitation rights enjoying his "access to the children."

Even those writers we may consider above or beyond detail, those who seem more concerned with oddities of language and aberrant states of consciousness than with creating naturalistic scenes and plausible dialogue, even Samuel Beckett wrote—in almost the same words Chekhov used half a century earlier—"In the particular is contained the universal." The details of the sixteen sucking stones Molloy transfers from pocket to pocket as he tries to suck each one equally, and the crutches he ties to his bicycle, rise like sharp peaked islands from that bleak and hilarious novel *Molloy*.

Like many writers, Chekhov filled his notebook not only with large observations about philosophy and life in general— ideas of the sort that never appear in his stories except in the mind of a character, the pompous, the self-deluded, the disappointed, or the hopeful about to be disappointed—but also with minute trivia of the sort that might have made it into one of his stories or plays: "A bedroom. The light of the moon shines so brightly through the window that even the buttons on his night shirt are visible" and "a tiny little schoolboy with the name of Tractenbauer." His letters stress the importance of the single, well-chosen detail:

> *In my opinion a true description of nature should be very brief and have the character of relevance. Commonplaces such as "the setting sun bathed the waves of the darkening sea, poured its purple gold, etc."—"the swallows flying over the surface of the water tittered merrily"—such commonplaces one ought to abandon. In descriptions of nature one ought to seize upon the little particulars, grouping them in such a way that, in reading, when you shut your eyes you get the picture.*
>
> *For instance you will get the full effect of a moonlit night if you write that on the milldam, a little glowing starpoint flashed from the neck of a broken bottle, and the round black shadow of a dog or a wolf emerged and ran, etc. . . .*
>
> *In the sphere of psychology, details are also the thing. God preserve us from commonplaces. Best of all is to avoid depicting the hero's state of mind; you ought to try to make it clear from the hero's actions.*
>
> *You understand it at once when I say, "The man sat on the grass." You understand it because it is clear and makes no demands on the attention. On the other hand it is not easily understood if I write, "A tall, narrow-chested, middle-sized man, with a red beard, sat on the green grass, already trampled by pedestrians, sat silently, shyly, and timidly looked about him." That is not immediately grasped by the mind, whereas good writing should be grasped at once—in a second.*

We cannot think of Chekhov's stories without thinking of their details: one of the most famous is the slice of watermelon that Gurov eats in Anna Sergeyevna's hotel room in "The Lady with the Dog." There is also, in that same story, the detail of

Gurov's wife's dark eyebrows; of the lorgnette Anna loses during the evening she spends with Gurov; the sturgeon that Gurov's friend says is a bit "off"; the numerous touches with which Chekhov describes the small-town theater where Gurov again sees Anna; the gray hair that Gurov notices when he regards his own reflection in the mirror; the fence outside Anna's house, and so forth.

Some of his lesser stories have the most stunning details, for example the ironing board, the iron, and the boiled potato in the climactic scene of "The Murder." Matvey, a poor factory worker and a religious fanatic, has been arguing about money and religion with his cousin Yakov, a poor tavern owner and another sort of religious fanatic. Matvey lives at the tavern with Yakov, Yakov's wife, Aglaia, and their retarded daughter, Dashutka, all of whom hate Matvey, and all of whom he hates. At a certain point in the story, we see Matvey in the kitchen, peeling some boiled potatoes, "which he had probably put away from the day before." A page later, Yakov has gone through a brief but hysterical spiritual crisis on the theme of faith and doubt and repentance, and we again catch up with Matvey, "sitting in the kitchen before a bowl of potato, eating. . . . Between the stove and the table at which Matvey was sitting was stretched an ironing-board; on it stood a cold iron."

Matvey asks Yakov's wife, Aglaia, for a little oil to put on his potatoes, a simple enough request except that this is Lent, and oil is one of the things restricted by the fast. Yakov screams that Matvey can't have oil; they call each other heretics and sinners, and order one another to repent. A scuffle ensues, and Yakov's wife, thinking her husband is in danger, picks up the bottle of oil

and with all her force brought it down straight on the skull
of the cousin she hated. Matvey reeled, and in one instant

his face became calm and indifferent. Yakov, breathing heavily, excited, and feeling pleasure at the gurgle the bottle had made, like a living thing, when it had struck the head, kept him from falling and several times (he remembered this very distinctly) motioned Aglaia towards the iron with his finger; and only when the blood began trickling through his hands and he heard Dashutka's loud wail, and when the ironing-board fell with a crash, and Matvey rolled heavily on it, Yakov left off feeling anger and understood what had happened.

"Let him rot. . . ." Aglaia cried . . . still with the iron in her hand. The white bloodstained kerchief slipped on to her shoulders and her grey hair fell in disorder. "He's got what he deserved!"

Everything was terrible. Dashutka sat on the floor near the stove with the yarn in her hands, sobbing, and continually bowing down, uttering at each bow a gasping sound. But nothing was so terrible to Yakov as the potato in the blood, on which he was afraid of stepping, and there was something else terrible which weighed upon him like a bad dream and seemed the worst danger, though he could not take it in for a minute. This was the waiter, Sergey Nikanoritch, who was standing in the doorway with the reckoning beads in his hand, very pale, looking with horror at what was happening in the kitchen.

"We think in generalities," wrote Alfred North Whitehead. "But we live in detail." To which I would add: We remember in detail, we recognize in detail, we identify, we re-create—cops rarely ask eyewitnesses for general vague descriptions of the perpetrator. In grade school, my son was trying to remember a Greek myth and kept referring to the story about the pomegranate seeds until at last we figured that he meant the story of Persephone: forget being kidnapped by Pluto, the half-life in the underworld, the months underground, forget the mother's grief intense enough to make the seasons change. My son was referring to a detail that I myself had forgotten: the number of months that Persephone agreed to spend with her husband underground was determined by the number of pomegranate seeds she ate while she was there.

One mark of the highly skilled and competent but less than first-rate writer is that we may vividly remember one detail from a novel but not the rest of the book, or even its title. We may recall the scene from an Elmore Leonard thriller in which Teddy Majestyk's mother feeds her parrot with food from her mouth without being able to remember if this was the book in which so many characters seem to get pushed from high windows.

If we doubt for a moment how our memory for detail can be trusted and used to pull us through a story, consider the detail of Julian's mother's hat in Flannery O'Connor's "Everything That Rises Must Converge": "It was a hideous hat. A purple velvet flap came down on one side of it and stood up on the other; the rest of it was green and looked like a cushion with the stuffing out." Again, it is the perfect detail, the perfect hat for Julian's mother, and just like her (as Julian decides) "less comical than jaunty and pathetic." All her hopes and dreams are concentrated in that hat, all her desperate efforts to maintain some pretense of style and social standing, to present herself as an aristocrat come down in the world and forced to live among the peasantry. After all, she is the proud granddaughter of a man who had a plantation with two hundred slaves who were "better off" than the black people with whom she must now ride the bus to her reducing class at the Y and who, she thinks, "should rise, yes, but on their own side of the fence."

A bit later in the story, our attention is again directed to "the preposterous hat" she wears "like a banner of her imaginary dignity." So when a black woman gets on the bus in a "hideous hat. A purple velvet flap came down on one side of it and stood up on the other; the rest of it was green and looked like a cushion with the stuffing out," we get the significance of the coincidence a few moments before

> *the vision of the two hats, identical, broke upon [Julian] with the radiance of a brilliant sunrise. His face was suddenly lit up with joy. He could not believe that Fate had thrust upon his mother such a lesson. He gave a loud chuckle so that she would look at him and see what he saw. She turned her eyes on him slowly. The blue in them seemed to have turned a bruised purple. For a moment he had an uncomfortable sense of her innocence, but it lasted only a second before principle rescued him. Justice entitled him to laugh. His grin hardened until it said to her as plainly as if he were saying aloud: Your punishment exactly fits your pettiness. This should teach you a permanent lesson.*

And of course, the lesson that Julian's mother is about to learn could hardly be more permanent.

But details needn't be extreme or unusual—a bloody potato or a hideous hat—in order for them to enrich a story or novel. Henrietta, the little girl in Elizabeth Bowen's *The House in Paris*, carries a stuffed toy monkey. How banal, we might think. But the monkey, whose name turns out to be Charles, becomes a character, always present, eliciting a range of responses from the other characters. And Charles's relationship with Henrietta tells us something that nothing else does about certain aspects of her inner life.

> *But Miss Fischer, making an effort, now touched one of the monkey's stitched felt paws. "You must be fond of your monkey. You play with him, I expect?"*
>
> *"Not nowadays much," said Henrietta politely. "I just always seem to take him about."*

"For company," said Miss Fisher, turning upon the monkey a brooding, absent look.

"I like to think he enjoys things!"

"Ah, then you do play with him!"

It was not in Henrietta's power to say: "We really cannot go into all that now."

If we want to write something memorable, we might want to pay attention to how and what we remember. The details are what stick with us, as I realized after watching a remarkable documentary called *Mob Stories*, a film in which five *mafiosi* took turns telling the story of their careers. Each story was preceded by a title—"Family," "Mutiny," "Revenge," etc.

Afterward, I recalled the following details. Trying to explain how "sick" his boss was, one man said, "He used to read about serial killers and be very impressed by how the guy had gotten away with whacking twenty-eight people. I mean, you hang around with wise guys, you never hear no one admiring serial killers . . . " A Rodney Dangerfield lookalike served as the lawyer for himself and his friends and won the case by endearing himself to the jury with dirty jokes about his wife. Now he is back in jail on another charge, and the camera showed this big man gracefully doing tai chi exercises in the prison garden.

The last man told the story of how he used to commit brutal acts in order to ingratiate himself with the bosses for whom he worked as a low-level debt collector. At forty, he got married and fell in love with his wife, had two kids, and redirected his life; he raised a quarter million to buy his way out of the mob, and now was a born-again preacher.

The detail he kept returning to was the worst thing he used to do: he'd chain a guy, some deadbeat, to the back bumper of his car and drag him along the street. The storyteller repeated this detail several times, amazed by his previous self, by the other life he used to lead, and with that edge of longing that always goes right along with nostalgia. And it was this detail—the man, the chain, the bumper—that made me believe every word of this guy's story of sin and repentance.

READING back through this chapter, I'm appalled by the details. A one-legged skier, a gangrenous cat bite, a game of dueling stories, a cut-out magazine photo beside the bed of a giant insect, a bloody potato on the kitchen floor, a wise guy driving down the road with a deadbeat tied to his bumper.

But why should I be surprised? It's not just God in the details, but the times in which we live. Details aren't only the building blocks with which a story is put together, they're also clues to something deeper, keys not merely to our subconscious but to our historical moment.

There is one more detail, one final detail, that I feel I should add. Several months after the Esalen workshop ended, and a few weeks before my friend told me the story of the dueling stories, he had gotten a letter from the woman, the one-legged skier. She wrote that for New Year's Eve she had gone out into the desert and thrown back her head and just screamed and screamed, and she wanted to tell him that, and to say that she felt much better.

NINE

Gesture

CHANNEL SURFING ONE NIGHT, I WATCHED THE LAST twenty minutes of a made-for-TV movie about a small-town girl who gets pregnant and gives up her baby and leaves her boyfriend. Decades later she is reunited with the baby's father when the baby (a grown man, a minister, about to become a father himself) locates his parents and brings them together. At the end of the film, the long-separated teen parents (now in late middle age) are married by their son, the reverend, after a brief scene in which the groom gets out of the car and goes to pick up his bride.

The groom straightens his tie, pats down his hair, paces, checks his reflection in the car mirror, straightens his tie, smoothes his hair, fixes his tie again. It's not as if a man in this situation might *not* straighten his tie and smooth his hair, but the familiarity of the gestures, amplified by repetition, shredded the already-fragile veil of illusion surrounding this tender scene.

Perhaps I should say that my definition of gesture includes

small physical actions, often unconscious or semi-reflexive, including what is called body language and excluding larger, more definite or momentous actions. I would not call picking up a gun and shooting someone a gesture. On the other hand, language—that is, word choice—can function as a gesture: the way certain married people refer to their spouses as *him* or *her* is a sort of a gesture communicating possession, intimacy, pride, annoyance, tolerance, or some combination of the above.

Mediocre writing abounds with physical clichés and stock gestures. Opening a mass-market thriller at random, I read: "Clenching her fists so hard she can feel her nails digging into the palms of her hand she forces herself to walk over to him. . . . She snuggled closer to Larry as she felt his arms tighten around her and his sweet breath warm the back of her neck. . . . She adjusted her cap as she crunched down the gravel driveway. . . . Tom bit his lip." All of these are perfectly acceptable English sentences describing common gestures, but they feel generic. They are not descriptions of an individual's very particular response to a particular event, but rather a shorthand for common psychic states. He bit his lip, she clenched her fists—our characters are nervous. The cap-adjuster is wary and determined, the couple intimate, and so forth.

Writers cover pages with familiar reactions (her heart pounded, he wrung his hands) to familiar situations. But unless what the character does is unexpected or unusual, or truly important to the narrative, the reader will assume that response without having to be told. On hearing that his business partner has just committed a murder, a man might be quite upset, and we can intuit that without needing to hear about the speed of his heartbeat or the dampness of his palms. On the other hand, if he's glad that his partner has been caught, or if he himself is the murderer, and he smiles . . . well, that's a different story.

Too often, gestures are used as markers, to create beats and pauses in a conversation that, we fear, may rush by too quickly without them.

> "Hello," she said, reaching for a cigarette.
> "Hello," he replied.
> "How are you?" She lit her cigarette.
> "Fine." He poured two glasses of wine.

One might ask why we need to linger over this conversation, why we can't just be permitted to hurry through it, though I suppose the gestures (cigarette, wine) are meant to communicate a certain portentousness. Or something. In any case, the catalogue of gestures will not be improved much if we learn that her hand shook as she lit her cigarette, but it might be given a bit of an edge if we learn that he poured one glass of wine, and then remembered and poured two, or that he poured his own—or her glass much fuller than the other.

If a character's going to light a cigarette, or almost light a cigarette, it should *mean* something, as it does in this scene from ZZ Packer's story "Drinking Coffee Elsewhere." A tense interview with a college student makes a psychiatrist nervous enough to reach for a smoke, and the question of whether he can light up or not leads to an exchange in which the student briefly takes control, and the doctor just as quickly grabs it back.

> "Tell me about your parents."
> I wondered what he already had on file. The folder was thick, though I hadn't said a thing of significance since Day One.
> "My father was a dick and my mother seemed to like him."
> He patted his pockets for his cigarettes. "That's some heavy stuff," he said. "How do you feel about Dad?" The man

couldn't say the word "father." "Is Dad someone you see often?"

"I hate my father almost as much as I hate the word 'Dad.'"

He started tapping his cigarette

"You can't smoke in here."

"That's right," he said, and slipped the cigarette back into the packet. He smiled, widening his eyes brightly. "Don't ever start."

Much about the relationship between age and youth, social position and suspicion is revealed by the anxious hesitation of the customers in Junot Diaz's story "Edison, New Jersey," which concerns some boys who work delivering card and pool tables:

Sometimes the customer has to jet to the store for cat food or a newspaper while we're in the middle of a job. I'm sure you'll be all right, they say. They never sound too sure. Of course, I say. Just show us where the silver's at. The customers ha-ha and we ha-ha and then they agonize over leaving, linger by the front door, trying to memorize everything they own, as if they don't know where to find us, who we work for.

One could say that everything that happens in Philip Roth's *Goodbye, Columbus* can be predicted, more or less accurately, from the succession of swift gestures that begins the novel. Much of what we need to know about the lovers at the book's center is succinctly telegraphed by the entitled, sexually confident insouciance with which the privileged Brenda Patimkin asks the novel's narrator—a stranger who is merely a day guest at her country club—to hold her glasses before she dives in the pool, and then, knowing he is watching, adjusts her bathing suit:

The first time I saw Brenda she asked me to hold her glasses. Then she stepped out to the edge of the diving board and looked foggily into the pool; it could have been drained, myopic Brenda would never have known it. She dove beautifully, and a moment later she was swimming back to the side of the pool, her head of short-clipped auburn hair held up, straight ahead of her, as though it were a rose on a long stem. She glided to the edge, and then was beside me. "Thank you," she said, her eyes watery though not from the water. She extended a hand for her glasses but did not put them on until she turned and headed away. I watched her move off. Her hands suddenly appeared behind her. She caught the bottom of her suit between thumb and index finger and flicked what flesh had been showing back where it belonged. My blood jumped.

A wealth of very different information comes to us through gesture in a scene that Raymond Chandler describes, one that took place in the 1940s, when men more often wore hats: A man and his wife are riding up in the elevator. The door opens. A pretty young woman gets on. The man takes off his hat. And observe how much is conveyed by the moment in Tolstoy's *Resurrection* when a society woman, conscious that she is aging and desperate to appear young, keeps turning from her festive lunch to eye the window through which a beam of unflattering sunlight has begun to shine.

Properly used gestures—plausible, in no way stagy or extreme, yet unique and specific—are like windows opening to let us see a person's soul, his or her secret desires, fears or obsessions, the precise relations between that person and the self, between the self and the world, as well as (in the Chandler story) the complicated emotional, social and historical male-female choreography that is instantly comprehensible, even in these hatless times.

Though we may associate Henry James with the complex, long-winded sentence, one of the crucial plot turns in *The Portrait of a Lady* occurs without any need for words. It happens during the famous scene in which Isabel Archer walks into her drawing room to find her husband, Gilbert Osmond, talking to Madame Merle. Their posture and gestures finally make Isabel see that the "friendship" between them has been more intimate than she'd imagined. And we too understand exactly what is going on even if we don't live in an era in which, if a gentleman is lounging while a woman stands, the woman is either his mother, his sister, his wife, or, in the case of Madame Merle, his mistress and the mother of his child.

Madame Merle was there in her bonnet, and Gilbert Osmond was talking to her; for a minute they were unaware she had come in. Isabel had often seen that before, certainly; but what she had not seen, or at least had not noticed, was that their colloquy had for the moment converted itself into a sort of familiar silence, from which she instantly perceived that her entrance would startle them. Madame Merle was standing on the rug, a little way from the fire; Osmond was in a deep chair, leaning back and looking at her. Her head was erect, as usual, but her eyes were bent on his. What struck Isabel first was that he was sitting while Madame Merle stood; there was an anomaly in this that arrested her. Then she perceived that they had arrived at a desultory pause in their exchange of ideas and were musing, face to face, with the freedom of old friends who sometimes exchange ideas without uttering them. There was nothing to shock in this; they were old friends in fact. But the thing made an image, lasting only a moment, like a sudden flicker of light. Their relative positions, their absorbed mutual gaze, struck her as something detected. But it was all over by the time she had fairly seen it. Madame Merle had seen her and

*had welcomed her without moving; her husband, on the other
hand, had instantly jumped up.*

Even in a surreal story, such as Kafka's "The Judgment,"
gesture can be used to anchor the fiction in a recognizable hu-
man context. As Georg Bendermann's father keeps shrinking
and growing, gaining and losing personal power, his gestures
(the playing with the watch-chain, the throwing off of the bed-
clothes) keep us apprised of his terrifyingly enlarged or dimin-
ished condition, even as Georg's gestures are those of a man
attempting to remain calm and reasonable and to make the best
of an extremely bizarre situation:

> *He carried his father in his arms to the bed. During his
> few steps toward it he noticed with a terrible sensation that
> his father, as he lay against his breast, was playing with his
> watch-chain. He could not put him down on the bed straight-
> away, so firmly did he cling to this watch-chain.*
>
> *But no sooner was he in bed when all seemed well. He
> covered himself up and drew the blanket extra high over his
> shoulders. He looked up at Georg with a not unfriendly eye.*
>
> *"There you are, you're beginning to remember it now,
> aren't you?" Georg asked, nodding at him encouragingly.*
>
> *"Am I well covered up now?" asked his father, as if he
> couldn't quite see whether his feet were properly tucked in.*
>
> *"So you're feeling quite snug in bed already," said Georg,
> and arranged the bedclothes more firmly around him.*
>
> *"Am I well covered up?" he asked once more, and seemed
> to await the answer with special interest.*
>
> *"Don't worry, you're well covered up."*
>
> *"No!" shouted his father, and, sending the answer re-
> sounding against the question, flung back the blanket with
> such force that for an instant it unfurled flat in the air, and he*

stood up erect on the bed. He steadied himself gently with one hand against the ceiling. "You wanted to cover me up, I know that, you young scoundrel, but I'm not covered up yet."

Among the most touching, compressed, and communicative gestures in all of literature occurs in Chekhov's "The Bishop." Our hero, the bishop, is dying. Despite his high position in the church, despite his servants and his ecclesiastical entourage, he is dying alone, cut off from his family, from his own humble origins, and especially from his mother who—quite by accident—comes to visit him, after a long separation. In this scene, the bishop is having lunch with his mother and her granddaughter, the bishop's eight-year-old niece, Katya. One gesture—the business with the drinking glasses—conveys the mother's social unease, her bewilderment in the presence of this important, successful stranger, her son, and a capsule history of the bishop's upward mobility.

> *He could see she was constrained as though she were un-certain whether to address him formally or familiarly, to laugh or not, and that she felt herself more a deacon's widow than his mother. And Katya gazed without blinking at her uncle, his holiness, as though trying to discover what sort of person he was. Her hair sprang up from under the comb and the velvet ribbon stood out like a halo; she had a turned up nose and sly eyes. The child had broken a glass before sitting down for dinner, and now her grandmother as she talked moved away from Katya first a wine glass and then a tumbler. The bishop listened to his mother and remembered how many, many years ago she used to take him and his brothers and sisters to relations whom she considered rich.*

Later, when the bishop is lying ill in bed, he hears from an adjoining room the sound of crockery breaking as Katya drops a cup or saucer, an action that makes us wonder if what we have observed is not only the grandmother's nervousness but the granddaughter's, as well. Eventually, the little girl summons all her courage and asks the bishop for some money because the family is very poor. So perhaps her clumsiness may not be simply a character trait, or even a result of her youth, but rather a situational response to her own anxiety about how to approach her distinguished uncle on this delicate matter.

Yet another famous literary gesture concludes the opening scene of Joyce's "The Dead"—the exquisitely uncomfortable exchange between the self-important Gabriel Conroy, arriving at his elderly aunts' house for their annual Christmas party, and the aunts' servant, Lily.

> —Tell me, Lily, he said in a friendly tone, do you still go to school?
>
> —O, no, sir, she answered. I'm done schooling this year and more.
>
> —O, then, said Gabriel gaily, I suppose we'll be going to your wedding one of these fine days with your young man, eh?
>
> The girl glanced back at him over her shoulder and said with great bitterness:
>
> —The men that is now is only all palaver and what they can get out of you.
>
> Gabriel coloured as if he felt he had made a mistake and, without looking at her, kicked off his goloshes and flicked actively with his muffler at his patent-leather shoes. . . .
>
> When he had flicked lustre into his shoes he stood up and pulled his waistcoat down more tightly on his plump body. Then he took a coin rapidly from his pocket.
>
> —O Lily, he said, thrusting it into her hands, it's Christmas-time, isn't it? Just . . . here's a little . . .

He walked rapidly towards the door.

—O no, sir! cried the girl, following him. Really, sir, I wouldn't take it.

Christmas-time! Christmas-time! said Gabriel, almost trotting to the stairs and waving his hand to her in deprecation.

The girl, seeing that he had gained the stairs, called out after him:

—Well, thank you, sir.

Gabriel's clumsily giving Lily the coin is the culmination of their awkward exchange; it underlines the inappropriate sexual suggestiveness of his half-flirtatious inquiry about the young man, his patronizing attitude, their mutual awareness of class difference, power, gender, etc. And it prepares us for what we will see Gabriel do throughout the story: take the wrong tone, misinterpret, draw the incorrect conclusions. The smaller gestures that punctuate Gabriel's talk with Lily—his polishing his shoes and straightening his waistcoat—are not the stock tics frequently used (as in the TV movie) as shorthand for anxiety but rather the natural reflexes of a man whose principal struggle is against the fragility of his own vanity, a man who can hardly see the world beyond his defensive self-regard. It's also a sublimely accurate presentation of the way that, following some petty embarrassment or after committing some faux pas, we may find ourselves hurrying to the mirror to gaze at the person who could have done such a thing and, if possible, ever so slightly to improve the face that this person presents to the world.

Gabriel reflects (as we all do) on the larger implications of his small social mistake and attempts to repair his pride with the comforts of his own importance:

He waited outside the drawing-room door until the waltz
should finish. . . . He was still discomposed by the girl's bitter
and sudden retort. It had cast a gloom over him which he tried
to dispel by arranging his cuffs and the bows of his tie. Then he
took from his waistcoat pocket a little paper and glanced at the
headings he had made for his speech. He was undecided about
the lines from Robert Browning, for he feared they would be
above the heads of his hearers. . . . The indelicate clacking of
the men's heels and the shuffling of their soles reminded him
that their grade of culture differed from his.

The economy with which gesture reveals the prickly con-
sciousness of social class reminds me of a story I heard about a
German theater troupe rehearsing a scene in which a boss was
supposed to hand a document to a worker in the plant. The ac-
tor playing the worker kept saying that he couldn't get the scene
right, that something felt incorrect about the way that the
worker was taking the document from his boss. At which point
the director—Bertolt Brecht, in the version I heard—called in the
theater's cleaning woman. Very politely, he said that they were
having a problem. Could she help them and hold their document
for a moment? The cleaning woman wiped her hands on her
apron and only then reached for the paper, thus demonstrating
for the actor what had been missing and what was required.

Unlike dialogue, gesture can delineate character when there
is only one character in the room. Charles Baxter's "The Cures
for Love" begins with a gesture that illuminates its protagonist's
domestic and romantic situation:

On the day he left her for good, she put on one of his
caps. It fit snugly over her light brown hair. The cap had the
manufacturer's name of his pickup truck embossed above
the visor in gold letters. She wore the cap backward, the way

he once had, while she cooked dinner. Then she kept it on in her bath that evening. When she leaned back in the tub, the visor hitting the tiles, she could smell his sweat from the inside of his headband, even over the smell of the soap. His sweat had always smelled like freshly-broiled whitefish.

And Katherine Mansfield's "The Fly" turns on a single gesture performed in solitude, or at least with no other humans present, an action that at first seems obvious in its meaning and import but that grows more complex the longer we think about it. The protagonist, identified only as "the boss," is visited by a friend who happens to mention the grave of the boss's son, killed six years before in the First World War, a death the boss never mentions and tries not to think about. Stricken with anguish, the boss suddenly notices that a fly has fallen into his inkpot:

> *The boss took up a pen, picked the fly out of the ink, and shook it on to a piece of blotting-paper. For a fraction of a second it lay still on the dark patch that oozed round it. Then the front legs waved, took hold, and, pulling its small, sodden body up, it began the immense task of cleaning the ink from its wings. Over and under, over and under, went a leg along a wing as the stone goes over and under the scythe. Then there was a pause, while the fly, seeming to stand on the tips of its toes, tried to expand first one wing and then the other. It succeeded at last, and, sitting down, it began, like a minute cat, to clean its face. Now one could imagine that the little front legs rubbed against each other lightly, joyful. The horrible danger was over; it had escaped; it was ready for life again.*
>
> *But just then the boss had an idea. He plunged his pen back into the ink, leaned his thick wrist on the blotting-paper, and as the fly tried its wings down came a great heavy blot. What would it make of that? What indeed! The little beggar seemed*

absolutely cowed, stunned, and afraid to move because of what would happen next. But then, as if painfully, it dragged itself forward. The front legs waved, caught hold, and, more slowly this time, the task began from the beginning.

He's a plucky little devil, thought the boss, and he felt a real admiration for the fly's courage. That was the way to tackle things; that was the right spirit. Never say die; it was only a question of . . . But the fly had again finished its laborious task, and the boss had just time to refill his pen, to shake fair and square on the new-cleaned body yet another dark drop. What about it this time? A painful moment of suspense followed. But behold, the front legs were again waving; the boss felt a rush of relief. He leaned over the fly and said to it tenderly, "You artful little b . . ." And he actually had the brilliant notion of breathing on it to help the drying process. All the same, there was something timid and weak about its efforts now, and the boss decided that this time should be the last, as he dipped the pen deep into the inkpot.

It was. The last blot fell on the soaked blotting-paper, and the draggled fly lay in it and did not stir. The back legs were stuck to the body; the front legs were not to be seen.

"Come on," said the boss. "Look sharp!" And he stirred it with his pen—in vain. Nothing happened or was likely to happen. The fly was dead.

The boss lifted the corpse on the end of the paper-knife and flung it into the waste-paper basket. But such a grinding feeling of wretchedness seized him that he felt positively frightened. He started forward and pressed the bell for Macey.

"Bring me some fresh blotting-paper," he said sternly, "and look sharp about it." And while the old dog padded away he fell to wondering what it was he had been thinking about before. What was it? It was . . . He took out his handkerchief and passed it inside his collar. For the life of him he could not remember.

It's easy to interpret this gesture over-simply: the boss's grief has moved him to do violence to a harmless fly. But the delicate shifts in the boss's emotions and his responses to the fly's struggle move us beyond this surface reading to consider the distractions of casual cruelty, the pleasures of playing god as a means of mediating one's own sense of powerlessness, and the perverse desire to pass pain on to anyone—anything—who is weaker and more helpless than we are.

Though both scenes involve the murder of insects, the boss's fatal encounter with the fly couldn't be more unlike this moment near the beginning of Edward St. Aubyn's *Some Hope.* This massacre is being carried out by the young hero's sadistic father, Doctor David Melrose, and observed by the family maid, Yvette, who is carrying a heavy load of laundry that she ironed the night before.

> *In his blue dressing gown, and already wearing dark glasses although it was still too early for the September sun to have risen above the limestone mountain, he directed a heavy stream of water from the hose he held in his left hand onto the column of ants moving busily through the gravel at his feet. His technique was well-established: he would let the survivors struggle over the wet stones, and regain their dignity for awhile, before bringing the thundering water down on them again. With his free hand he removed a cigar from his mouth, its smoke drifting up through the brown and gray curls that covered the jutting bones of his forehead. He then narrowed the jet of water with his thumb to batter more effectively an ant on whose death he was wholly bent.*
>
> *Yvette had only to pass the fig tree and she could slip into the house without Doctor Melrose knowing she had arrived. His habit, though, was to call her without looking up from the ground just when she thought she was screened by the tree.*

Yesterday he had talked to her for long enough to exhaust her arms, but not for so long that she might drop the linen. He gauged such things very precisely.

Unlike the boss, who does not begin his spontaneous little contest with the fly until the insect has suffered an unfortunate accident, Doctor Melrose (and by now the close reader will have admired the way St. Aubyn has found to apprise us of the doctor's age and social class) is employing a well-established technique. The ants have done nothing to deserve their fate, nor do their struggles move him to the sort of admiration felt by the boss in the Mansfield story. In fact, he prolongs and intensifies their death, on which he is "wholly bent." So it hardly comes as a surprise when, in the next paragraph, we see him tiring of his game with the ants and redirecting his cruelty higher up the evolutionary ladder, tormenting a fellow human as he calculates the exact length of conversation required to make Yvette's arms ache from holding the heavy laundry but without causing her to drop it.

Usually we think of dialogue and physical description as the principal ways in which characters are created, but there are some writers who—when we stop and analyze their narrative strategies—turn out to rely heavily on gesture and on semiconscious action, especially when they are dealing with semirational and irrational fictive personalities. In the first chapter of Flannery O'Connor's novel *Wise Blood*, the God-haunted preacher Hazel Motes finds himself among the more ordinary travelers in the dining car of a train. Notice how dialogue is used to punctuate the lengthy catalogue of small actions, how dialogue serves as the punch line for the running jokes set up by gesture:

The steward beckoned and Mrs. Hitchcock and the women walked in and Haze followed them. The man stopped him and said, "Only two," and pushed him back to the doorway.

Haze's face turned an ugly red. He tried to get behind the next person and then he tried to get through the line to go back to the car he had come from but there were too many people bunched in the opening. He had to stand there while everyone around looked at him. No one left for awhile. Finally a woman at the far end of the car got up and the steward jerked his hand. Haze hesitated and saw the hand jerk again. He lurched up the aisle, falling against two tables on the way and getting his hand wet in somebody's coffee. The steward placed him with three young women dressed like parrots.

Their hands were resting on the table, red-speared at the tips. He sat down and wiped his hand on the tablecloth. He didn't take off his hat. The women had finished eating and were smoking cigarettes. They stopped talking when he sat down. He pointed to the first thing on the menu and the steward, standing over him, said, "Write it down, sonny," and winked at one of the women; she made a noise in her nose. He wrote it down and the steward went away with it. He sat and looked in front of him, glum and intense, at the neck of the woman across from him. At intervals her hand holding the cigarette would pass the spot on her neck; it would go out of his sight and then it would pass again, going back down to the table; in a second a straight line of smoke would blow in his face. After it had blown at him three or four times, he looked at her. She had a bold game-hen expression and small eyes pointed directly at him.

"If you've been redeemed," he said, "I wouldn't want to be." Then he turned his head to the window. He saw his pale reflection with the dark empty space outside coming through it. A boxcar roared past, chopping the empty space in two, and one of the women laughed.

"Do you think I believe in Jesus?" he said, leaning toward her and speaking almost as if he were breathless. "Well I wouldn't even if He existed. Even if He was on this train."

"Who said you had to?" she asked in a poisonous Eastern voice.

He drew back.

The waiter brought his dinner. He began eating slowly at first, then faster as the women concentrated on watching the muscles that stood out on his jaw when he chewed. He was eating something spotted with eggs and livers. He finished that and drank his coffee and then pulled his money out. The steward saw him but he wouldn't come total the bill. Every time he passed the table, he would wink at the women and stare at Haze . . . Finally the man came and added up the bill. Haze shoved the money at him and then pushed past him out of the car.

Often, gestures betray the unconscious, but in fact there are many cases in which we are all too conscious of our gestures—and that consciousness too is a sort of revelation. In Beckett's work, characters are painfully aware of every move they make or don't make, just as they are conscious of everything— and nothing—about themselves. And much of Turgenev's novella *First Love*, is told through the characters' gestures, countless tiny actions that the narrator is too young and innocent to interpret correctly or understand.

The first time the narrator sees Zinaida, his neighbor, a beautiful young woman with whom he will fall in love, she is surrounded by four suitors. She is tapping them on the forehead with small gray flowers, a gesture that defines Zinaida's character (at least at that moment) and her relations with the men who adore her.

The young men presented their foreheads so eagerly, and there was in the movements of the young girl . . . something so fascinating, imperious, caressing, mocking and charming that I nearly cried out with wonder and delight and would, I

believe, have given everything in the world at that moment to
have those lovely fingers tap me on the forehead too.

That night, the newly infatuated boy finds himself, without
knowing why, spinning around three times before going to bed.
Soon after, his friendship with Zinaida deepens—she draws him
into her web, so to speak—when she asks him to hold the skein
of red wool she is winding into a ball.

In one wordless scene, the narrator, strolling in his garden,
coughs to attract his pretty neighbor's attention, then watches as
she puts down the book she is reading to watch his father go by.
The next day, Zinaida and her mother come for dinner, during
which the strong current of attraction between Zinaida and the
narrator's father becomes apparent to everyone but the narra-
tor. Again, nothing needs to be said, no dialogue is required or
reported. All that the narrator's mother has to observe in order
to conceive an instant dislike for Zinaida is the way the young
guest and her host behave at the table:

> *My father sat beside her during dinner and entertained*
> *his neighbor with his usual exquisite and calm courtesy. From*
> *time to time he glanced at her, and she too looked at him now*
> *and again, but so strangely, almost with hostility. Their con-*
> *versation was carried on in French; I remember I was surprised*
> *by the purity of Zinaida's pronunciation.*

Subsequently, all of Zinaida's gestures—mysterious smiles,
enigmatic sighs, fevered handclasps—will be examined by the
narrator for signs of love and favor, even as the reader knows
that they are the actions of a woman in love with the father of
a boy whose eyes remind her of his father's. And when the boy
tells his father about a visit to Zinaida, we read a similar subtext
in the father's response:

He listened to me half attentively and half absently, sit-
ting on a bench and drawing in the sand with the end of his
riding crop. From time to time he would chuckle, look at me
in a sort of bright and amused way, and he egged me on with
short questions and rejoinders.

That evening, the narrator visits Zinaida, who refuses to see him and merely stares at him from her room, softly closes the door, and refuses to respond when her mother calls her. And the narrator's fate is sealed: "My passion began from that day."

Zinaida bites a blade of grass, asks to hear poetry read aloud, blushes over a line of verse, twists the narrator's hair till it hurts, asks him to jump down from a high wall, flings her parasol into the dust, covers his face with kisses, pulls down her window-shade late one night after the narrator has seen his father disappear in the direction of her house. Unbeknownst to the boy, each of these gestures charts the trajectory of her affair with his father. And all of it culminates in the celebrated scene that the narrator watches from a distance, in silence. The interlude plays out almost as if it were being performed in pantomime, conducted entirely through gestures except for one line of over-heard dialogue.

It begins when the boy observes his father standing at an open window of a small wooden house, talking to Zinaida, who sits inside the window:

My father seemed to be insisting on something. Zinaida
would not agree. . . . She did not raise her eyes but just smiled,
submissively and obstinately. It was by this smile alone that
I recognized my Zinaida as I used to know her. My father
shrugged and set his hat straight on his head, which was al-
ways a sign of impatience with him. Then I heard the words:
"Vous devez vous séparer de cette". . . Zinaida drew herself

up and stretched out her hand. . . . Suddenly something quite unbelievable took place before my very eyes; my father all of a sudden raised his riding crop, with which he had been flicking the dust from the skirts of his coat, and I heard the sound of a sharp blow across her arm, which was bared to the elbow. I just managed to restrain myself from crying out, while Zinaida gave a start, looked at my father without uttering a word, and, raising her arm to her lips, kissed the scar that showed crimson on it. My father flung away the crop and, running up the steps rapidly, rushed into the house. Zinaida turned round, tossed back her head, and, with arms outstretched, also moved away from the window.

This gesture—Zinaida kissing the welt on her arm—is what the narrator realizes will remain forever imprinted on his memory, together with the sexually charged reconciliation suggested by the father's haste and his mistress's outstretched arms. And that is certainly what remains with the reader.

Even the greatest writers may use stock gestures or employ gesture badly. Dickens sometimes includes gestures that are not so much revelations of personality as handy mnemonic devices designed to help us to keep track of a large cast of characters: this one blinks, that one twitches, this one limps, that one repeats the same phrase again and again. And of course, it's possible to write without describing gesture. One notices how rarely—almost never—Jane Austen uses physical gesture; perhaps her attention is so attuned to the shifts in a character's sensibility that she simply can't be bothered to lower her gaze and record the silly or pointless self-betrayals that the character's hands and feet, knees and elbows are performing.

If we are to use gesture—and why wouldn't we use this practical tool, this shortcut, this neat way of circumventing brain and mouth and proceeding directly to the heart—how can we use it more effectively? First of all, it's important, as with every word we write, to be careful and sparing. If a gesture is not illuminating, simply leave it out, or try cutting it and see if you later miss it or even remember that it's gone. Do we really need that cigarette lit, that glass of wine poured? Is it merely a way of passing time, of making space in dialogue, of telegraphing mood and emotion? Does it tell us something specific about the character or the situation we are attempting to recreate on the page?

And how do we find these telling gestures? The answer is, simply, by observation: by paying attention to the world. Watch people, watch them closely, and write down or remember what you see. (It might be argued that the recording of small gesture rather than the Big Idea is a more worthwhile use for one's empty notebook.) Notice that woman across from us on the subway compulsively fingering the tiny, almost imperceptible roll of flesh at her middle. Watch the young couple in the car pulled alongside us at the stop sign, the man performing an elaborate ballet with his head and hands to the rap song on the radio, the woman turned away from him, staring out the window.

In pursuit of what he called "the poetry of gesture," Proust cultivated what his housekeeper, Celestine Albert, called his

fabulous powers of observation and a tenacious memory. For example, each of the two or three times he looked through the kitchen window of rue Hamelin at Mme. Standish and her family at dinner, he made only a brief appearance, as if he were just passing by. But in thirty seconds everything was recorded, and better than a camera could do it, because behind the image itself there was often a whole character analysis based on a single detail—the way someone picked up a salt cellar, an inclination of the head, a reaction he had caught on the wing.

Since I started off by criticizing bad actors and their stagy gestures, perhaps I should conclude by praising good actors, who are, after all, students of physical motion. Actors are always watching, and writers can learn by watching actors: the very different gestures that, let's say, Robert DeNiro uses to portray Jake LaMotta or Travis Bickle or any of the kindly priests that he so often winds up playing. An actor once told me that years ago he had watched an old man caught in the rain without an umbrella, and that he had later used the old man's hunched, defensive walk in portraying a father bowed by grief over the sudden death of a child.

Finally, I'd like to quote a story about gesture, about the attention a director might pay to the way that humans reveal their secrets in every move they make. The story, which is from a memoir by the actress Isabella Rossellini, is interesting to compare with a similar situation in fiction, one from L. P. Hartley's novel, *The Go-Between*. In both cases, the use of gesture involves an action that betrays or conceals a secret love affair.

The Hartley passage concludes a scene in which an aristocratic young Englishwoman is accompanying, on the piano, a post–cricket-match serenade sung by a local farmer, who, unbeknownst to the other guests, happens to be her lover:

> At the conclusion of the song there was a call for the accompanist, and Marian left her stool to share the applause with Ted. Half turning, she made him a little bow. But he, instead of responding, twice jerked his head round towards her and away again, like a comedian or a clown wisecracking with his partner. The audience laughed and I heard Lord Trimingham say, "Not very gallant, is he?" My companion was more emphatic. "What's come over our Ted," he whispered across me to our other neighbour, "to be so shy with the ladies? It's because she comes from the Hall, that's why." Meanwhile

Ted had recovered himself sufficiently to make Marian a bow. "That's better," my companion commented. "If it weren't for the difference, what a handsome pair they'd make!"

By contrast, Rossellini describes how an outer *show* of affection (rather than restraint) can be employed to conceal a passion. Shocked and grief-stricken at having been abandoned by her lover, David Lynch, the actress called her former husband Martin Scorsese to tell him what had happened:

> *"Martin, David left me," I said on the phone.*
>
> *"I knew it," he announced to my complete surprise.*
>
> *"How did you know? None of us knew—none of my friends, none of my family expected it, and it was the furthest thing from my mind. How did you know?"*
>
> *"I knew it when I saw you and David on the news, at the Cannes Film Festival. When David won the Palme d'Or for* Wild At Heart, *he kissed you on the lips in front of the press."*
>
> *"So what?"*
>
> *"Well, you've both been so very discreet about your relationship, even if everybody knew you were together—there haven't been any photos, any declarations. If David chose to display his love to you in front of the press after the five years you were together, he obviously had something to hide."*

TEN

Learning from Chekhov

IN THE LATE 1980S, I TAUGHT AT A COLLEGE TWO AND A half hours from my home. I traveled down once a week, stayed overnight, came back. Through most of the winter I commuted by bus. The worst part was waiting in the New Rochelle Trailways Station. The bus was often late, so I wound up being in the station, on the average, forty minutes a week.

Although the bus station was a glassed-in corner storefront, none of the windows opened, so the only time air moved was when someone came through the door. There was a ticket counter, a wall of men's magazines, a phone, a rack of dusty candy. The station was never crowded, which was hardly a comfort when half the people who were there looked like they'd happily blow my brains out on the chance of finding a couple of Valiums in my purse.

Usually, I bought a soda and a greasy sugar cookie to cheer myself up and read *People* magazine because I was scared to lose touch with my surroundings for any longer than it took to read a

People magazine article. Behind the counter worked a man about sixty and a woman about fifty, and in all the time I was there I never heard them exchange one word that was not about their jobs. Behind them was a TV, on constantly, and it will give you an idea of what kind of winter I had when I say that the first ten times I saw the *Challenger* blow up were on the bus station TV. I was having a difficult time in my life, and every minute that kept me from getting home to my family was painful.

Finally the bus came, and the two drivers who alternated— the nasty younger one who seemed to slip into some kind of trance between Newburgh and New Paltz and went slower and slower up the thruway, and the kindlier older one who looked like the villain in a Victorian melodrama and had a fondness for an aerosol spray that smelled like a cross between cherry candy and insect repellent. The bus made Westchester stops for half an hour before it even got to the highway.

As soon as I was settled and had finished my soda and cookie and magazine, I began reading the short stories of Anton Chekhov. It was my ritual, and my reward. I began where I'd left off the week before, through volume after volume of the Constance Garnett translations. And I never had to read more than a page or two before I began to think that maybe things weren't so bad. The stories were not only profound and beautiful, but also involving, so that I would finish one and find myself, miraculously, a half hour or so closer to home. And yet there was more than the distraction, the time so painlessly and pleasantly spent. A sense of comfort came over me, as if in those thirty minutes I myself had been taken up in a spaceship and shown the whole world, a world full of sorrows, both different and very much like my own, and also a world full of promise. It was as if I had been permitted to share an intelligence large enough to embrace bus drivers and bus station junkies, a vision so piercing it would have kept seeing those astronauts long after that fiery plume disappeared from the screen. I began to think that maybe nothing was wasted, that someday I could do something with what was happening to me, to use even the New Rochelle bus station in some way in my work.

Reading Chekhov, I felt not happy, exactly, but as close to happiness as I knew I was likely to come. And it occurred to me that this was the pleasure and mystery of reading, as well as the answer to those who say that books will disappear. For now, books are still the best way of taking great art and its consolations along with us on a bus.

IN the spring, at the final meeting of the course I was commuting to teach, my students asked: If I had one last thing to tell them about writing, what would it be? They were half joking, partly because by then they knew that whenever I said anything about writing, and often when we'd gone on to some other subject completely, I could usually be counted on to come up with qualifications and even counterexamples proving that the opposite could just as well be true. And yet they were also half serious. We had come far in that class. From time to time, it had felt as if, at nine each Wednesday morning, we were shipwrecked together on an island. Now they wanted a souvenir, a fragment of a seashell to take home.

Still it seemed nearly impossible to dredge up that one last bit of advice. Often, I have wanted somehow to get in touch with former students and say: Remember such and such a thing I told you? Well, I take it back, I was wrong! Given the difficulty of making any single true statement, I decided that I might just as well say the first thing that came to mind, which was this: The most important things, I told them, were observation and consciousness. Keep your eyes open, see clearly, think about what you see, ask yourself what it means.

After that came the qualifications and counterexamples: I wasn't suggesting that art necessarily be descriptive, literal, autobiographical, or confessional. Nor should the imagination be overlooked as an investigative tool. "The Distance of the Moon," Italo Calvino's story about a mythical time when the moon could be reached by climbing a ladder from the earth, has always seemed to me a work of acute observation and accuracy. If clear-sightedness—meant literally—were the criterion for genius, what should we do about Milton? But still, in most cases the fact remains: the wider and deeper your observational range, the better, the more interestingly and truthfully you will write.

My students looked at me and yawned. It was early in the morning; they'd heard it before. And perhaps I would not have repeated it, or repeated it with such conviction, had I not spent the year reading all that Chekhov, all those stories illuminated with the deepest and broadest—at once compassionate and dispassionate—observation of life that I know.

I have already described what reading the Chekhov stories did for me, something of what they rescued me from and what they brought me to. But what I have to add now is that after a while I started noticing an odd thing. Let's say that I had just come from telling a creative writing student that one reason the class may have had trouble telling his two main characters apart is that they were named Mikey and Macky. I wasn't saying that the two best friends in his story *couldn't* have similar names. But, given the absence of other distinguishing characteristics, it might be better—in the interests of clarity—to call one Frank, or Bill. The student seemed pleased with this simple solution to a difficult problem. I was happy to have helped. And then, as my bus pulled out of New Rochelle, I began Chekhov's "The Two Volodyas."

In that story, a young woman named Sofya deceives herself into thinking that she is in love with her elderly husband, Volodya, then deceives herself into thinking she is in love with a childhood friend, also named Volodya. In the end, we see her being comforted by an adoptive sister who has become a nun, and who tells her "that all this is of no consequence, that it would all pass and God would forgive her." That the two men have the same name is not the point of the story. Here, as in all Chekhov's work, there is never exactly "a point." Rather, we feel that we are seeing into this woman's heart and what she perceives as her "unbearable misery." That she would be in love—or not in love—with two men named Volodya is simply a fact of her life.

The next week, I suggested to another student that what made her story so confusing was the multiple shifts in point of view. It's only a five-page story, I said. Not *Rashomon*. And that afternoon I read Chekhov's "Gusev," which concerns a sailor who dies at sea. The story begins in the sailor's point of view, then shifts into long stretches of dialogue between him and another dying man. When Gusev dies—another "rule" I was glad I hadn't told my students was that you can't write a story in which the narrator or point-of-view character dies—the perspective shifts to that of the sailors burying him at sea and then to that of the pilot fish who see his body fall, then to the shark who comes to investigate, until finally, as a student of mine once wrote, we feel we are seeing through the eyes of God. It's nearly impossible to describe or summarize the end of this story. So I will quote the last few paragraphs to point out what probably needs no pointing out: how much would have been lost had Chekhov followed the "rules":

> He went rapidly towards the bottom. Did he reach it? It was said to be three miles to the bottom. After sinking sixty or seventy feet, he began moving more and more slowly, swaying rhythmically, as though he were hesitating, and, carried along by the current, moved more rapidly sideways than downwards.

Then he was met by a shoal of the fish called harbour pilots. Seeing the dark body the fish stopped as though petrified, and suddenly turned round and disappeared. In less than a minute they flew back swift as an arrow to Gusev, and began zig-zagging round him in the water.

After that another dark body appeared. It was a shark. It swarmed under Gusev with dignity and no show of interest, as though it did not notice him, and sank down upon its back, then it turned belly upwards, basking in the warm transparent water, and languidly opened its jaws with two rows of teeth. The harbour pilots are delighted, they stop to see what will come next. After playing a little with the body the shark nonchalantly puts its jaws under it, cautiously touches it with its teeth, and the sailcloth is rent its full length from head to foot; one of the weights falls out and frightens the harbour pilots, and, striking the shark on the ribs, goes rapidly to the bottom.

Overhead at this time the clouds are massed together on the side where the sun is setting; one cloud like a triumphal arch, another like a lion, a third like a pair of scissors. . . . From behind the clouds a broad, green shaft of light pierces through and stretches to the middle of the sky; a little later another, violet-coloured, lies beside it; next to that, one gold, then one rose-coloured. The sky turns a soft lilac. Looking at this gorgeous enchanted sky, at first the ocean scowls, but soon it, too, takes on tender, joyous, passionate colours for which it is hard to find a name in human speech.

Around the same time, I told my class that we should, ideally, have some notion of whom or what a story is about—in other words, as they so often say in workshops, whose story is it? To offer the reader that simple knowledge, I said, wasn't really giving much. A little clarity of focus cost the writer nothing and paid off, for the reader, a hundredfold. And it was about this same time that I first read "In the Ravine," in which we don't realize that the peasant girl Lipa is our heroine until almost halfway through. Moreover, the story turns on the death of a baby, just the sort of incident I advise students to stay away from because it is so difficult to write well and without sentimentality. Here—I have no pedagogical excuse to quote this, but am only including it because I so admire it—is the extraordinarily lovely scene in which Lipa plays with her child:

> Lipa spent her time playing with the baby which had been born to her before Lent. It was a tiny, thin, pitiful little baby, and it was strange that it should cry and gaze about and be considered a human being, and even be called Nikifor. He lay in his swinging cradle, and Lipa would walk away towards the door and say, bowing to him: "Good day, Nikifor Anisimitch!"
>
> And she would rush at him and kiss him. Then she would walk away to the door, bow again, and say: "Good day, Nikifor Anisimitch!" And he kicked up his little red legs, and his crying was mixed with laughter like the carpenter Elizarov's.

By now I had learned my lesson. I began telling my class to read Chekhov instead of listening to me. I invoked Chekhov's name so often that a disgruntled student accused me of trying to *make* her write like Chekhov. She went on to tell me that she was sick of Chekhov, that plenty of writers were better than Chekhov, and when I asked her who, she said Thomas Pynchon. I said I thought both writers were very good, suppressing a wild desire to run out in the hall and poll the entire faculty on who was better, Chekhov or Pynchon, and only stopping myself because—or so I'd like to think—the experience of reading Chekhov was proving not merely enlightening, but also humbling.

Still there were some things I thought I knew. A few weeks later I suggested to yet another student that he might want to think twice about having his character pick up a gun in the very last paragraph of his story and blow his head off for no reason. It wasn't that something like that couldn't happen, but it just seemed so unexpected, so melodramatic. Perhaps if he prepared the reader, ever so slightly, hinted that his character was, if not considering suicide, then at least capable of it. A few hours later I got on the bus and read the ending of "Volodya":

> *Volodya put the muzzle of the revolver to his mouth, felt something like a trigger or a spring, and pressed it with his finger. . . . Then he felt something else projecting, and once more pressed it. Taking the muzzle out of his mouth, he wiped it with the lapel of his coat, looked at the lock. He had never in his life taken a weapon in his hand. . . .*
>
> *"I believe one ought to raise this . . ." he reflected. "Yes, it seems so . . ."*
>
> *Volodya put the muzzle in his mouth again, pressed it with his teeth, and pressed something with his fingers. There was the sound of a shot. . . . Something hit Volodya in the back of his head with terrible violence, and he fell on the table with his face downwards among the bottles of glasses. Then he saw his father . . . in a top-hat with a wide black band on it, wearing mourning for some lady, suddenly seize him by both hands, and they fell headlong into a very deep, dark pit.*
>
> *Then everything was blurred and vanished.*

Until that moment we'd had no indication that Volodya was troubled by anything more than the prospect of school exams and an ordinary teenage crush on a flirtatious older woman. Nor had we heard much about his father, except that Volodya blames his frivolous mother for having wasted his father's money.

What seemed at issue here was far more serious than a question of similar names and divergent points of view. For, as anyone who has ever attended a writing class knows, the bottom line of the fiction workshop is motivation. We complain, we criticize, we say that we don't understand why this or that character says or does something. Like Method actors, we ask: What is the motivation? Of course, all this is based on the comforting supposition that things, in fiction as in life, are done for a reason. But here was Chekhov telling us that, as we may have noticed, people often do terrible and irrevocable things for no good reason at all.

No sooner had I assimilated this critical bit of information than I happened to read "A Dull Story," which convinced me that I had been not only overestimating but also oversimplifying the depth and complexities of motivation. How could I have demanded to know exactly how a certain character felt about another character when, as the narrator of "A Dull Story" reveals on every page, our feelings for each other can be elusive, changing, contradictory, hidden in the most clever disguises even from ourselves?

Chekhov was teaching me how to teach, and yet I remained a slow learner. The mistakes and the revelations continued. I had always assumed and probably even said that insanity was not an especially happy state. And maybe this is mostly true, but as Chekhov is always reminding us, "most" is not "all."

For Kovrin, the hero of "The Black Monk," the visits from an imaginary monk are the sweetest and most welcome moments in his otherwise unsatisfactory life. And what about the assumption that, in life and in fiction, a crazy character should "act" crazy, or at least do something that might hint at a certain degree of imbalance? Not Kovrin, who, aside from these hallucinatory attacks and a youthful case of "upset nerves," is a university professor, a husband, a functioning member of society, a man whose consciousness of his own "mediocrity" is relieved only by his conversations with the phantasmagorical monk, who assures him that he is a genius.

Reading another story, "The Husband," I remembered asking: What is the point of writing a story in which everything is rotten and all the characters are terrible and nothing much happens and nothing changes? In "The Husband," Shalikov, the tax collector, watches his wife enjoying a brief moment of pleasure as she dances at a party, has a jealous fit, and blackmails her into leaving the dance and returning to the prison of their shared lives. The story ends:

> *Anna Pavlovna could scarcely walk. . . . She was still under the influence of the dancing, the music, the talk, the lights, and the noise; she asked herself as she walked along why God had thus afflicted her. She felt miserable, insulted, and choking with hate as she listened to her husband's heavy footsteps. She was silent, trying to think of the most offensive, biting, and venomous word she could hurl at her husband, and at the same time she was fully aware that no word could penetrate his tax-collector's hide. What did he care for words? Her bitterest enemy could not have contrived for her a more helpless position.*
>
> *And meanwhile the band was playing, and the darkness was full of the most rousing, intoxicating dance-tunes.*

The "point"—and, again, there is no conventional "point"—is that in just a few pages, the curtain concealing these lives has been drawn back, revealing them in all their helplessness and rage and rancor. The point is that lives go on without change, so why should fiction insist that major reverses should always, conveniently, occur?

And finally, this revelation: In a fit of irritation, I told my class that the sufferings of the poor are more compelling and worthy of our attention than the vague discontents of the rich. So it was with some chagrin that I read "A Woman's Kingdom," a delicate and moving story about a rich, lonely woman—a factory owner, no less—who finds herself attracted to her foreman until a casual remark by a member of her own class awakens her to the impossibility of her situation. By the time I had finished the story, I felt that I had been challenged, not only in my more flippant statements about fiction but also in my most basic assumptions about life. The truth was what Chekhov had seen and what I—with all my fancy talk of observation—had somehow overlooked: If you cut a rich woman, she bleeds just like a poor one. Which isn't to say that Chekhov didn't know and know well: the world being what it is, the poor are cut more often and more deeply.

And now, since we are speaking of life, a brief digression about Chekhov's. By the time Chekhov died of tuberculosis at the age of forty-four, he had written, in addition to his plays, approximately six hundred short stories. He was also a medical doctor. He supervised the construction of clinics and schools, he was active in the Moscow Art Theater, he married the famous actress Olga Knipper, he visited the infamous prison on Sakhalin Island and wrote a book about that. Once, when someone asked him his method of composition, Chekhov picked up an ashtray.

"This is my method of composition," he said. "Tomorrow I will write a story called 'The Ashtray.'"

His letters are filled with revealing and immensely useful reflections on writing in general and, in particular, on the writer's need for objectivity, the importance of seeing clearly, without judgment, certainly without prejudgment, the necessity that the writer be "an unbiased observer."

*That the world "swarms with male and female scum" is
perfectly true. Human nature is imperfect. But to think that*

the task of literature is to gather the pure grain from the muck heap is to reject literature itself. Artistic literature is called so because it depicts life as it really is. Its aim is truth—unconditional and honest. A writer is not a confectioner, not a dealer in cosmetics, not an entertainer; he is a man bound under compulsion, by the realization of his duty and by his conscience. To a chemist, nothing on earth is unclean. A writer must be as objective as a chemist.

It seems to me that the writer should not try to solve such questions as those of God, pessimism, etc. His business is but to describe those who have been speaking or thinking about God and pessimism, how and under what circumstances. The artist should be not the judge of his characters and their conversations, but only an unbiased observer.

You are right in demanding that an artist should take an intelligent attitude to his work, but you confuse two things: solving a problem and stating a problem correctly. It is only the second that is obligatory for the artist.

You abuse me for objectivity, calling it indifference to good and evil, lack of ideas and ideals, and so on. You would have me, when I describe horse thieves, say: "Stealing horses is an evil." But that has been known for ages without my saying so. Let the jury judge them; it's my job simply to show what sort of people they are. I write: you are dealing with horse thieves, so let me tell you that they are not beggars but well-fed people, that they are people of a special cult, and that horse stealing is not simply theft but passion. Of course it would be pleasant to combine art with a sermon, but for me personally it is impossible owing to the conditions of technique. You see, to depict horse thieves in 700 lines I must all the time speak and think in their tone and feel in their spirit. Otherwise, the story will not be as compact as all short stories ought to be. When I write, I reckon entirely upon the reader to add for himself the subjective elements that are lacking in the story.

And now, one final quotation, which, given my record for making statements and having to retract them a week later, struck me with particular force:

> *It is time for writers to admit that nothing in this world makes sense. Only fools and charlatans think they know and understand everything. The stupider they are, the wider they conceive their horizons to be. And if an artist decides to declare that he understands nothing of what he sees—this in itself constitutes a considerable clarity in the realm of thought, and a great step forward.*

Every great writer is a mystery, if only in that some aspect of his or her talent remains forever ineffable, inexplicable, and astonishing. The sheer population of Dickens's imagination, the fantastic architecture Proust constructs out of minutely examined moments. We ask ourselves: How could anyone do that? And of course, different qualities of the work will mystify different people. For me, Chekhov's mystery is first of all one of knowledge: How does he know so much? He knows everything we pride ourselves on having learned, and much more. "The Name Day Party," a story about a pregnant woman, is full of observations about pregnancy that I had thought were secrets known only to pregnant women.

The second mystery is how, without ever being direct, he communicates the fact that he is not describing the world or how people should see the world or how he, Anton Chekhov, sees the world, but only the world that one or another character inhabits for a certain span of time. When the characters are unattractive, we never feel the author hiding behind them, peeking out from around them to say, "This isn't me, this isn't me!" We never feel that Gurov, the hero of "The Lady with the Dog" is Chekhov, though, for all we know, he could be. Rather we feel that we are seeing Gurov's life—and his life transformed. Chekhov is always, as he says in his letters, working from the particular to the general.

But to me the greatest mystery is this matter he keeps alluding to in his letters: the necessity of writing without judgment. Not saying, "Stealing horses is an evil." Not to be the judge of one's characters and their conversations but rather the unbiased observer. Surely, Chekhov didn't live without judgment. I don't know if anyone does, or if it is even possible except for psychotics and Zen monks who've trained themselves to suspend all reflection, moral and otherwise. My sense is that living without judgment is probably a bad idea. Nor, again, is any of this required of the writer. Balzac judged everyone and found nearly all of them wanting; their smallness and the ferocity of his outrage is part of the greatness of his work. But what Chekhov believed and acted on more than any writer I can think of is that judgment and prejudice were incommensurate with a certain kind of literary art. It is why, for reasons I still can't quite explain, his work comforted me in ways that Balzac's simply could not.

Before I finish, I'd like to quote Vladimir Nabokov's summation of his lecture on Chekhov's story "The Lady with the Dog":

> *All the traditional rules of storytelling have been broken in this wonderful story of twenty pages or so. There is no problem, no climax, no point at the end. And it is one of the greatest stories ever written.*
>
> *We will now repeat the different features that are typically for this and other Chekhov tales.*

First: The story is told in the most natural way possible, not beside the after-dinner fireplace as with Turgenev or Maupassant, but in the way one person relates to another the most important things in his life, slowly and yet without a break, in a slightly subdued voice.

Second: Exact and rich characterization is attained by a careful selection and careful distribution of minute but striking features, with perfect contempt for the sustained description, repetition, and strong emphasis of ordinary authors. . . .

Third: There is no special moral to be drawn and no special message to be received.

Fourth: The story is based in a system of waves, on the shades of this or that mood. In Chekhov, we get a world of waves instead of particles of matter.

Sixth: The story does not really end, for as long as people are alive, there is no possible and definite conclusion to their troubles or hopes or dreams.

Seventh: The storyteller seems to keep going out of his way to allude to trifles, every one of which in another type of story would mean a signpost denoting a turn of the action. But just because these trifles are meaningless, they are all-important in giving the real atmosphere of this particular story.

Let me repeat one sentence which seems to me particularly significant. "We feel that for Chekhov the lofty and the base are not different, that the slice of watermelon and the violet sea and the hands of the town governor are essential points of the beauty plus pity of the world." And what I might add to this is: the more Chekhov we read, the more strongly we feel this. I have often thought that Chekhov's stories should not be read singly but as separate parts of a whole. For like life, they present contradictory views, opposing visions. Reading them, we think: How broad life is! How many ways there are to live! In this world, where anything can happen, how much is possible! Our whole lives can change in a moment. Or: Nothing will ever change—especially the fact that the world and the human heart will always be wider and deeper than anything we can fathom.

And this is what I've come to think about what I learned and what I taught and what I should have taught. Wait! I should have said to the class: Come back! I've made a mistake. Forget observation, consciousness, clear-sightedness. Forget about life. Read Chekhov, read the stories straight through. Admit that you understand nothing of life, nothing of what you see. Then go out and look at the world.

ELEVEN

Reading for Courage

WHEN WE THINK ABOUT HOW MANY TERRIFYING THINGS people are called on to do every day as they fight fires, defend their rights, perform brain surgery, give birth, drive on the freeway, and wash skyscraper windows, it seems frivolous, self-indulgent, and self-important to talk about writing as an act that requires courage. What could be safer than sitting at your desk, lightly tapping a few keys, pushing your chair back, and pausing to see what marvelous tidbit of art your brain has brought forth to amuse you?

And yet most people who have tried to write have experienced not only the need for bravery but a failure of nerve as the real or imagined consequences, faults and humiliations, exposures and inadequacies dance before their eyes and across the empty screen or page. The fear of writing badly, of revealing something you would rather keep hidden, of losing the good opinion of the world, of violating your own high standards, or of discovering something about yourself that you would just as soon not know—those are just a few of the phantoms scary enough to make the writer wonder if there might be a job available washing skyscraper windows.

All of which brings up yet another reason to read. Literature is an endless source of courage and confirmation. The reader and beginning writer can count on being heartened by all the brave and original works that have been written without the slightest regard for how strange or risky they were, or for what the writer's mother might have thought when she read them.

Often, when I teach, I like to draw up a reading list composed entirely of masterpieces that, for one reason or another, might have been thoroughly trashed by the more conventional newspaper review or the writing workshop. Much of the work I've mentioned so far in this book might run afoul of some of today's amateur or professional critics. And actually, many things that we *ourselves* consider indispensable for a work of fiction may turn out, the more we read, to be superfluous. If the culture sets up a series of rules that the writer is instructed to observe, reading will show you how these rules have been ignored in the past, and the happy outcome. So let me repeat, once more: literature not only breaks the rules, but makes us realize that there *are none*.

Let's say we've been struggling to find some subtle way of letting our reader know what a character looks like. Should we have Miss X admire her lovely blond hair in the mirror? Or should Mr. Y's neighbor say, "Why, Mr. Y, how blue your eyes look this morning!" Or should we reread *The Marquise of O—* and decide that hair and eye color may be Too Much Information?

But appearance is, as we know, superficial. What about everything that lies beneath the visible façade, the polished veneer? What happens when we return to our desks after attending the literature seminar in which our fellow students have acted like a team of psychiatrists convened in the asylum staff-room to discuss the case and the prognosis of a character in a short story? What are we to think after the workshop in which the author has been asked for a character's lifetime employment résumé? Or after the writers' group in which it is pointed out that we cannot hope to understand anything Mrs. Z. does if we don't know the full history of how she was treated by her mom and dad? What good does it do us to protest that, in life, we are constantly being called upon to figure out why people act the way they do before we hear one word about their childhood? None. All we can conclude is that we have failed at one of the most elemental jobs of the fiction writer.

Alternately, we can read Samuel Beckett's "First Love," in which we learn almost no physical details about the narrator, whose background is equally murky and who stubbornly resists any attempts to judge his personality or his behavior by the standards of anything resembling normality. For all the cues we are given about how to visualize our speaker, his voice could be that of a brain in formaldehyde, talking to us from a jar. Indeed, the story consistently refuses to provide any of the information, the consolations, or the surface niceties of structure and form that we are used to expecting from fiction

The opening paragraph is remarkable for many reasons, one of which is the speed with which it alerts us to the strangeness of the reading experience that lies ahead:

> I associate, rightly or wrongly, my marriage with the death of my father, in time. That other links exist, on other planes, between these two affairs, is not impossible. I have enough trouble in trying to say what I think I know.

The fact that we get sex and death in the very first sentence is the least of it, somehow. What's startling is the voice, as unsettling now as it must have been when the story was written in

1950, though it did not appear in English translation until almost twenty-five years later. By now, we've grown used to seeing, on the page, the operations of human consciousness, the interior rat-tat-tat that monitors and responds to the world. But rarely before (one notable exception is Dostoyevsky) have we heard a voice we recognize from our own darkest hours, our own most uncertain, disassociated, and alienated moments, a mind that, from the opening sentence, begins correcting itself and expressing doubt about the most basic facts. So far the narrator has spent more time telling us what he cannot say and doesn't know than saying what he does know.

If narrative authority comes from our sense that the writer is in control, part of what's so mysterious and encouraging about Beckett is how much authority he achieves in the process of telling us about confusion and doubt. And he manages to make it funny, to make us see the comedy in crankiness, misanthropy, solitude, and despair. We feel that the voice comes from a region of the psyche deeper than self-censorship; it never occurs to the narrator not to tell us, in detail, why he enjoys hanging out in graveyards.

> The smell of corpses, distinctly perceptible under those of grass and humus mingled, I do not find unpleasant, a trifle on the sweet side perhaps, a trifle heady, but how infinitely preferable to what the living emit. . . . And when my father's remains join in, however modestly, I can almost shed a tear. The living wash in vain, in vain perfume themselves, they stink. Yes, as a place for an outing, when out I must, leave me my graveyards and keep—you—to your public parks and beauty spots. My sandwich, my banana, tastes sweeter when I'm sitting on a tomb, and when the time comes to piss again, as it so often does, I have my pick.

By now we will have noticed that one of the things that's holding our attention—in addition to the outrageousness of what's being said—is precision of language, and language's power to create this weirdly fascinating narrator. Sentence by sentence, his personality emerges in one paradoxically schizoid and astute association after another. Nearly everything we hear contradicts whatever impression we have been forming. At one moment, he seems not to know the difference between constipation and diarrhea, and in the next he tells us that he has read romances in six or seven languages, under the guidance of a tutor. However bizarre his thinking might seem, he is a philosopher and a bit of a writer himself, though he is "revolted" by his own writings. He has even composed his own epitaph:

Hereunder lies the above who up below
So hourly died that he survived till now.

The second and last or rather latter line limps a little perhaps, but that is no great matter, I'll be forgiven more than that when I'm forgotten. Then with a little luck you hit on a genuine interment, with real live mourners and the odd relict rearing to throw herself into the pit. And nearly always that charming business with the dust, though in my experience there is nothing less dusty than holes of this type, verging on muck for the most part, nor anything particularly powdery about the deceased, unless he happened to have died, or she, by fire. No matter, their little gimmick with the dust is charming.

By now the reader may be wondering if Beckett worried about what his mum and her friends might think if they read this. Would they decide that Sam was not a *nice person*? We can assume that Beckett, like his mentor Joyce, either put these demons to rest long enough to write, or that the need to drown out their voices provided one reason for writing.

Which brings up a related matter: Is our narrator *sympathetic*?

On this subject, I imagine, readers will disagree. No doubt, many will wish to shut the book and silence the voice of this fellow who tells us far more than we need to know about his bodily fluids, a man who is capable of having such vile thoughts in the graveyard. So what does it say about me that I so enjoy spending time in his company? One of the things it may mean is that I have read to the end of the story, when this exotic individual with such unpleasant attitudes about sex, women, love, and human connection is shown to be capable of feeling recognizably human heartbreak and grief. Or perhaps I find his humor and intelligence attractive, to say nothing of his goofy honesty and his gift of gab. If I consider him sympathetic perhaps it's ultimately because he so often seems to speak in the voice of that secret part of the self that we would just as soon keep quiet.

Not long ago, I met two young writers who had collaborated on a very successful first novel. In the process of publishing it, and a subsequent novel, they were summoned to editing conferences at which, they said, they were constantly being urged to rewrite their characters for greater *likability*.

It's one of the things that writers are most commonly being told these days: their characters should be *likable* and *sympathetic* so the reader can *care* about them. And what does *care* mean, exactly? Too often, I'm afraid, it's being used as a synonym for *identify*. But what's even more unsettling is the possibility that, in order for us to identify with them, characters in modern fiction are supposed to be nice people, like us, having the exact same experiences that we have had. We want to read about a high school student, maybe with a few problems, one who is going through precisely what we went through in high school. Consequently, we sympathize. We identify. We care.

In fact, most writers would like you to identify and sympathize with their characters, even if you don't particularly want to. Tolstoy's *The Death of Ivan Ilych* works its terrifying magic by bringing us in steadily closer to its protagonist, luring us from the safe courthouse steps on which the story begins into the airless confines of Ivan Ilyich's sickroom. As the world drops away in stages, as it does for the dying, we move deeper into its hero's psyche. So that when at last he wonders if he has led his whole life wrongly, the clammy chill we feel comes partly from being compelled to imagine ourselves in a similar situation. And our response has nothing to do with how *nice* Ivan Ilyich is.

It's always gratifying to be moved by a character's fate, even if it means being moved to sadness. I remember how long it took me to get through the last hundred pages of Gabriel García Márquez's *Love in the Time of Cholera*; I kept having to put the book down because my eyes kept welling with tears.

To read the literature of the past is to be reminded that, while we have always cared about, and sympathized with, fictional characters, the *insistence* that we do so is a relatively new one. It would seem absurd to dismiss *Moby Dick* because the standoffish Ishmael never tells us one more word about himself than he absolutely has to. And perhaps we don't know enough about Queequeg's background to care about him? Do we identify with the vengeful, monomaniacal Captain Ahab?

What might hearten the beginning writer who feels compelled to create a succession of puppy-dog heroes and heroines is that masterpieces survive in which all that's expected of us is that we be *interested* in the characters, engaged by their fates, intrigued by their complexities, curious about what will happen to them next. Moreover, as you read these novels, you begin to see that writers have often found it a little too *easy* to make the reader sympathize with characters who are beautiful and true and good, a little too simple to make us care about the innocent and the charitable.

How much more of a challenge it is to attempt what Dostoyevsky accomplished in *Crime and Punishment*. We might not automatically expect to empathize with Raskolnikov, a student who brutally kills two old women. So what an achievement it represents not only to make us care about him but also to find ourselves hoping, just as he does, that he can be redeemed. Reading all of Patricia Highsmith's novels in succession, as I did one summer, provides a sustained, enthralling descent into the dark crannies of the minds of a group of appalling psychopaths. I read one book, and then the next, sorry when I had finished each one. Not for one second did it occur to me to stop reading because so many of her protagonists are not only loners and misfits, but cold-blooded killers. William Trevor is another writer who immerses us in the psyches of the marginal and the demented; the hero of his novel, *The Children of Dynmouth*, is an adolescent voyeur who blackmails his neighbors into helping him fulfill his antisocial desires.

At the same time, reading makes you realize that writers may always have felt that they might be more popular and successful if they stayed away from such unsavory and unpleasantly "real" characters and rewrote for *likability*. Gogol, who himself created a lengthy roll call of eccentrics and oddballs (a man who loses his nose only to see it walking toward him down the street: another whose life is ruined by an overcoat) mused in *Dead Souls* on the very different fates of writers who create angels, and those who describe human beings:

> *Happy is the writer who omits these dull and repulsive characters that disturb one by being so painfully real. . . . The delicious mist of the incense he burns dims human eyes; the miracle of his flattery masks all the sorrows of life and depicts*

only the goodness of man. . . . He is called a great universal poet, soaring high above all other geniuses of the world even as an eagle soars above other high flying creatures. The mere sound of his name sounds a thrill through ardent young hearts; all eyes greet him with radiance and responsive tears . . .

But a different lot and another fate awaits the writer who has dared to evoke all such things that are constantly before one's eyes . . . the shocking morass of trifles that has tied up our lives, and the essence of cold, crumbling, humdrum characters with whom our earthly way, now bitter, now dull, fairly swarms. . . . Not for him will be the applause, no grateful tears will he see . . . not to him will a girl of sixteen come flying, her head all awhirl with heroic fervor. Not for him will be that sweet enchantment when a poet hears nothing but the harmonies he has engendered himself; and finally, he will not escape the judgment of his time, the judgment of hypocritical and unfeeling contemporaries who will accuse the creatures his mind has bred of being base and worthless, will allow a contemptible nook for him in the gallery of those authors who insult mankind, will ascribe to him the morals of his own characters, and will deny him everything, heart, soul, and the divine flame of talent.

Flaubert might have concluded something similar when his Madame Bovary received the following review from the esteemed literary critic Sainte-Beuve: "There is no goodness in the book. Not a character represents it. In these provincial existences, which abound in bickerings, minor persecutions, mean ambitions, and pinpricks of all kinds are also to be found good and beautiful souls . . . why not indicate them, as well? Son and brother of eminent doctors, M. Gustave Flaubert holds the pen as others hold the scalpel. Anatomists and physiologists, I find you on every page!"

Reading can give you the courage to resist all of the pressures that our culture exerts on you to write in a certain way, or to follow a prescribed form. It can even persuade you that it might not be necessary to give your novel or story a happy ending. In Robert Altman's film, *The Player*, a sleazy producer says that what a film needs to get made in Hollywood is "Stars, laughs, violence, nudity, sex, and happy endings. Especially happy endings." And as publishing gets more like Hollywood, or tries, it may become more important to raise the volume of the background music and show the joyous couple united in a kiss. Probably, the happy ending is taken for granted in an editing conference at which the authors are being told to revise for likability. First you create the likable heroine, and then you throw her under a train?

Every so often a book review or literary magazine will ask several authors to rewrite the endings of famous works of literature. Often, these fanciful revisions involve the sort of wishful thinking that rescues the characters from whatever sad fate they meet in the book and instead lets them live happily ever after. Anna Karenina gets over Vronsky, Romeo and Juliet marry and have a couple of kids. And yet the fact is that these endings—the suicide of Anna Karenina, the deaths of Romeo and Juliet—are the endings we remember, as opposed to the happier solution some clever revisionist has suggested. Which doesn't mean that fiction is *better* if it ends in disaster. We want, we deserve, those satisfying marriages that end the novels of Jane Austen.

Nor, you may discover, is it necessary to have an ending in which every loose thread is neatly tied up, every problem resolved, and the characters tracked into the future as far as the mind's eyes can see. To quote Chekhov one more time, here is the ending of "The Lady with the Dog," an ending which, I have always thought, could serve as the final few lines of every work of modern fiction. As the story concludes, the aging adulterous lovers are contemplating their future.

*And it seemed as though in a little while the solution
would be found, and then a new and glorious life would be-
gin; and it was clear to both of them that the end was still far
off, and that what was to be most complicated and difficult for
them was only just beginning.*

Reading can show you how capacious and stretchy fiction
is, how much it can accommodate, and how far it has expanded
beyond the straight and narrow path from point A to point B.
Along with the Beckett story, I like teaching Juan Rulfo's short
novel *Pedro Páramo*. The atmosphere of the book (to say nothing
of its "plot") is as hard to convey as that of a poem, though you
may get some idea of what it is like from the novel's startling
beginning:

*I came to Comala because I was told that my father, a
certain Pedro Páramo, was living here. My mother told me
so, and I promised her I would come to see him as soon as she
died. I pressed her hand so that she'd know I would do it, but
she was dying and I was in the mood to promise her anything.
"Be sure you go and visit him," she told me. "I know he'll be
pleased to see you." So all I could do was to keep telling her I
would do it, and I kept on saying it until I had to pry my hand
loose from her dead fingers.*

*Before that she told me, "Don't ask him for anything that
isn't ours. Just for what he should have given me and didn't.
Make him pay for the way he forgot us."*

"All right, Mother."

*I didn't intend to keep the promise. But then I began to
think about what she told me, until I couldn't stop think-
ing and even dreaming about it, and building a whole world
around that Pedro Páramo. That's why I came to Comala.*

It was in the dog-days, when the hot August wind is poi-

soned by the rotten smell of the saponaria, and the road went up and down, up and down. They say a road goes up or down depending on whether you're coming or going. If you're going away it's uphill, but it's downhill if you are coming back.

"What's the name of that village down there?"

"Comala, señor."

"You're sure it's Comala?"

"Yes, señor."

"Why does it look so dead?"

"They've had bad times, señor."

I expected it to look the way it did in my mother's memories. She was always sighing for Comala, she was homesick and wanted to come back, but she never did. Now I was coming back in her place, and I remembered what she told me: "There's a beautiful view when you get to Los Colimotes. You'll see a green plain. . . . It's yellow when the corn is ripe. You can see Comala from there. The houses are all white, and at night it's all lighted up." Her voice was soft and secret, almost a whisper, as if she were talking to herself.

"And why are you going to Comala?" *I heard him ask me.*

"To see my father."

"Oh," *he said.*

And we were silent again.

We were walking downhill, hearing the steady trot of the burros. Our eyes were half-closed, we were so tired and sleepy in the August heat.

"They'll give you a fine party," *he said.* "They'll be glad to see somebody again. It's been years since anybody came here."

Then he added: "It's you, so they'll be glad to see you."

The heat shimmered on the plain like a transparent lake. There was a line of mountains beyond the plain, and beyond that, nothing but the distance.

"What does your father look like?"

"I don't know," I said. "I just know that he's called Pedro Páramo."

"Oh."

But the way he said it, it was almost like a gasp. I said, "At least that's what they told me his name was."

I heard him say, "Oh," again.

I met him in Los Encuentros, where three or four roads come together. I was just waiting there, and finally he came by with his burros.

"Where are you going?" I asked him.

"That way, señor," he said, pointing.

"Do you know where Comala is?"

"That's where I'm going."

So I followed him. I walked along behind, keeping up with his steps, until he understood I was following him and slowed down a little. After that we walked side by side, almost touching shoulders.

He said, "Pedro Páramo is my father too."

A flock of crows flew across the empty sky, crying caw, caw, caw.

After we crossed the ridge we started downhill again. We left the warm air up there and walked down into pure heat without a breath of air in it. Everything looked as if it were waiting for something.

"It's hot here," I said.

"This is nothing. Just wait, you'll be a lot hotter when you get to Comala. That town's the hottest place in the world. They say when somebody dies in Comala, after he arrives in Hell he goes back to get his blanket."

"Do you know Pedro Páramo?" I asked him. I dare to ask him questions because I had an idea I could trust him.

"Who is he?" I asked.

"He's hate. He's just pure hate."

He lashed the burros even though he didn't need to, because they were keeping ahead of us down the slope.

I had my mother's picture in my shirt pocket and I could feel it warming my heart, as if she were sweating too. It was an old picture, all frayed at the edges, but it was the only one I knew about. I found it in the kitchen in a box full of herbs, and I've kept it ever since. My mother hated to have her picture taken. She said pictures were for witchcraft, and maybe she was right, because the picture was full of holes, like needle holes. Near the heart there was a hole so big you could put your middle finger into it.

It's the same picture that I have with me now. I hope it'll help me with Pedro Páramo when he recognizes who it is.

"Look," he said, stopping. "See that mountain, the one that looks like a pig's bladder? Good. Now look over there. See that ridge of that mountain? Now look over there. See that mountain way off there? Well, all that's the Media Luna, everything you can see. And it all belongs to Pedro Páramo. He's our father, but we were born on a petate on the floor. And the real joke is that he took every one of us to be baptized. He took you didn't he?"

"I don't know."

"You go to hell."

"What did you say?"

"I said we are almost there, señor."

"I know. But what about the village? It looks deserted."

"That isn't how it looks. It is. Nobody lives there any more."

"And Pedro Páramo?"

"Pedro Páramo died a long time ago."

Reading even this brief passage, you may begin to intuit one of the odd things about the novel, which is that you don't exactly know if its characters are living or dead, or if it makes any difference. Throughout, the twists and turns in the road keep coming as fast as they do in this section, upsetting whatever we thought we knew about the novel's premise or its characters, causing us to rethink such basic questions as whether the inhabitants of Comala are fantasies or real, presences or memories. Saying this risks making the novel sound like a work of science fiction or magical realism, which it is not. It is a work of art, and there is nothing else like it.

But the first chapter of *Pedro Páramo* will not necessarily help you during a bad writing day, or after a few days in which you are constantly fighting what William Burroughs described as the temptation to tear up your work in little pieces and throw it in someone else's wastepaper basket. And reading a masterpiece may be even less of a consolation when you first figure out, or are reminded for the thousandth time, of how much *work* writing is, of how much patience and solitude it demands from the writer who wants to write well, and of how the compulsion to spend long hours writing can deform a "normal" life. And, as awful as they are, these doubts and terrors pale beside the question of whether your writing will be any good, or of whether you will succeed enough to be able to do it in the first place. Those are the moments when it can help to read the lives and letters of great writers.

In the same interview in which he talks about the lightning flash of the paragraph break, Isaac Babel has this to say about the hard labor of revision:

> "I work like a pack mule, but it's my own choice. I'm like a galley slave who's chained for life to his oar but who loves the oar. Everything about it . . . I go over each sentence, time and again. I start by cutting all the words it can do without. You have to keep your eye on the job because words are very sly, the rubbishy ones go into hiding and you have to dig them out—repetitions, synonyms, things that simply don't mean

anything. . . . I go over every image, metaphor, comparison, to see if they are fresh and accurate. If you can't find the right adjective for a noun, leave it alone. Let the noun stand by itself. A comparison must be as accurate as a slide rule, and as natural as the smell of fennel. . . . I take out all the participles and adverbs I can. . . . Adverbs are lighter. They can even lend you wings in a way. But too many of them make the language spineless. . . . A noun needs only one adjective, the choicest. Only a genius can afford two adjectives to one noun. . . . Line is as important in prose as in an engraving. It has to be clear and hard. . . . But the most important thing of all . . . is not to kill the story by working on it. Or else all your labor has been in vain. It's like walking a tight-rope. Well, there it is. . . . We ought all to take an oath not to mess up our job."

Babel's literary career coincided with the height of Stalin's madness. The attention his work attracted was, by definition, too much, and he may have hastened his own doom by having some kind of writerly research-flirtation with the secret police. Under pressure from the government to be a mouthpiece for party propaganda (in an address to the 1934 Soviet Writers Congress, he praised Stalin's literary style), he wrote less and less. He referred to himself in one speech as a master of the art of silence. In 1939 he was arrested by the secret police and died (it was said) in a labor camp, a few years later. Now we know that Babel was never sent to a labor camp, but was shot in prison after his arrest, a fact that the government hid from his family until decades later.

It does seem like quite a price to pay for the freedom to sit in your room and think about metaphors and paragraph breaks. But Babel's crime and his punishment had something to do with the fact that art implies a kind of freedom, the freedom of choice, of possibility, of the individual imagination. Which is why dictators—and big corporations—tend not to like art and artists, except those of a highly predictable and malleable sort. If art demanded Babel's life, we can certainly handle whatever inconvenience or effort it seems to require from us.

Isaac Bashevis Singer once said, "If Tolstoy lived across the street, I wouldn't go meet him." And you know what he means. The work is the work, what exists on the page is what matters, and we need not have tea with the writer in order to understand and love the writing. But whether or not we can understand and love Tolstoy's work without meeting him, there is much that is heartening about his life. To read his biography is to watch a writer destroying the printer's plates of *Anna Karenina* because he wanted to make some last-minute revisions, and one who had started out imagining the novel as something more in the manner of a sermon against an adulterous woman. The less admirable parts of his biography—the long, nightmarish marriage, the selfish ideologue he became, the cruel (to his family) way he chose to die—also have a strangely liberating aspect: how orderly and thoughtful our own lives seem, by comparison.

Nor do you have to go meet Flaubert to read his letters and be warmed by the heat of the obsessive mania he expended on every detail of *Madame Bovary*, as he struggled with the feeling that he was "like a man playing the piano with leaden balls attached to his fingers." His correspondence is a litany of suffering and complaint, like the following: "I feel as dreary as a corpse, completely stupefied. My accursed *Bovary* torments and confounds me. . . . There are moments when it all makes me want to die like a dog." In Dostoyevsky's letters, you can hear him realizing that he has just wasted a year of his life on something that was no good. And you can read the Flannery O'Connor letters in which she finally gives in and goes to Lourdes because her mother is hoping for a miracle to cure O'Connor's multiple sclerosis. When she gets there, she winds up praying that her novel will go well. Like the work of these writers, such details provide little jolts of inspiration, that is, if you are a person who finds the torment of others inspiring.

Reading can even offer the writer courage during those moments when (given how much suffering there is in the world, the dangers looming around us) the very act of writing itself begins to seem suspect. Who can be saved by a terrific sonnet? Whom can we feed with a short story?

At times, questions such as those have sent me straight to Czeslaw Milosz's translation of Zbigniew Herbert's poem "Five Men."

1.
They take them out in the morning
to the stone courtyard
and put them against the wall

five men
two of them very young
the others middle-aged
nothing more
can be said about them

2.
when the platoon
level their guns
everything suddenly appears
in the garish light
of obviousness

the yellow wall
the cold blue
the black wire on the wall
instead of a horizon

that is the moment
when the five senses rebel
they would gladly escape
like rats from a sinking ship

before the bullet reaches its destination
the eye will perceive the flight of the projectile
the ear record the steely rustle

the nostrils will be filled with biting smoke
a petal of blood will brush the palate
the touch will shrink and then slacken
now they lie on the ground
covered up to their eyes with shadow
the platoon walks away
their buttonstraps
and steel helmets
are more alive
than those lying beside the wall

3.
I did not learn this today
I knew it before yesterday

so why have I been writing
unimportant poems on flowers
what did the five talk of
the night before the execution
of prophetic dreams
of an escapade in a brothel
of automobile parts
of a sea voyage
of how when he had spades

he ought not to have opened
of how vodka is best
after wine you get a headache
of girls
of fruits
of life
thus one can use in poetry
names of Greek shepherds
one can attempt to catch the colour of morning sky
write of love
and also
once again
in dead earnest
offer to the betrayed world
a rose

Recently, a friend told me that her fears and concerns about the current state of the world were making it hard for her to write. I e-mailed her a copy of Herbert's poem and suggested it might help her problem, perhaps just a little.

A few hours later, she called back. "But that *is* the problem," she said. "He's talking about a rose. But how do you know if you've created a rose—or just a weed?"

She's right. That *is* the problem. So one final reason for reading is to confront this problem of roses versus weeds in the company of geniuses, and with the pleasure of looking at the roses that have actually been produced, against all odds. If we want to write, it makes sense to read—and to read like a writer. If we wanted to grow roses, we would want to visit rose gardens and try to see them the way that a rose gardener would.

BOOKS TO BE READ IMMEDIATELY

Akutagawa, Ryunosuke. M. Kuwata and Tashaki Kojima (translators), *Rashomon and Other Stories*
Alcott, Louisa May, *Little Women*
Anonymous. Dorothy L. Sayers (translator), *The Song of Roland*
Austen, Jane, *Pride and Prejudice*
Austen, Jane, *Sense and Sensibility*
Babel, Isaac. Walter Morrison (translator), *The Collected Stories*
Baldwin, James, *Vintage Baldwin*
Balzac, Honoré de. Kathleen Raine (translator), *Cousin Bette*
Barthelme, Donald, *Sixty Stories*
Baxter, Charles, *Believers: A Novella and Stories*
Beckett, Samuel, *The Complete Short Prose, 1929–1989*
Bowen, Elizabeth, *The House in Paris*
Bowles, Jane, *Two Serious Ladies*
Bowles, Paul, *Paul Bowles: Collected Stories and Later Writings*
Brodkey, Harold, *Stories in an Almost Classical Mode*
Brontë, Emily, *Wuthering Heights*
Calvino, Italo, *Cosmicomics*
Carver, Raymond, *Where I'm Calling From: Selected Stories*

Carver, Raymond, *Cathedral*

Cervantes, Miguel De. Tobias Smollett (translator), *Don Quixote*

Chandler, Raymond, *The Big Sleep*

Cheever, John, *The Stories of John Cheever*

Chekhov, Anton. Constance Garnett (translator), *A Life in Letters*

Chekhov, Anton. Constance Garnett (translator), *Tales of Anton Chekhov: Volumes 1–13*

Diaz, Junot, *Drown*

Dickens, Charles, *Bleak House*

Dickens, Charles, *Dombey and Son*

Dostoyevsky, Fyodor. Constance Garnett (translator), *Crime and Punishment*

Dybek, Stuart, *I Sailed With Magellan*

Eisenberg, Deborah, *The Stories (So Far) of Deborah Eisenberg*

Eliot, George, *Middlemarch*

Elkin, Stanley, *Searches and Seizures*

Fitzgerald, F. Scott, *The Great Gatsby*

Fitzgerald, F. Scott, *Tender Is the Night*

Flaubert, Gustave. Geoffrey Wall (translator), *Madame Bovary*

Flaubert, Gustave. Robert Baldick (translator), *A Sentimental Education*

Fox, Paula. Jonathan Franzen (introduction), *Desperate Characters*

Franzen, Jonathan, *The Corrections*

Gallant, Mavis, *Paris Stories*

Gaddis, William, *The Recognitions*

Gates, David, *The Wonders of the Invisible World: Stories*

Gibbon, Edward, *Decline and Fall of the Roman Empire*

Gogol, Nikolai. Richard Pevear and Larissa Volokhonsky (translators), *Dead Souls: A Novel*

Green, Henry, *Doting*

Green, Henry, *Loving*

Hartley, L. P., *The Go-Between*

Hemingway, Ernest, *A Moveable Feast*

Hemingway, Ernest, *The Sun Also Rises*

Herbert, Zbigniew. Czeslaw Milosz and Peter Dale Scott (translators), *Selected Poems*

James, Henry, *The Portrait of a Lady*

James, Henry, *The Turn of the Screw*

Jarrell, Randall, *Pictures from an Institution*

Johnson, Denis, *Angels*

Johnson, Denis, *Jesus' Son*

Johnson, Diane, *Le Divorce*

Johnson, Diane, *Persian Nights*

Johnson, Samuel, *The Life of Savage*

Joyce, James, *Dubliners*

Kafka, Franz. Malcolm Pasley (translator), *The Judgment* and *In the Penal Colony* and *Metamorphosis and Other Stories*

Kafka, Franz. Willa and Edmund Muir (translators), *The Trial*

Le Carré, John, *A Perfect Spy*

Mandelstam, Nadezdha, *Hope Against Hope: A Memoir*

Mansfield, Katherine, *Collected Stories of Katherine Mansfield*

Márquez, Gabriel García. Gregory Rabassa (translator), *One Hundred Years of Solitude*

Márquez, Gabriel García. Gregory Rabassa (translator), *The Autumn of the Patriarch*

McInerney, Jay, *Bright Lights, Big City*

Melville, Herman, *Bartleby the Scrivener* and *Benito Cereno*

Melville, Herman, *Moby Dick*

Milton, John, *Paradise Lost*

Munro, Alice, *Selected Stories*

Nabokov, Vladimir, *Lectures on Russian Literature*

Nabokov, Vladimir, *Lolita*

O'Brien, Tim, *The Things They Carried*

O'Connor, Flannery, *A Good Man Is Hard to Find and Other Stories*

O'Connor, Flannery, *Collected Stories*

O'Connor, Flannery, *Wise Blood*

Packer, ZZ, *Drinking Coffee Elsewhere*

Paustovsky, Konstantin. Joseph Barnes (translator), *Years of Hope: The Story of a Life*

Price, Richard, *Freedomland*

Proust, Marcel. Lydia Davis (translator), *Swann's Way*

Pynchon, Thomas, *Gravity's Rainbow*

Richardson, Samuel, *Pamela: Or Virtue Rewarded*

Roth, Philip, *American Pastoral*

Roth, Philip, *Philip Roth: Novels and Stories 1959–1962*

Rulfo, Juan. Margaret Sayers Peden (translator), *Pedro Páramo*

Salinger, J. D., *Franny and Zooey*

Shakespeare, William, *King Lear*

Shteyngart, Gary, *The Russian Debutante's Handbook*

Sophocles. Sir George Young (translator), *Oedipus Rex*

Spencer, Scott, *A Ship Made of Paper*

St. Aubyn, Edward, *Mother's Milk*

St. Aubyn, Edward, *Some Hope: A Trilogy*

Stead, Christina, *The Man Who Loved Children*

Steegmuller, Francis, *Flaubert and Madame Bovary: A Double Portrait*

Stein, Gertrude, *The Autobiography of Alice B. Toklas*

Stendhal. Roger Gard (translator), *The Red and the Black*

Stout, Rex, *Plot It Yourself*

Strunk, William and E. B. White. Maira Kalman (illustrator), *The Elements of Style, Illustrated*

Taylor, Peter, *A Summons to Memphis*

Tolstaya, Tatyana, *Sleepwalker in a Fog*

Tolstoy, Leo. Constance Garnett (translator), *Anna Karenina*

Tolstoy, Leo. Aylmer Maude (translator), *The Death of Ivan Ilych and Other Stories*

Tolstoy, Leo. David McDuff (translator), *The Kreutzer Sonata and Other Stories*

Tolstoy, Leo. Rosemary Edmonds (translator), *Resurrection*

Tolstoy, Leo. Constance Garnett (translator), *War and Peace*

Trevor, William, *The Children of Dynmouth*

Trevor, William, *The Collected Stories*

Trevor, William, *Fools of Fortune*

Turgenev, Ivan Sergeevich. Isaiah Berlin (translator), *First Love*

Twain, Mark, *The Adventures of Huckleberry Finn*

Von Kleist, Heinrich. Martin Greenberg (translator) and Thomas Mann (preface), *The Marquise of O— and Other Stories*

West, Rebecca, *The Birds Fall Down*

West, Rebecca, *Black Lamb and Grey Falcon: A Journey Through Yugoslavia*

Williams, Joy, *Escapes*

Woods, James, *Broken Estate: Essays on Literature and Belief*

Woolf, Virginia, *On Being Ill*

Yates, Richard, *Revolutionary Road*

ACKNOWLEDGMENTS

WRITING THIS BOOK, I OFTEN JOKED THAT I FELT LIKE Tom Sawyer painting the fence, conning a number of my friends and fellow writers into helping me, or actually, doing the work. Throughout, I've drawn on their experience and wisdom, quoted them, and told their stories, without naming them or giving them proper credit. So I'd like to thank them by name, not only for their advice and suggestions, but for the friendship and for the support that makes it possible to keep on painting the fence. Thank you, Russell Banks, Deborah Eisenberg, David Gates, Richard Price, Charles Simic, Scott Spencer, Mark Strand.

About the author

About the book

Insights,
Interviews
& More . . .

Read on

Meet Francine Prose

© Lisa Yuskavage

FRANCINE PROSE was born and raised in Brooklyn, New York. The daughter of two physicians, she experienced literacy at an early age. "I was a big reader—that's what I did, I just read all the time," she says. "I learned to read before I went to kindergarten, so that was sort of a problem. I started off in a big public school, and I was probably a pain in the ass because I was bored. I loved to read, but my early years in school weren't that great because of it." Her reading was fairly unsystematic. "I read anything I could get my hands on. I didn't know there was such a thing as good books, so I read all the children's classics. As I got older I would read these big crappy novels—I didn't care . . . I would just read anything. I would read the back of a cereal box, it didn't matter."

She wrote stories and poems during high school. The summer of her fifteenth year was the occasion of her most unusual job. "My father was a pathologist, and he got me a job as lab assistant in the Bellevue morgue," she says. "I worked next door to the autopsy room, and

" My father was a pathologist, and he got me a job as lab assistant in the Bellevue morgue. "

I loved it. It was my favorite job, ever, because that was when the medical examiner's office was still at Bellevue. There were people there who knew the history of murders in New York in a kind of firsthand way, and who loved talking to me because I had never heard their stories before. It was just a great job."

She attended college at Radcliffe (1964–1968), where she majored in English and completed her reading and writing assignments quickly enough to enjoy an uncommon amount of leisure time. ("I've always been able to write fairly quickly.") Her alma mater, she recalled in a *New York Times* Op-Ed, was a place where "a genteel girls'-school ethos prevailed, enforcing a baroque set of rules about curfews and male visitors, strictures not imposed on our luckier pals at Harvard. We were not allowed to wear jeans on the ground floor of the dorm, where we attended high teas. . . . By the time I left Cambridge, drugs had replaced pre-dinner sherry, and female students broke curfew to occupy University Hall during an anti-Vietnam demonstration."

She attended Harvard graduate school for one year and soon thereafter began work on her first novel. "I was so unemployable," she says. "I just wasn't good at anything else." *Judah the Pious* was published in 1973. "[T]hings were different then," she wrote in an online chat sponsored by the *Washington Post*. "There were more small publishing houses. I wrote [the novel] and sent it to an editor who was a friend of a friend. The fee was $1,000 which seemed like a fortune then."

She developed an intense literary routine. Indeed, there is a fearful point of agreement ▶

> **❝** There is a fearful point of agreement between her surname and her career, the output of which includes not only fiction but criticism, translation, travel writing, and reportage—from children's books to controversial polemics. **❞**

between her surname and her career, the output of which includes not only fiction but criticism, translation, travel writing, and reportage—from children's books to controversial polemics.

"Francine Prose is a keen observer," noted *The Atlantic Monthly*, "and her fiction is full of wryly delivered truths and sardonic witticisms that come from paying close attention to the world. . . . But Prose's fiction does not ease into a fashionable cynicism; instead, it tends toward irony with heart." Her journalism, added the periodical, "covers a remarkably wide range of contemporary topics. . . . Very little . . . escapes her sharply honed perceptions."

Her second career, teaching, took her to Utah, Arizona, and Iowa. She has recently taught in New York, at the New School and Bard. She told the *Toronto Star* about one exceptional hindrance to an otherwise agreeable profession. "He [her student] was just out to give me a bad time. Everything I said, he contradicted—if I said 'black' he said 'white.' Finally, after the third class—and it was exhausting—I called him up and said to him, 'It's perfectly fine with me to fight with you for the entire semester but the thing is, a lot of your fellow students have paid money to attend this class and they're not really here to listen to you argue with me. I'll make a deal with you. I'll give you an 'A' if you don't show up.' . . . The funny thing is that he did show up later, and he was as good as gold. Perfectly co-operative. He was just looking for a showdown."

Of her physical appearance, *Los Angeles*

Times book critic Susan Salter Reynolds once observed: "Prose looks like a cross between (Virginia) Woolf and Frida Kahlo, which perhaps adds to the impression of intellectual ferocity."

Does she have any writerly quirks? "Like most writers," she says, "I'm a real perfectionist. Last night I woke up at two a.m. because I realized I had sent off an essay and had made the plural of a word completely wrong—I was horrified." Anything else? "I love my computers. I just completely love them, they're the love of my life. . . . I play a lot of computer solitaire. You know what? I could, without thinking for half a second, tell you about a half dozen writers I know who are completely addicted. Computer solitaire—it's the dirty little secret of the literary world."

Do any beverages stimulate her writing? "I have to have very strong coffee."

Her enthusiasms are many. "I write about art a lot," she says. "My husband is a painter. I have a huge garden. Right now I have this gourmet agrobiz vegetable garden, and so I work in that a lot. This year it just swelled to such incredible proportions that I really could have had a farm stand if I wanted. We're growing soy beans and fava beans and tiny little yellow-and-green pinwheel squashes. There are chickens and roosters."

The mother of two adult sons, she lives in New York with her husband; they divide their time between the city and the country. ⌒

> ❝Computer solitaire—it's the dirty little secret of the literary world.❞

Reading and Writing
A Conversation with Francine Prose

The following interview, conducted by Jessica Murphy, appeared in The Atlantic online, July 18, 2006.

The title of your new book, Reading Like a Writer: A Guide for People Who Love Books and for Those Who Want to Write Them, *indicates that your audience is twofold. Why did you decide to address both readers and aspiring writers?*

If I had to really characterize the book I'd say it's about the pleasure of reading and about learning to write. I gave the book in galleys to this wonderful young writer, maybe the second or third person to see it at that stage, and he read it and said to me, "It's like Harold Bloom, but written by and for human beings." And that made me so happy. It's what I had in mind. That is—Bloom's obvious passion for literature, but on a more human, approachable, engaged level; less lofty but, I would like to think, not especially less intelligent.

I'm considering using it for one of my writing classes.

Yeah, well that's my hope. It really is my hope that people will use it in classes—and not just for the obvious reasons. For me, writing this

> 66 I gave the book in galleys to this wonderful young writer, and he read it and said to me, 'It's like Harold Bloom, but written by and for human beings.' 99

book was a pretty passionate endeavor. What I'm hoping is that some of that passion gets through. Because it seems to me that the most important thing in any discussion of reading and writing is that *intense* commitment to the whole process.

While I was preparing for this interview, I noticed that you were interviewed for The Atlantic *in 1998 by Katie Bolick. You said in that conversation that you became a writer because you were an avid reader and that you were often perplexed by the fact that some of your students who wanted to be writers weren't reading—or weren't reading passionately.*

That hasn't gotten any better, let me tell you. In fact, I can look back and identify a few incidents that led up to my writing the book. Several of them took place in classrooms. In one instance, I was at a graduate MFA colloquium and a student asked me, "How do you spell Turgenev?" And I thought, *Uh-oh. We're in trouble here.* Another time, in yet another graduate classroom, the students asked, as they sometimes do, "What are you reading?" I said, "I'm rereading *Crime and Punishment.*" And there's this feeling you get when there's nothing coming back at you from the room. That's the feeling I was getting. So I said, "Have any of you read *Crime and Punishment*?" Silence. "Have any of you read anything by Dostoevsky?" More silence. And these were *graduate* students.

I don't quite get it. On a very basic level, I can't figure out why people would want to write unless they like to read. I mean, what ▶

> ❝ So I said, 'Have any of you read *Crime and Punishment*?' Silence. 'Have any of you read anything by Dostoevsky?' More silence. And these were *graduate* students. ❞

would be the point? For the incredibly glamorous fast track lifestyle? I don't think so.

Do you think that reading is not being stressed enough in MFA programs, or is it something that's happening before that?

I think it's happening before that. In most MFA programs, or certainly the ones I've taught at, there's usually a literature seminar that goes along with the writing workshop. One of the sad things that I think partly accounts for the decline of the audience for reading and books is that people aren't being encouraged to read for pleasure. As I say somewhere in the book, book clubs have had both a positive and negative effect. On the one hand, they do get people reading and talking about reading. But on the other hand, when you're reading for a book club, the whole time you're thinking, *I have to have an opinion and I'm going to have to defend it to these people.* The whole notion of being swept away by a book pretty much goes out the window.

I've noticed that high school students can have a certain resistance to reading if it's something that's imposed on them, whereas if they can discover a book on their own, they're more apt to be passionate about reading and to love the book.

I think it's partly that teachers are teaching books that they themselves find boring to students who are bored by them. And they're teaching them in a way that bores the students. It's just this cycle of boredom that goes on and on and round and round. Whereas reading is the least boring thing you can do. It's so engaging and it's so endlessly satisfying, really. The idea of it becoming associated in people's minds with tedium is kind of tragic.

This raises the question about "how" to read. There have been any number of people who have weighed in on this. Joyce Carol Oates, in her essay "To a Young Writer," advises aspiring writers to read without design. Elizabeth Bishop, in one of her letters to a young writer, advised reading everything by a certain poet and then moving on—starting with the past and progressing to one's contemporaries. What's your advice on the "how"?

I think the most important thing—and it's what I say in the book over and over—is to focus on what's directly in front of you on the page; to read especially for the language. Too often students are being taught to read as if literature were some kind of ethics class or civics class—or worse, some kind of self-help manual. In fact, the important thing is the way the writer uses the language. I think there are writers who would be read more—and, conversely, writers who would never be read at all—if people actually looked at how well or how badly they wrote. In most cases, I would rather read something that's written ▶

> " Too often students are being taught to read as if literature were some kind of ethics class or civics class—or worse, some kind of self-help manual. In fact, the important thing is the way the writer uses the language. "

Reading and Writing: A Conversation with Francine Prose *(continued)*

beautifully and doesn't grapple with grand themes than something apparently slighter that actually has a kind of marvelous and fresh and invigorating approach to the language.

You begin Reading Like a Writer *with the age-old, often very divisive question: Can creative writing be taught? I wonder if you might expound on what you get into in the book and why, in your view, this is a particularly difficult question to answer.*

Well, I think certain things can be taught. I think editing can be taught. Once you've written something, it's very hard to assess what you've done. But the first time or the second time or the fourth time that someone says to you, "Look, you don't need these ten words; one word will do perfectly well," or, "This whole sentence or this whole paragraph can be cut," that's a learning experience, and it's certainly the most important thing that can be taught in a writing class. I also think you can teach writing through literature. You can say, "Look, James Joyce has written the greatest party scene that has ever been written," or "Tolstoy has written the most marvelous horse racing scene. And if it happens to be that you want to write a party scene or a horse racing scene, you might want to go look and see how geniuses have done it and take a lesson." But can talent be taught? I don't think so.

I cringed when I read this passage in your book: "Imagine . . . Kafka enduring the seminar in which his classmates inform him that, frankly, they just don't believe the part about the guy waking up one morning to find he's a giant bug." As someone who's been through an MFA program, I can just hear that happening. It's frightening! People often make the claim that one of the dangers of the workshop setting is that it produces cookie-cutter stories, and styles that are too similar, or too similar to the tastes of the instructor. Have you seen this happen? How, as a teacher of writing, do you avoid it?

For one thing, I think that the idea of writing by committee, or learning to write by committee is insanity. It's just simply insanity. I mean, writing is a very solitary process. It's all about being different from everything else—not the same. So when you're writing to satisfy the tastes of a group, and presumably you know those tastes after a while, that's actually quite dangerous. One of the things I do when I'm teaching a literature class to MFA students—and I much prefer teaching a literature class to a writing workshop—is make up a reading list based on masterpieces that would just wither and die in a workshop setting. Things like Beckett's *First Love* or "The Metamorphosis." The list is endless. You can just hear the workshop saying something like, "I think we should know what his mother looked like." When I'm teaching one of these classes I actually can't stop myself from ▶

66 I think that the idea of writing by committee, or learning to write by committee is insanity. It's just simply insanity. I mean, writing is a very solitary process. It's all about being different from everything else—not the same. 99

saying the things that I imagine would be said
about the books in a workshop, and this kind
of whining, querulous tone creeps into my
voice.

***Would you advise a young writer to go to
an MFA program or would you say that
thoughtful reading is a better way to go?***

I'll tell you quite frankly what I would advise:
If you're getting money or some kind of
scholarship, I would go without a question,
because it gives you two years to write. That's
two years where you don't have to wait tables;
two years to take your work seriously. And if
you're really gifted, it's pretty hard to lose that
in the course of a workshop. On the other
hand—and perhaps I shouldn't say this
because so many of my friends, and I myself
at many points, have been so dependent on
workshops for making a living—if you're
going to spend two years [in an MFA
program] and come out the other end $80,000
in the hole, I'd think a million times before
doing it. But an MFA program does do many
things for you. You do form a community. I
have friends now who are even older than
I am who went to the Iowa Writers' Workshop
before I even knew there was such a thing
as a workshop, and who studied with John
Berryman and Donald Justice and other great
writers, and who made friends who they're
still friends with forty years later. That
seems to me invaluable. You make lifelong
friendships, and you find people who will be

> 66 If you're
> going to spend
> two years [in an
> MFA program]
> and come out the
> other end $80,000
> in the hole, I'd
> think a million
> times before
> doing it. 99

your readers long after you're out of the workshop—people whose voices and opinions you depend on. But that's quite different from taking everything that every idiot in your class says seriously.

Why do you prefer teaching literature to the fiction workshop?

Well, in literature workshops the writer isn't in the room. In many cases, the writer isn't in the world at all anymore, so Tolstoy isn't going to get his feelings hurt by what gets said about his work in my class. Beyond that, I only pick things that I think are masterpieces and have been around for hundreds of years for a reason. They can be learned from and can fill you with a desire to write and to be part of whatever universe those works exist in. Also, I would like to flatter myself that if for whatever reason, God forbid, a student comes out of an MFA program and doesn't become a writer, he or she will still know better how to read as a result of having been in my class. So I don't feel those twinges of conscience that I sometimes feel in a fiction workshop, teaching young writers who may not end up becoming writers.

How do your students respond to the close reading that you do? At one point in your book you mention that in some of your classes you've only gotten through two pages in a two-hour class because you've been going over it so closely. ▶

You'd think it would be the most tedious thing that ever happened. You would really imagine that this would be the most boring class you've ever taken in your entire life. But in fact, it's surprisingly lively because students kind of "get it" right away. When you're doing a John Cheever story and looking at the brilliance of each word choice and how much every sentence is telling you without *telling* you and—that dreadful word—"unpacking" a sentence for what it communicates, there's something kind of exhilarating about it and energizing. Four or five weeks into every semester I find myself thinking—*Oh my God they're so smart, I had no idea they were all such geniuses*—because it's something that you just *get* how to do. It's a great thing to see happen in students, undergraduates too. It's equally, if not more exhilarating, to teach undergraduates because in most cases they haven't been taught to read that way, and it's thrilling for them. I'd be equally happy teaching a class in an old age home, because it's not as if it's some special arcane thing that only someone who wants to write can do. In fact, anyone who loves to read might be incredibly relieved to be told, "Look, pay attention to the language. You don't have to have this grand opinion and you don't have to read this with a view to figuring out how the writer screwed up in some way." It's just about the pleasure of language.

I had to laugh as I was reading the many workshop classroom scenes in your novel

> When you're doing a John Cheever story and looking at the brilliance of each word choice and how much every sentence is telling you without *telling* you[,] there's something kind of exhilarating about it and energizing.

14

Blue Angel. *It seemed the perfect match to looking at* **Reading Like a Writer.**

Well, you know that's the writing class from hell. It's the worst-case scenario. Some of those students were based on students I had— but from over many years. I just basically took the most difficult students I'd ever had and put them all in the same class, the most personality disordered, the most dysfunctional.

The writing workshop and the way it's structured, is something that's pretty easy to poke fun at. When Swenson, the writing teacher in **Blue Angel,** *is trying to stop someone from ripping somebody's heart out and saying, "No we're going to say something nice first—"*

I can't remember if I come right out and say it in the novel, but there's something essentially sadistic about the whole process. I mean, to sit there and have the love of your life—your work—something that close to your heart and soul, just ripped apart by strangers. . . .

And not to be able to say anything.

Yes—and not be able to *say* anything. Who thought *that* up? It's so cruel. And everybody essentially knows it's so cruel, but that's one of the many things you're not allowed to say. This whole language of euphemism has sprung up around the inability to be honest. You can't say, "This just bored the hell out of me." So ▶

> 66 There's something essentially sadistic about the whole process [of the writing workshop]. 99

instead you say, desperately, "I think you should *show* instead of *tell*." Where'd *that* come from? I mean, tell that to Jane Austen!

There is this common vocabulary that comes out of the MFA program—the "show don't tell."

"Whose story is this?"

"What's the occasion?"

"What's at stake here for the characters?"

If you go into an MFA program you're going to come out with this vocabulary, even if you don't necessarily become a better writer.

Well, yeah, because the fact is that when someone says, "What's at stake here?" what they may mean is, "Why would anyone waste their time writing this crap?" but no one's going to say that, thank God. Occasionally I've taught at writers' conferences or in programs where two writers teach together. Sometimes it's fantastic. I've taught with Stuart Dybeck, for example, and Diane Johnson, and I've thought, *Gee, I would pay to be in this workshop because hearing what this person has to say about writing is so fascinating and enlightening.* But other times I've co-taught with people who just mouth all the platitudes of the workshop. That's a very difficult position because you're sitting there listening to your colleague say, "Whose story is this?" and you're

66 I've co-taught with people who just mouth all the platitudes of the workshop. That's a very difficult position because you're sitting there listening to your colleague say, 'Whose story is this?' and you're trying not to say, 'Well whose story is *The Brothers Karamazov*?' 99

16

trying not to say, "Well whose story is
The Brothers Karamazov?"

*That's exactly what you do in Chapter 10,
your chapter on Chekhov. I read this Chekhov
chapter and I thought, Oh this is so brave.
You go to the moments when your knee-jerk
reaction would be to give these rules to a
student—a person can't commit suicide for
no good reason or you can't just switch point
of view on a whim—and you find a story by
Chekhov that disproves them.*

Rules that are out of *nowhere,* that just have
nothing to do with anything.

*As a teacher, how do you run a workshop? Do
you have techniques for saving yourself from
those knee-jerk reactions?*

I do. Instead of saying something like, "I think
we should know more about what his mother
was like," I try to come up with some examples
from literature that that might be helpful for
the writer to look at. And there are certain
things that I feel the compulsion to point out
every so often about reading and writing.
For example, I often hear myself telling the
class, "You know we're not the character's
therapists. And we shouldn't function as sort
of a group therapy session for the characters in
the story; they're characters in a story."

*That speaks to another of these writing
program truisms that you take issue with* ▶

Reading and Writing: A Conversation with Francine Prose *(continued)*

in the final chapter: that the reader has to sympathize with the characters.

Yeah, sympathy for the characters is not a requirement.

Presumably, for a reader to make it through an entire novel, they have to care about the character—but not have to like them?

I don't know. I mean, I don't know what you have to do. Again, Beckett is an example I always come up with because do you care about Molloy? I don't know that you do. Maybe in the sense that everything he says is incredibly interesting and weird and amusing and strange. But that's not the same as wanting to go for a drink with him. You end up admiring the incredible gift Beckett has for using language to express a unique and very particular and perceptive and strange idea about the world. But that's not the same as caring about Molloy.

At one point in the book you say, "I discovered how reading a masterpiece can make you want to write one." You've given countless examples in the book of places where there's inspired word choice, brilliant sentences, telling literary gestures and dialogue. I wonder if you could offer up an example of a masterpiece that really made you want to write one.

The first time I read *One Hundred Years of Solitude*. Not that I could ever imagine writing

> **❝** Sympathy for characters is not a requirement. **❞**

anything that extraordinary myself. But it's hard to read that without becoming just infected by the *joy* of storytelling. I mean, seeing what it's like to create an entire world and have things come back around and characters appear and disappear and what you can do on the page. That was a real revelation for me.

Or reading *Anna Karenina*, in which on practically every page there's something that you've noticed about character and the world or that you've seen someone do, and that you never thought anyone else had ever noticed before. And here's this Russian nutcase who's been dead all these years capturing it all perfectly.

You dropped out of a PhD program and essentially left the life of the academic for the life of a novelist/short-story-writer/ journalist.

I've never looked back.

What made you choose the life of the writer over the life of the academic?

I don't really feel that I had a choice. Graduate school was driving me quite literally insane. I wanted a different approach to the work. I just felt that the passion I felt as a reader was not being reflected by my professors and by my future colleagues. I don't know what they were doing, but it wasn't what I was doing. And I don't know how they were reading, but it ▶

> 66 On practically every page [of *Anna Karenina*] there's something that you've noticed about character and the world or that you've seen someone do, and that you never thought anyone else had ever noticed before. 99

wasn't the way I was reading. When I look at the list of papers presented at an MLA convention, I still get that same feeling of *What are these people talking about?* It was extremely alienating, because in theory we were all talking about the same (as they would say) "texts," but I really, literally could not understand. I had never thought of myself as the stupidest person in the room, but suddenly that's what I had become. Nothing anyone was saying made any particular sense to me. Which isn't to say that I didn't have great teachers. I did. The book is dedicated to three of them, one of whom was my teacher both in college and graduate school. But they certainly weren't in the majority.

As a teacher, journalist, and writer, you've had your thumb on the pulse for some time now. Have you been struck by any recent trends in the literary world?

I will say one thing. For one reason or another, I get sent a lot of new books. I don't know what they're hoping—reviews or blurbs I guess. So I see a lot of what's being published. And plenty of it is pretty dull. But quite a bit of it is actually really interesting. Every so often you hear these gloomy predictions about the death of the novel or the death of fiction and the end of literary culture, blah, blah, blah. But, you know, my friend the novelist Richard Price said the novel will be around at our funeral. And I think he's right; it's alive and well.

> 66 Every so often you hear these gloomy predictions about the death of the novel[.] But, you know, my friend the novelist Richard Price said the novel will be around at our funeral. And I think he's right; it's alive and well. 99

What are you reading these days?

Because I'm reviewing so much I often tend to read books on assignment more than for sheer pleasure, but let me look at my desk and see what's on it. Okay I'll just tell you what's on my desk. *The Collected Works of Jane Bowles.* A collection of essays by Janet Malcolm. The new book by Daniel Mendelsohn which I just reviewed called *The Lost*, about a search for his relatives lost in the Holocaust. *Huckleberry Finn*. A book called *Stuart: A Life Backwards*, by Alexander Masters, which is a strange and terrific biography of a homeless person. That's what's on my desk. It's a range. But one of the reasons I'm glad I wrote this book and I'm glad there's the bibliography at the end is that whenever anyone asks you for a book recommendation or what you're reading, everything just flies out of your mind; you just can't think of a single book you've ever read.

That's true.

You know that experience. So now at least I have this list and I can say, "Go look at the list. Don't ask me. Read the list!"

More from Francine Prose

A CHANGED MAN

On an unseasonably warm spring afternoon, a young neo-Nazi named Vincent Nolan walks into the Manhattan office of World Brotherhood Watch, a human rights foundation headed by a charismatic Holocaust survivor, Meyer Maslow. Vincent announces that he wants to make a radical change in his life. But what is Maslow to make of this rough-looking stranger who claims to have read Maslow's books, who has Waffen-SS tattoos under his shirtsleeves, and who says that his mission is to save guys like him from becoming guys like him?

As he gradually turns into the sort of person who might actually be able to do that, Vincent also transforms those around him: Maslow, who fears that heroism has become a desk job; Bonnie Kalen, the foundation's fund-raiser, a divorced single mother and a devoted believer in Maslow's crusade against intolerance and injustice; and Bonnie's teenage son, Danny, whose take on the world around him is at once openhearted, sharp-eyed, and as fundamentally decent as his mother's.

Masterfully plotted, darkly comic, *A Changed Man* illuminates the everyday transactions in our lives, exposing what remains invisible in plain sight in our drug-addled and media-driven culture. Remarkable for the author's tender sympathy for her characters, the novel poses the essential

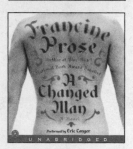

**A CHANGED MAN
CD UNABRIDGED**

Available on CD from HarperAudio, this unabridged audio edition of Francine Prose's novel is performed by Eric Conger.

questions: What constitutes a life worth living? Is it possible to change? What does it mean to be a moral human being?

"Powerful, funny, and exquisitely nuanced. . . . This story has a continental sweep."
—*New York Times Book Review*

BLUE ANGEL

It's been years since Swenson, a professor in a New England creative writing program, has published a novel. It's been even longer since any of his students have shown promise. Enter Angela Argo, a pierced, tattooed student with a rare talent for writing. Angela is just the thing Swenson needs. And, better yet, she wants his help. But, as we all know, the road to hell is paved with good intentions.

"*Blue Angel* is a smart-bomb attack on academic hypocrisy and cant, and Francine Prose, an equal-opportunity offender, is as politically incorrect on the subject of sex as Catullus and twice as funny. What a deep relief it is, in these dumbed-down Late Empire days, to read a world class satirist who's also a world class story-teller."   —Russell Banks

"An engaging comedy of manners. . . . Prose once again proves herself one of our great cultural satirists."
—*Kirkus Reviews* (starred review)

CARAVAGGIO: PAINTER OF MIRACLES
(Eminent Lives)

Caravaggio defied the aesthetic conventions of his time; his portrayal of ordinary people—street boys, prostitutes, the aged—was a revolutionary innovation that left its mark on generations of artists. His insistence on painting from nature, on rendering the emotional truth of experience, makes him an artist who speaks across the centuries to our own time. His life itself is among the most intriguing of any artist, for Caravaggio, though promoted and protected by the influential Cardinal del Monte, remained a man of the streets who couldn't seem to free himself of its brawls and vendettas—a man who would flee Rome (apparently after killing another man in a dispute), produce masterpieces in exile, and eventually receive a papal pardon . . . only to die under mysterious circumstances. Francine Prose evokes the genius of this great artist through a brilliant reading of his paintings, rendering his brief but tumultuous life with passion and acute sensitivity.

"Racy, intensely imagined and highly readable. . . . Prose brings to Caravaggio a fresh and unflinching eye."
                    —*New York Times Book Review*

LEOPOLD, THE LIAR OF LEIPZIG: A CHILDREN'S BOOK

Every Sunday the people of Leipzig marvel at Leopold's amazing tales about wondrous things—like the green gorilla governor in the galaxy of Gelato and the lizard ladies in the land of Lusitana. For generations everyone has believed his stories were true. That is, until a great scientist and explorer arrives in Leipzig and accuses Leopold of being a liar.

Francine Prose teams up with artist Einav Aviram for this brand-new fable about the magic of storytelling.

"The silliness, the rhythm of the words, and the magic realism of the brilliantly colored pictures . . . affirm what kids know: the exciting truth of imaginative play."
—*Booklist*

THE LIVES OF THE MUSES: NINE WOMEN AND THE ARTISTS THEY INSPIRED

All loved, and were loved by, their artists, and inspired them with an intensity of emotion akin to Eros.

In a brilliant, wry, and provocative book, Francine Prose explores the complex relationship between the artist and his muse. In so doing, she illuminates with great sensitivity and intelligence the elusive emotional wellsprings of the creative process.

"A book of serious ideas that is also addictively juicy."   —*Boston Globe*

More from Francine Prose *(continued)*

PRIMITIVE PEOPLE: A NOVEL

What are these barbaric rituals that pass for social and family life? Who are these fearsome creatures who linger in decaying mansions and at glittery malls, trendy weddings and dinner parties? These are the questions that trouble Simone, a beautiful, smart young Haitian woman. She has fled the chaotic violence of Port-au-Prince only to find herself in a world no less brutal or bizarre—a seemingly civilized landscape where dead sheep swing from trees, lightbulbs are ceremonially buried, fur-clad mothers carve terrifying goddesses out of pumice . . . and where learning to lie is the principal rite of passage into adulthood. The primitive people of this darkly satiric novel are not, as one might expect, the backward denizens of some savage isle, but the wealthy inhabitants of the Hudson Valley in upstate New York.

"Francine Prose has a wickedly sharp ear for pretentious American idiom, and no telling detail escapes her observation."
                                    —*New York Times Book Review*

WOMEN AND CHILDREN FIRST: STORIES

These bright and entertaining tales display Prose's special gift for revealing the mysteries and contradictions at the heart of contemporary life; beneath their humorous, acerbic surface, they deal seriously and compassionately with that most modern discovery: nothing is as we've foreseen—not even our own desires.

"Reading *Women and Children First* is like driving down the road with a companion who is so smart and funny and insightful that her conversation transforms the landscape. I loved reading these stories."   —Jane Smiley

HOUSEHOLD SAINTS: A NOVEL

The setting is New York's Little Italy in the 1950s—a community closely knit by gossip and tradition. This is the story of an extraordinary family, the Santangelos. There is Joseph, the butcher, who cheats in his shop and at pinochle, only to find the deck is stacked against him; his mother, Mrs. Santangelo, who sees the evil eye everywhere and who calls on her saints; and Catherine, his wife, whose determination to raise a modern daughter leads her to confront ancient questions. Finally, there is Theresa, Joseph, and Catherine's daughter, whose astonishing discovery of purpose moves the book toward its unpredictable conclusion.

"Prose brings off a minor miracle . . . in the rare sympathy and detachment with which

More from Francine Prose *(continued)*

she gives life to this poignant story. She writes equally well about sausages and saints, documenting the madness and the grace of God in everyday life." —*Newsweek*

AFTER: A YOUNG ADULT NOVEL

School has become a prison. No one knows why. There's no way to stop it. Francine Prose's hard-hitting children's book deals with the aftermath of a high-school shooting in Massachusetts.

"Chillingly plausible. The drama raises all-too-relevant questions."
  —*Publishers Weekly* (starred review) ∾